'Jeremy Jones has written a penetrating and timely rebuttal to assumptions that Middle Eastern political societies are unusually resistant to change and even democratisation. With an intimate knowledge of the Middle East and an engaging style, he takes us through a shifting landscape that has never been as static as one set of stereotypes had it, nor as inherently unstable as others made it. Discerning judgement and informed commonsense are found on every page, and all those who hope to understand this vital region of the world should welcome it as an indispensable and lively guide.'

James Piscatori, *Oxford University*

'Jeremy Jones has written the book that Secretary of State Condoleezza Rice and every member of our Congress should read ... it challenges the preconceptions of the political elite of America on what should constitute democracy in the Middle East and how best to attain it. He has based his meticulous examination of the political structure in every major Arab country and Iran on the realities in each country and on the cultural and historical underpinnings of these disparate regimes. ... I have not read a better introduction to the complexities of Middle East politics in places like Iran, Iraq and Lebanon in my 35 years of concentration on this region. This book is a major contribution.'

Edward Walker, Former Ambassador to Israel and President, *Middle East Institute*, Washington DC

NEGOTIATING CHANGE

The New Politics of the Middle East

Jeremy Jones

I.B. TAURIS

LONDON · NEW YORK

Published in 2007 by I.B.Tauris & Co Ltd
6 Salem Road, London W2 4BU
175 Fifth Avenue, New York NY 10010
www.ibtauris.com

In the United States of America and Canada distributed by Palgrave Macmillan
a division of St Martin's Press 175 Fifth Avenue, New York NY 10010

Library of Modern Middle East Studies 58

HB   ISBN: 978 1 84511 269 1

PB   ISBN: 978 1 84511 270 7

A full CIP record for this book is available from the British Library
A full CIP record is available from the Library of Congress

Library of Congress Catalog Card Number: available

Printed and bound in Great Britain by TJ International Ltd, Padstow, Cornwall
From camera-ready copy edited and typeset by Oxford Publishing Services, Oxford

Contents

Acknowledgements

This book would not have been written without the research fellowship given me at the Belfer Center for Science and International Affairs, Kennedy School of Government, Harvard University. I am very grateful for the support and encouragement of many colleagues there, as well as for the Center's generous help with the substantial travel costs my research entailed. Subsequently, I have benefited from the support and encouragement of colleagues at the Oxford Centre for Islamic Studies, for which I am also very grateful.

Many people have given up their time to discuss the themes of this book with me. Many of them would prefer to remain anonymous, and indeed some of them have shown a good deal of trust, in depending on my discretion when talking candidly about sensitive issues off the record. I offer my warmest thanks to them all.

Finally, I would like to thank Nick Ridout, who has been an invaluable colleague in my consulting practice for 17 years of happy collaboration. More than anything, this book is the result of the ideas he and I have pushed to and fro over these years. He has worked with me on it from the beginning, and without him it could not have been done.

Jeremy Jones, Oxford, 28 June 2006

Introduction

T he title of a conference held at an Ivy League University in the spring of 2005 was 'Democracy in the Middle East. Is it possible?'[1] The tone is almost incredulous: it is as though someone had just caught sight of a phenomenon so unexpected, so unlikely, that they could hardly believe their eyes. It is widely held, and not just in America, that the Middle East – with the exception of Israel – is the one region of the world that remains untouched by democracy. Since the wave of democratic change that transformed central and Eastern Europe starting in 1989, democracy has enjoyed, it seems, a global reach. It would scarcely have been imaginable before 1989, and quite inconceivable only 60 years earlier, when some of Europe's most advanced nations seemed to have abandoned democracy altogether in favour of modern ideologies of fascism and communism. Democratic government had actually established itself as a global norm. Governments that were not democratic had started to look out of step with the times. Governments in the Middle East – apparently a mixture of royal autocracies, military dictatorships and even one theocracy – seemed especially anomalous. They continued stubbornly to resist the global embrace of democracy, and advocates of reform found their message falling on stony ground.

The poster used to promote the conference told a slightly different story. The scene is a hillside at night. It is the kind of hillside on which, 2000 years ago, they say, Middle Eastern shepherds, watching their flocks by night, were astonished to see an angel appear in the sky and transfigure the darkness with a celestial light. In the poster the angel takes the form of Liberty, instantly recognizable from the famous statue in New York harbour. She carries a ballot box in one hand, while with the other she pours a glorious river of light from a huge ceramic jar, so that where it falls the desert hillside brings forth verdant life. The lower part of her face is covered, in what can only be the designer's gesture towards Islamic conventions of female dress, but the scarf that covers her mouth is transparent, presumably so as to avoid any suggestion that this angel of democracy might be silenced. Glad tidings of great joy are carried to the Middle East, and the bearer of these tidings, for all her claims to universal status – she is Liberty, after all – is also unmistakeably American, and, given the setting of this allegory, representative of a distinctly Christian tradition. By coincidence, this conference took place immediately after the death of Pope John Paul II, whose contribution to the promotion of democracy in Europe was warmly invoked by speakers inaugurating the conference and held out as an example of what might be achieved in the Middle East.

The message communicated by the poster – and by the rather parochial failure to see how inappropriate its images might be in the eyes, say, of Muslim advocates of democracy – is fortunately no longer a dominant one in the discussion of democracy in the Middle East. The idea of a region redeemed by the healing power of a liberty-loving Christian world carries very little weight today outside the radical Christian right. One might object that it is precisely that radical Christian right that has come to dominate the thinking of the United States government on this topic. While that may be the case, at least as far as the presentation of the issue to a sympathetic domestic public in the United States is concerned, it would be deeply misleading to claim that such simplistic views are actually shaping the formulation of policy. The makers of foreign policy in the Bush administration may be idealists, they may genuinely believe in the promotion of democracy as work on behalf of a universal good, but they do not, at least with very rare exceptions, subscribe to a genuinely messianic mission. They are not really returning to the Holy Land to redeem its people by means of democracy.

There has been a historical shift, however, in the approach of the United States: the centre of gravity has moved, perhaps decisively, away from a policy of non-intervention, and towards a policy in which the promotion of democracy is an openly acknowledged objective. This shift took place during the first years of the twenty-first century. Supporters of this shift who can continue to dream without having to submit to the day-to-day realities of government can still subscribe to the messianic notion that this policy constitutes 'a Cold War, a crusade, a campaign'.[2] But they also acknowledge that, although they have won the argument in Washington and achieved this shift, no one actually engaged in trying to promote democracy in the region is likely to use this kind of language any more, or adopt their own more radical proposals for its realization, such as more invasions and covert operations to force regime change. Once is probably enough, for, as we shall see, the ongoing crisis in Iraq has been a difficult encounter with regional reality.

In the debate over democratic reform in the Middle East nearly everyone involved is now careful to show they understand there can be no 'one size fits all solution' imposed upon the region from outside. It is widely, if not universally, recognized that the imposition of a standard political system would be both impossible and counter-productive. In order to support regional advocates for change the United States government, too, acknowledges that the diversity of the countries and peoples engaged in the process must be respected. However, this does not prevent many policy makers and commentators conducting comparative exercises in which the progress towards democracy is evaluated either in relation to political systems already accepted as being democratic, or in relation to one another, or both. In many instances surveys of the region ask which countries are ahead and which behind in their progress towards the goal of democracy.

These judgements are missing the point. They assume, for example, there is a common destination. The comparative evaluation of progress assumes a finishing line, which marks the point at which a country becomes democratic. It also assumes a finishing line demarcated according to the values, institutions and social practices of existing, mainly Western, democracies. It does not accommodate the possibility that the process of political development currently underway in the countries of the region may be going in different directions. If one size is not enough for all, then neither is one finishing line. In some cases, the process of political development is both gradual and experimental, and therefore there may be no specific finishing line in mind. While it would perhaps be wrong to characterize such gradual and cautious processes as continual revolution, it might be equally misleading to suppose that each is headed towards a common goal, and, further, that the common goal in question is either identical to or even closely resembles the kind of democratic systems with which we are familiar in the West.

Other factors that might be used in the countries in question to evaluate the political process are not considered, partly, perhaps, because they would not produce a measurement of how far there still might be to go before the finishing line is reached. There is an assumption, widely held in the West, that political reformers in the Middle East are measuring their progress in this way, whereas, in reality, many may be evaluating political practices in wholly other terms. They may in fact be asking questions such as: do they work? Who benefits? What kinds of specific outcomes do they produce? Are they consistent with cultural values? Is the country better governed as a result?

If we think of political development as an organic process, arising out of interactions between living people in specific social and cultural environments, it might be useful, in seeking to meet the requirement that we respect the uniqueness of each country engaged in such a process, to imagine ourselves promoting and protecting a kind of political biodiversity. In the biodiversity approach to the study of political ecology, then, we want to be attentive to the kind of micro climates of everyday social interaction in which political action takes place. This is one way of moving inside the abstract frameworks in which much political science is conducted, and avoiding the trap of thinking of the Middle East, either as it is, or as it might be, as just one political system.

This approach is not, however, a way of slipping straight into an extreme cultural relativism in which there is no attempt to discriminate between one form of government and another on ethical terms. It is not to deny the possibility of achieving agreement on some universal values, such as those expressed within documents such as the Universal Declaration of Human Rights. This was a document shaped by historical circumstances and informed by the values of its authors, but that does not deny its usefulness in establishing a basic framework within which people of diverse social, cultural and political traditions can articulate their aspirations to freedom and justice. Former Secretary of State Henry Kissinger, who is generally associated with an approach to foreign policy that avoids idealistic considerations such as the promotion of democracy, articulates the tension between an approach based on abstract principle and one based on respect for diversity. 'The advocates of the important role of a commitment to democracy in American foreign policy have won their intellectual battle. But institution-building requires not only doctrine but a vision recognizing cultural and historical circumstance. Such humility is not an abdication of American values; it is the only way to implement these values effectively.'[3]

But it is not simply a matter of recognizing that 'cultural and historical circumstances' might impede the process of introducing 'American values' to societies in the Middle East. It is also vital to recognize that those 'cultural and historical circumstances' are neither a political blank slate nor inherently resistant to democratic politics. In the assumption that democracy – and along with it the associated ideas of civil and political rights – is a Western idea, pure and simple, there is a failure to recognize the possibility that there may be forms of democratic practice that are completely different, not only in cultural origin, but in the forms they take. Both those who advocate the democratization of the Arab Middle East and those who decry such a project as a gambit of cultural imperialism are making the same fundamental error. Democracy in the Middle East may not only be possible, it may already be under construction. In the diverse institutions and conversations, the traditions and experiments with which the people of the region conduct their daily lives, manage their social relations and organize their politics there might be all kinds of practices that ought to be recognized as democratic in nature. It may be these practices, rather than those that have developed in the West, or anywhere else for that matter, that will form the foundations for the further development of democratic political institutions in the Middle East. One tradition many of the people and countries in the region share is hospitality, a concept that extends to hospitality to new ideas. The people of the Middle East have a long history of the practice of assimilation, and will make their own particular accommodations with democratic practices they encounter from elsewhere. The idea that there is a particular problem associated with the assimilation of democratic practices in countries where the population is largely Muslim is manifestly untenable, although it continues to feature in some analyses of the region's politics. As scholars like Khaled Abou El Fadl and James Piscatori have persuasively shown, there is ample scope within the Islamic tradition for democratic practice to root itself in that tradition itself. At the same time, the evidence of the last few years in the region – where activists and political leaders who speak in the name of Islam have been among the most committed supporters of democracy – testifies that there is no incompatibility whatever between the practice of Islam and the practice of democracy. They can coexist and even mutually reinforce one another.

Noah Feldman has made the persuasive point that democracy is what he calls 'a mobile idea', that is to say that, despite its specific and contingent historical origins, it is capable of being understood as a universal. It is sufficiently flexible to be accommodated within a great diversity of different cultural situations. It belongs, as it were, to everyone and to no one.[4] This is one helpful way of looking at the situation as it stands at this particular historical moment. It is however, vulnerable to the charge that its supposed 'universality' is merely a historical effect of political power. Democracy is universal, now, because it is an idea developed in one specific cultural setting that has been effectively universalized because it is

one of the leading ideas or most profound ideological commitments of the most powerful nations in the world at this historical
moment. Perhaps a more useful formulation, as a modification of
Feldman's concept, is to suggest that democracy is not actually an
idea at all, or at least it is always something more than an idea,
something more concrete: it is a political, social and cultural
practice. Or rather, democracy is a term we give to a range of
different political, social and cultural practices, which, while they
arise out of specific cultural situations and take different forms in
each situation, have certain key features in common, or might be
seen to share close family resemblances. That there is not a single
democratic 'idea' but rather a range of democratic practices, which
are themselves adaptable, flexible and always in processes of
development, is perhaps just another way of casting Feldman's
concept of the 'mobile idea'. At the heart of this range of democratic practices, there is one simple practical requirement.
Democracy is a way of organizing society in such a way that the
people have a genuine say in how they are governed and by whom,
and in such a way that this right is preserved as a matter of first
priority. From this follow a whole range of institutions and
practices. In the early twenty-first century it has become more or
less axiomatic that democracy will involve elections, because
elections have proven to be an effective method of realizing and
preserving democratic principles as well as of negotiating change.

The 13-month period, from January 2005 to January 2006,
roughly the period in which this book was researched and written,
saw significant elections in Egypt, Iran, Palestine, Lebanon and
Iraq. These elections will therefore offer vantage points from which
analysis and insight are offered. But elections are not everything: in
this book I also explore some of the other less obvious ways in
which the new politics of the Middle East is taking shape, other
places and practices through which political change is constantly
being negotiated – negotiations over new social formations and
political parties, negotiations over the role of women in public life,
and negotiations with the challenges of a globalizing economy.

Negotiation is the order of the day. The era of regime change is at an ignominious end. Regime change was part of an anti-democratic logic of totalization. Your political opponent is removed, in order that your own values may prevail instead. The slate is wiped clean and a new order is written in its place. It is a simple matter of good and evil, in which any change is invariably good because what it replaces was so irredeemably bad. This was the gamble the United States took over Iraq. The gamble was lost, and the people of Iraq are now paying a heavy price for the failure of the flawed logic of regime change.

The logic of negotiation is completely different. To negotiate is to recognize, from the start, that those who disagree with you have a point. Negotiation is a process through which those who disagree with one another work out ways of living together and accommodating themselves to their mutual differences. To negotiate change, then, means to enter into an uncertain process with people with whom you have profound differences. In the new politics of the Middle East, negotiating change will require, not that these differences be set aside, nor that one ideology or vision of democratic politics be adopted universally, but rather that all parties to the process make a genuine effort to understand one another's values and aspirations.

In its efforts to promote democracy in the Middle East the United States has tended to assume that its own values and aspirations are both clearly understood and universally shared; that if the people of the Middle East were given the chance they would surely choose freedom, democracy and the pursuit of happiness; that these are straightforwardly universal values – a kind of default mode of human existence to which all societies will naturally revert the moment they are freed from tyranny. It has failed to take into account the extent to which many of the people of the region have different and equally compelling visions of what a just world might be like. We in the West too often think of these alternative visions of a just world as impediments to democracy. Religion, for example, stands in the way of enlightened secularism. Traditional social values retard the forward march of modernity.

When Westerners talk of the region in these terms it is hardly surprising that its ordinary citizens fear cultural and political domination. Instead of an offer of negotiation they hear the threat of regime change. It seems to them that they are being asked to renounce fundamental aspects of their social, political and religious identity in order to achieve democracy. The majority of ordinary people – from Morocco to Iran – are Muslims with a powerful sense of the validity and appropriateness of their own social values and practices. They are not going to negotiate away their own identity, as individuals and communities, for a share in a Western liberal tradition that many of them view with suspicion. But too often the Western approach seems to demand that they should do so, that the only path to democracy lies in renouncing an indigenous tradition and embracing the alien values of liberalism. This is not, should not and need not be the case.

A proper negotiation on the subject of democratic change in the region can only take place if all parties are prepared to accept the legitimacy of the others' values and traditions. That means, in simple political terms, that the West must stop talking only to its liberal secular friends in the region and instead engage meaningfully with those whom it has tended, rightly or wrongly, to identify as its enemies. After all, you do not negotiate with people who already agree with you. You negotiate where there is disagreement. That means – as this books seeks to show – that change in the region will only be negotiated if and when the West is prepared to sit down and talk directly with Hamas, with Hizballah, with the Muslim Brotherhood, and with the Iranian government, as well as with more apparently congenial interlocutors such as liberal politicians and human rights activists. For, like it or not, it is Hamas, Hizballah, and the Muslim Brotherhood that currently stand as the most effective representatives of mainstream opinion in the Arab world, and the Iranian government gains popular credibility at home with every day that the United States refuses to deal with it.

A new politics for the Middle East can only come about with the active participation of these important players. Refusing to acknowledge their existence, their social and political legitimacy and the credibility of their vision for a more just society is a policy for failure and stagnation. If one message emerges with greater clarity than any other from the last few years spent listening to people talk politics in the Middle East, it is that the negotiating has to begin here, where it will be most difficult. If the leaders of the West either cannot or will not negotiate with the likes of Hamas and Hizballah, then, for all their democratic rhetoric, they are ducking the challenge of negotiating change.

This urgent requirement is part and parcel of a broader challenge for Western policy makers, which is to accept and understand at least some of the diversity of the region's politics. Western policy makers are only going to be effective negotiators of change in the region if they are prepared to do the serious work necessary to understand the specifics of each particular situation. We must pay attention to the particular, to the complex consequences of historical experience, cultural practice and social relations. We must deal not only with facts and realities on the ground, but with questions of perception and perspective – our own and those of the diverse peoples of the Middle East.

Chapter 1
Egypt: Mosque and State

O f all the countries considered in this book, Egypt is the largest. With a population of nearly 80 million, it is larger than either Turkey or Iran, each of which has a population of around 70 million. Among the region's Arab states it is the largest by a far wider margin, with Morocco at around 32 million the next largest. The combined population of three of the most significant core Arab states – Iraq, Syria and Saudi Arabia – is roughly equivalent to the population of Egypt. Egypt has also and for a very long time played a leading role in the politics and culture of the Arab world. In the modern period alone, Egypt has been a regional political leader, providing the Arab world, in President Nasser, with perhaps its first and most prominent global political representative. It has been a centre for culture, too, with major novelists, essayists, playwrights and poets winning audiences throughout the Arabic public, and beyond. Its universities, its publishing, its film and television industries, have been the largest and most productive in the Arab world. In Sayyid Qutb and Hassan al-Banna, Egypt provided Muslims with two of their most important modern thinkers, whose influence on contemporary 'Islamist' movements has been a key element in the emergence of 'political Islam' in the last decades of the twentieth century and the beginning of the twenty first.

For these, and for many other reasons, what happens in Egypt matters throughout the region. Egypt may not dictate or shape what happens, as a conscious strategy of regional hegemony (much as it might, sometimes, wish it could), but despite the emergence of other centres of regional power and influence, either competitive or cooperative (such as Iran or Saudi Arabia) Egypt and Egyptians continue to offer the observer of the region a way of getting to grips with what is going on by concentrating on one country. It is a key claim of this book that each country in the region has its own indigenous political culture, that there is no homogeneous regional political space (not even among the Arab countries), and that political developments in each will follow their own course. But it is also true to say that many of the problems, challenges and opportunities facing the political leaders and people of the region are to be found in Egypt. Egypt is neither representative nor exemplary, but, by virtue of its own size and history, it contains within it much of what this book seeks to investtigate and understand. That is why we begin there.

We begin with two elections, both held in 2005. The first was a presidential election in which the incumbent won 88.7 per cent of the vote and his nearest challenger just 7 per cent. The challenger is currently in prison. The second was a parliamentary election in which the ruling National Democratic Party (NDP) won a two-thirds majority, but which also saw the resurgence as the largest other party in parliament (with an unprecedented 88 seats) of an avowedly 'Islamist' political party, which is still, technically, illegal. These events point to a complex, contested and difficult political situation. In identifying the factors at work in shaping this situation and rendering it so difficult, some of the most significant problems for political change in the region as a whole will be broached.

The Egyptian sociologist and dissident Saad Eddin Ibrahim likes to point out that President Hosni Mubarak of Egypt is now his country's second longest serving leader in over 3000 years of recorded history, with only Pharaoh Ramses II outlasting him (so far) with a reign of 66 years. Mubarak has been president of Egypt since 1981, when he took office after the assassination of Anwar Sadat. A typical Arab joke about Mubarak will involve the presentation of a list of imaginary news headlines from the future, which show how radically the world has changed – 'Sierra Leone agrees to bail out the United States economy with a further loan of $500 billion' – followed by the announcement that President

Mubarak has been re-elected president of Egypt. Mubarak is now in his late seventies, and when his current term of office comes to an end in 2011, he will be 83. This kind of political longevity is repeated across the region. Among current heads of state, Colonel Qadhafi took power in Libya in 1969, Sultan Qaboos of Oman in 1970, while the recently deceased president of the UAE, Sheikh Zayed, ruled for 33 years, King Hussein of Jordan for 47 and King Hassan of Morocco for 38. President Asad of Syria was in power for 29 years and Saddam Hussein was president of Iraq for 24 (making him something of a lightweight, assuming he does not make a comeback). President Mubarak has not named a vice president (which is generally seen as the way in which he would indicate his intended successor). There was some speculation during the late 1990s that Mubarak might not stand for re-election in 2005. There was also considerable speculation that he was grooming his son, Gamal Mubarak, to succeed him, thereby repeating the move towards dynastic republicanism enacted in Syria, when Bashar al-Asad assumed the presidency following the death of his father in 2000. Mubarak has repeatedly denied that he intends to control the succession, in favour of his son or anyone else, preferring to suggest that the choice will lie with the Egyptian people.

Egypt in 2005

The first step towards making such a choice possible may have been taken. In February 2005 Mubarak announced he would ask parliament to agree to a constitutional change allowing for a contested, multi-candidate presidential election to replace the referendum on the president's sole candidacy – the form taken by previous elections. It was approved and Mubarak duly won the election, held in September, defeating the leader of al-Ghad (Tomorrow), Ayman Nour and the leader of the traditional liberal opposition the Wafd, Numan Gomaa. Mubarak appears to have taken a decision to resume a gradual process of political reform in around 2002, and the new government appointed in 2004 was notable for the introduction into key economic posts of figures from outside the hierarchy of Mubarak's National Democratic

Party. If Mubarak is planning a long, slow transition, perhaps concluding with a presidential election in 2011 that would be a genuine contest between two or more credible candidates, this kind of long view would be typical of the way in which many of the region's incumbents view the process of political change.

This is an important consideration, especially when thinking about Western, particularly American, support for democratic change in the region. History is imagined and experienced differently. Tell someone in the Arab world you are interested in recent or contemporary history, and there is a good chance that he or she will respond with well-informed comments about events in the early eighteenth century, before the United States even existed. The disjunction between these senses of historical duration is exacerbated in Washington by the sheer speed of the political process there: no president can serve for more than eight years, many administrations last no longer than four, and within those administrations the careers and political fortunes of key officials ensure there is rarely much opportunity to take a long view. If someone's career depends on the success with which they handle a specific brief – the promotion of democracy in the Middle East, for example – they will be under intense pressure to produce results within a year or two. At a practical level this disjuncture is often experienced as an encounter between a culture that likes to get things done, and one that prefers to see how things will develop. It is also sometimes experienced more negatively as a clash between a kind of unreflective bullying on one side and a maddening resistance to any kind of change on the other. The dynamics of this differential temporality are just one of the difficulties that beset all Western attempts to intervene in the processes of political change in the Middle East. Recognizing that this problem exists is an important prerequisite for being able to make meaningful collaborations on this question. As the jokes about Mubarak show, it is not only Westerners in a hurry who suspect that Mubarak's preference for the *longue durée* speaks of an inflexible determination to keep everything under control, but Egyptians too. Mubarak's decision to open up the presidential election in 2005 was attributed, at least in part, to the very visible and voluble frustrations of such people, gathered under the intensely time-conscious slogan of *Kifaya* (Enough).

In appearance, the Kifaya protesters who first started to appear on the streets of Cairo towards the end of 2004 looked to many observers as though they could be the first authentically Arab manifestation of a phenomenon that had attracted a great deal of attention in the previous year or so – the return of 'people power'. First associated with popular demonstrations against the Philippines dictatorship of Ferdinand Marcos but, at least in Western minds, inevitably linked to the fall of the communist regimes in central and eastern Europe in 1989, 'people power' had reappeared in Serbia (with the overthrow of Slobodan Milosevic in 2000) and, perhaps most relevantly here, in Georgia and Ukraine. In both Georgia and Ukraine the form of the protest included as a vital part of its internal strategy and its external representation, a deliberate referencing of the 1989 movements. Coining names clearly derivative of the phrase 'velvet revolution' used for the successful popular movement that overthrew communist rule in Czechoslovakia, the 'Rose Revolution' of Georgia and the 'Orange Revolution' in Ukraine mobilized popular coalitions in which the young and well-educated played a prominent role. These young activists, wise to the ways of the global media, and fluent speakers of English, made for great television in the West as well as powerful opponents for the regimes they sought to overthrow. Their use of vivid one word slogans (in Ukraine it was '*Pora*', in Georgia '*Kmara*', both, like *Kifaya*, meaning 'Enough') and the smooth planning of their protest was readily traced to links between the protesters and largely American pro-democracy NGOs, although claims that the activists in Georgia and Ukraine were merely pawns in some global conspiracy betrayed a startling failure to recognize the possibility that educated, active students and young professionals might exist and take autonomous action outside the West. Undoubtedly there were strong links and practical collaboration between members of the various movements (including others in Albania, Belarus and Kyrgyzstan), often based on the fact that members had received training and support from veterans of Serbia's Otpor.

In a declaration to the nation issued in August 2004, Kifaya called for 'concrete steps' to be taken towards establishing a new Egyptian political system. The steps required included the end of the emergency law, and all laws that 'constrain public and individual freedoms', the direct election of the president and vice president in a competitive election, a limit of two terms for the presidency, separation of legislative, executive and judicial powers, unconstrained freedom of association, and free and fair parliamentary elections under full judicial scrutiny at every stage.[1] Although Mubarak might claim to have met, at least in part, two of these demands during 2005, Kifaya is clear that the limited reforms embodied in the elections of 2005 do not constitute a genuine response. Indeed, Kifaya called for a boycott of the presidential election, with one of its co-founders, George Ishaq, describing it as 'illegal'.[2] Kifaya is thus one voice among many to claim that Mubarak's democratization is a façade, what Amr Hamzawy has called a 'theatre of democratization.'[3]

Interest in Kifaya outside Egypt was further aroused by the events of March 2005 in Beirut, when far larger protests, once again with young educated people very much to the fore, created what rapidly became known as Lebanon's 'Cedar Revolution' and, to the astonishment of many, led to the resignation of the government. This popular mobilization created conditions in which international pressure on Damascus helped force the withdrawal of Syrian troops from the country. Kifaya may have faltered, for its protests are relatively small, and its critics accuse the movement of failing to offer a coherent programme and ask why it does not simply form a political party. Alongside Kifaya, and in some ways equally visible in the Western media during 2005, was the founder of the new Hizb al-Ghad (Tomorrow), Ayman Nour. Nour, a 41 year-old former member of the Wafd Party who left it to became an independent member of parliament, founded al-Ghad in October 2004 and, despite being arrested in January 2005 and stripped of his parliamentary immunity, stood against President Mubarak in the 2005 presidential election. Kifaya organized a protest against the conduct of this election, drawing over 10,000 people onto the streets of Cairo. Ayman Nour, however, has since been convicted on charges widely regarded as having been trumped up, and is serving a five-year prison term. Al-Ghad performed very poorly at the 2005 parliamentary elections, winning just one seat. In short, despite the visibility of Kifaya and Nour, secular political forces appear to have made no significant political gains during Egypt's tumultuous 2005.

The big winners of the 2005 election were the Muslim Brotherhood, which, despite being illegal as a political party, were permitted to field independent candidates. Everyone knew full well that they were Brotherhood candidates and their campaign made no secret of the fact. Their campaign presented the familiar and ubiquitous slogan (seen also in Palestine from Hamas) of 'Islam is the Solution'. Despite and because of the simplicity of this slogan, despite and because their leaders were detained and many of their supporters and potential voters intimidated or worse (especially in rounds two and three when the authorities had become aware of their likely success) the Muslim Brotherhood won 88 seats in parliament, which not only made them the largest opposition bloc by far, but also gave massive reinforcement to their claim – and the claim of similar movements elsewhere – to represent an authentic popular and democratic voice.

The process of political change in Egypt looks likely to continue, but it is unlikely to do so smoothly. Predictions about the fragility of the regime that tended to make headlines in the early 1990s, during the period of the most sustained attacks by Islamist terrorists, have proven to be exaggerated. There remains, however, considerable uncertainty about the direction of Egyptian political change, and who will exert the strongest influence on the process. It is already clear that the experimental and perhaps rather tentative, and even merely defensive and responsive steps taken in 2005 by Mubarak and the NDP will continue to have unintended consequences. Perhaps one of the most striking of these, so far, has been the emergence into public consciousness of the judiciary. The role of judicial scrutiny in both the presidential and parliamentary elections of 2005 was significant, and where the judges were obstructed in their work they have made their position and their criticism very public. They have also directly challenged the integrity of the presidential elections commission in four court rulings against it.

The activism of the judiciary in this regard has actually been a feature of Egyptian life for a long time, but the fact that it has become a matter of such prominent public discussion introduces a new element into the political process. It means that questions relating to the constitution (whose revision or replacement is the central demand of nearly all opposition movements and parties), the status of the emergency law (in force, more or less con-tinuously since 1967) and the legality of political parties will be addressed in a context in which the judiciary are less and less likely to succumb to executive interference. It is most unlikely that Mubarak intended to create this opportunity, but the result of his adjustments to the constitution, permitting a contested presidential election, may turn out to be more extensive than the negligible effect of bringing his own personal vote down below the 90 per cent mark. In effect, the judiciary has created a new and significant political space in which it will be increasingly able to limit the government's freedom of operation in election matters, and which at least one observer who has commented at length on the role of the judiciary in recent Egyptian politics is happy to welcome with enthusiasm. 'Completely unbeknownst to Mubarak and his hench-men, the elections have exponentially increased the audience interested in this previously obscure affair, exposing the regime's tactics of infiltration, co-optation, and corruption of the judicial community. … What strikes me is how government ploys have this pesky habit of going awry, thanks to the actions of citizens and judges with other ideas.'[4]

Negotiating opposition
Ambivalence towards political parties is, as we shall see, characteristic of the region as a whole, and is most strongly marked in the Arab countries. While Turkey enjoys a fairly robust party

political system, there are few Arab countries in the region in which political parties operate other than under very tight constraints. Iraq is an exception, though only very recently so. The monarchies of the Arab Gulf all limit the scope for the formation of parties, although it is not entirely accurate to claim that they are actually prohibited, and in both Kuwait and Bahrain there are groupings both inside and outside the parliaments that may as well be political parties. Parties are an active part of political life in both Jordan and Yemen, although Jordan suffers from a familiar regional problem in which most parties are little more than temporary vehicles for individual ambitions within an elite group, and Yemen's ruling General People's Congress (GPC) has not yet demonstrated a willingness to allow political competition among parties to threaten its own control of government. Only in Morocco has control of government actually passed from one party to another. Even here, it is widely felt that this stage-managed 'alternance' lacked authenticity, and it is suspected that if all practical restrictions on party activity were to be lifted, it is the Islamist Justice and Development Party that would emerge as the big winner, just as Hamas has done in Palestine and, as some suspect, the Muslim Brotherhood might do in Egypt if elections really represented public opinion fully. This possibility is certain to be used (either legitimately or opportunistically) as an argument against extending political participation.

The situation in Egypt wonderfully combines elements of nearly all these situations. There is (as in Yemen, and the non-pluralist republics of Syria and Tunisia, for instance) a ruling party, of which the president is the leader. The National Democratic Party holds 311 of the parliament's 454 seats, and, by virtue of its size and its position as the party of government, has gradually lost any sense of a clear ideological identity. As a ruling party its main aim remains to rule. It is also, therefore, divided internally, essentially around the vital though non-ideological issue of how best to maintain itself in power. This means that it does possess some potential to be an agent of political change, and cannot be dismissed out of hand as a part of the problem that must be removed before anything meaningful can be done. In this respect it offers rather more promise than Syria's Ba'ath Party, and perhaps resembles more closely President Saleh of Yemen's GPC. Elements within the NDP could decide to take the lead in opening up the political system, aware that in so doing they could be preparing the scene for their own exit from power. Others will be reluctant to help create a scenario that leads to the end of the NDP monopoly on power. Even though the party is rhetorically committed to political reform, and it is common to hear its members and supporters talk about how much work it still has to do in this regard, there is a widespread tendency to imagine only the possibility of political change managed by the NDP. The idea that political change might depend on the NDP relinquishing its position as the self-proclaimed 'party of the majority' does not appeal, obviously, to many within the NDP.

This confusion between the interests and future of the party and those of the country as a whole is evident in various forms elsewhere in the region. Neither the Syrian Ba'ath Party nor the monarchs of the Gulf, Jordan or Morocco are seriously contemplating having themselves replaced, at least not in the foreseeable future. This situation is complicated by the fact that in some of these countries it is the government that is itself an advocate and agent of political change. In at least some of the Gulf Cooperation Council (GCC) states (Qatar, Oman) it is apparent that the government is, at least to some extent, out ahead of a politically conservative population. The idea that a process of political change might lead not to greater openness and a recognizable 'modernization' of institutions, but to some kind of 'regression' does carry weight in some parts of the region. It is precisely on this basis that some within Egypt's NDP will insist on the importance of their retaining control of the process (for fear of what the 'Islamists' might bring). It is, however, a dubious general proposition resting on the notion of a unilinear process towards ever greater modernity, which we have already suggested is untenable. But all the same, the NDP shares attitudes held in common in government circles in the region, that the unintended consequences of an imperfectly managed process of change will be entirely negative. They reckon without two alternative possibilities – that managed change will throw up unintended consequences and that the unintended consequences of a less tightly managed process may turn out to be benign.

Ambivalence towards political parties takes a particular form in Egypt. A limited multi-partyism since 1977 has allowed the participation of a number of genuine opposition parties, all of them, so far, secular in their politics (though the Labour Party has traditionally been a place where Islamist opinion has found a legal space). The formation of new political parties is very strictly controlled. A new party must demonstrate that it offers, in its manifesto, something distinctively different from the options already made available by existing parties. Party registration is also closed to any movement deemed to be primarily religious in nature. This is the stipulation that prevented the Muslim Brotherhood forming a party and that therefore led to the strange paradox of an illegal party winning 88 seats in parliament in 2005. A Muslim Brotherhood splinter group called Hizb al-Wasat (the Moderate Party) has twice sought and been refused registration, and will seek to do so again. It was the formation of Hizb al-Ghad in 2004 that led to the charges against Ayman Nour of which he was convicted in December 2005 (it was alleged that he had forged documents associated with the registration of the party).

It is clear that, whatever the stated intentions of the government, there is a highly politicized control exercised over the legal issue of party formation. The law on political parties is implemented (many would say manipulated) to serve the interests of the NDP. Additional legal restrictions on public gatherings also function in a direct way to limit the scope for effective opposition parties. Without a licence it is not possible to hold even modest-sized meetings in public. Political parties are therefore reduced to holding their meetings in their own headquarters, severely limiting their capacity to reach out to a broader public. Low levels of participation in the political process generally mean that party activism is very modest indeed. No one seriously interested in wielding power and implementing policy (the very things that drive most political activists) would join an opposition party under such circumstances, particularly while there exists a large, welcoming and well-resourced government party to join instead. Without activists, a party cannot reach out to ordinary people and hope to build a constituency for itself. Party activists in Egypt seem to spend much of their time contributing to party newspapers, which tend to communicate mainly to a narrow section of the already active (even converted), and which make no contribution at all to the far more urgent task of party organization. Organization, by contrast, is the great political strength of the Muslim Brotherhood. The mainstream legal secular opposition parties are therefore caught in a vicious circle of impotence, and have suffered serious erosion in their support over the last ten years or so. Their inability to offer a credible alternative, or even really a meaningful space in which to articulate policy differences, is a major contributor to the lack of political participation that renders such groups feeble in the first place. The failure of such parties has also been a factor in the emergence of both Hizb al-Ghad and Kifaya, as well as continuing talk of the need to come up with new parties.

Without structural and legal change, however, it is hard to see what a new party could do that the old ones have not already demonstrably failed to do. Ultimately, in Egypt and elsewhere political parties other than those of an 'Islamist' complexion are unlikely to attract participation, build popular support and mobilize a social base until they can be regarded as credible alternatives to current governments. This means that political systems have to allow for change to come about as a result of what parties do, and how they perform at elections. The disconnection between parliamentary elections and the formation of governments even in a relatively pluralist polity such as Jordan's more or less ensures that political parties remain small and ineffectual. They have no incentive to merge or form coalitions, nor, indeed, to do anything much other than manoeuvre for limited and short-term gains in political position.

Members of both the Jordanian and Egyptian establishment speak of their desire to see two, three or perhaps four political parties (rather than the proliferation currently seen in Jordan, say) actively competing with one another, based on policies and programmes. Members of these establishments tend to be less forthcoming when it comes to enabling such politics, since to do so would have to involve contemplating a radical shift in their own position from monopoly holder to equal competitor (and likely loser). Islamist political parties enjoy a special advantage in these closed or blocked polities, in that they have aims and objectives beyond the purely political sphere. It is possible to build a powerful Islamist social and political movement, ready to enter the political sphere at the drop of a hat should it choose to do so, because such a social movement has its own *raison d'être* outside the pursuit of political power. In both Jordan and Egypt (as well as in Palestine) the Muslim Brotherhood could build mass participation and create the basis for political organization precisely because they were either excluded from or chose to remain outside the purely political arena. People like Ayman Nour in Egypt or Mustapha Barghouti in Palestine work at an acute disadvantage in such situations, a fact that some of their Western enthusiasts, baffled at how poorly they seem to perform in elections, often fail to recognize. The deck is stacked against them by the structure of the political systems in which they operate.

Most important of all is the position of the Muslim Brotherhood in this limited pluralism. Again Egypt's experience contains much that will be found in other countries in the region, where it is the Islamists who appear to constitute the major opposition to a secular government. Leaving aside the question of Turkey, where this might be said to have been the case but where the nature of the political environment and of the so-called Islamist party are distinct enough for comparisons to mislead, Islamist parties or movements appear to constitute the most significant opposition group in Jordan, Morocco, and Yemen (where Islah enjoys an uneasy partnership with the ruling GPC), as well as being major forces within powerful political coalitions in Iraq, and probably enjoying substantial popular support despite working underground in Syria, Saudi Arabia and perhaps even Libya. The victory of Hamas (or more accurately the Change and Reform list that Hamas led) in the elections for the Palestinian Legislative Council in January 2006 has demonstrated the appeal and effectiveness of the Islamists beyond any shadow of a doubt. The issue of where to allow the Islamists to position themselves in a more or less pluralist political space will therefore be one of the questions to which this book will repeatedly return.

Negotiating change with Islamists

The causes and effects of Egyptian Islamism will be familiar to many in the region, although, again, specific local differences will determine the extent to which any or all of the issues around Egypt's Muslim Brotherhood are central to thought and experience elsewhere in the region. In Egypt, analysts repeatedly point to a combination of factors that have led to the 'Islamization' of Egyptian politics in apparent defiance of its generally accepted secular political environment. The capacity to organize socially, rather than as a political party pure and simple, is, as already discussed, a key factor in the success of the Muslim Brotherhood. This organization or mobilization of support for the Brotherhood rests upon a range of social and political circumstances that present themselves in acute forms in Egypt, but that are present also in other countries in the region. The success of the Muslim Brotherhood, followed so soon afterwards by the outright victory achieved by Hamas in Palestine (see Chapter 3), puts the issue of the identity, intentions and potential of democratic Islamist movements right at the heart of contemporary debate about political change in the Middle East.

The possibility that the Muslim Brotherhood might be the party with which the Egyptian government will have to negotiate political change is a source of anxiety, not just within Egypt, but elsewhere in the region. Because secular-minded liberals have historically taken the lead – often courageously and at personal cost – in efforts to engage in meaningful negotiation over political change, they are understandably very concerned that a negotiation in which parties like the Muslim Brotherhood take a leading role will lead to political settlements that are radically different from those imagined by liberal democrats. Governments, too, fear that the Brotherhood and their ilk will prove unreliable partners in a negotiation over change. Both governments and their secular opposition sometimes maintain that the strength of the Muslim Brotherhood and other similar movements is overstated, that recent elections have in fact demonstrated the limits rather than the power of the Islamists. In this respect they echo the vision of writers like Olivier Roy, who are convinced of the 'failure of political Islam'.[5]

In Egypt, it is noted, the Muslim Brotherhood obtained its 88 seats – roughly 20 per cent of the total seats contested – on the basis of an overall turnout of between 20 and 25 per cent. Some claim that this indicates that the Muslim Brotherhood only won one-fifth of the votes of eligible voters, and that its support is only about 5 per cent of the electorate. This may be consoling to the NDP, but it masks the fact that the Muslim Brotherhood only fielded about 130 candidates, and that its success rate was therefore over 60 per cent. Unless the government really believes that the people who constitute the silent majority of 75 per cent of the electorate who did not vote are radically different in their views and aspirations from the 25 per cent of them who did, popular support for the Muslim Brotherhood is probably somewhere between the 20 per cent indicated by its parliamentary representation and the 60 per cent indicated by its success rate in the seats it contested.

The fact that Hamas clearly exceeded the predictions of opinion polls in the January 2006 legislative elections in Palestine should discourage political predictions based on low estimates of popular support for Islamist groups. If this kind of electoral outcome is failure, perhaps this is not really 'political Islam'. There is a protest vote at work here – in Egypt as well as Palestine – but that is no basis for dismissing it. Although not everyone who voted for the Muslim Brotherhood, or for Hamas, for that matter, really believes that 'Islam is the Solution', the vast majority of such voters seem fairly certain that the Islamist movements are better fitted for government than Fatah or the NDP. That may be a temporary sentiment, but it is unlikely to go away until someone other than Fatah and the NDP is given a chance to make its own mess of governing. The fact that Hamas now has that chance probably means that Palestine is one step ahead of Egypt, that in Egypt the protest vote can be expected to continue to grow, and that as it does, so will the strength of the Muslim Brotherhood. The idea that their support is over-reported is probably self-deluding.

Thus, the fears of the secularists, those in opposition as well as those in government, start to circulate around the obvious questions. Have these Islamists really renounced violence? Are they simply pretending to be legitimate politicians? Are they not, in fact, simply the acceptable face of a secret militant organization? If they are allowed to take power will they respect religious diversity? Will they try to enforce shari'a, repealing social liberties that secular forces have fought for many years to establish? These are also some of the questions I shall seek to address in the chapters that follow. In Egypt, the answers may be a long time coming. In some of the other countries in the region clarity may come sooner and offer some genuine hope that, for those willing to do so, negotiating change with the Islamists will be a democratic process worth entering.

Egypt is neither exemplary nor representative. But as well as maintaining an influential role in the wider politics and culture of the region, it has experienced political phenomena that are to be found in many other countries. As far as these aspects of Egypt are concerned, then, it may offer some pointers to developments elsewhere. It has a government that enjoys a monopoly on power; its secular opposition parties are small and weak; political participation is at a low level; it has faced politically motivated violence in the name of religion; it has a large mainstream Islamist movement whose power is based in social mobilization; its government has conceded political space to Islamism in a defensive reaction over many years; its government is also, at least rhetorically, committed to both economic and political reform; actions in pursuit of political reform, in particular, have been limited and tentative; it faces political challenges from a large and young population that faces unemployment and poor education; the public sphere in which political change might be openly discussed and negotiated is in a state of disrepair.

Other countries in the region face radically different challenges and enjoy very different opportunities. Egypt does not have a significant Shia population; it is not ruled by a monarch (at least not in name); it is not under occupation; it is not divided on confessional lines, though it has some religious diversity; it is not a military dictatorship (quite); it does not suffer from acute political instability threatening the integrity of the state; it is not engaged in civil war and has not recently had one; there are no significant unresolved issues regarding its territorial integrity; it has neither a significant non-Arab minority nor a large non-citizen population; its economy is not primarily dependent on oil; and it is not under acute external pressure for 'regime change'.

So as we move on from Egypt, to look at the politics of Iran – another large regional power, very different in its history, culture and even its language – we will wish to hold simultaneously in mind the possibility that one country can learn from the experiences of another, and also that any attempt to understand the nature of political change in the region must respect its political and cultural diversity. Part of doing this, at least for those of us who live and work in the West, will involve opening ourselves to the unavoidable reality that all kinds of different groups – including Islamists whose politics we may find difficult to understand or accept – will be involved in negotiating change.

Chapter 2
Iran: Innovation Impeded

There is one country in the Middle East that has enjoyed over 25 years of regular elections. Its president is elected by universal suffrage every four years. The president appoints a cabinet that is subject to a stringent approval process by parliament. The parliament itself is also elected every four years. Political parties campaign vigorously in parliamentary elections. The parliament frequently offers critical opposition to the policies of the president and the government, sometimes forcing the resignation of ministers or rejecting presidential appointments. Political debate is lively and partisan. Parliamentary and presidential elections are fiercely contested and have produced surprising results on several occasions. This is also a country with a remarkably rich culture of political, scientific, philosophical and religious thought. This culture has meant that the country has long been one of the most open and innovative in the region, a place where one might reasonably imagine the conditions for democratic politics – based on the idea that independent human thought might be the basis for collective decision-making – to be particularly propitious. There might be a connection, then, between this cultural tradition and this country's recent experience of electoral politics. This country could be one of those places in the region where the roots of democracy are genuinely and firmly established. This country is Iran. Because it is, like Egypt, one of the largest and most powerful countries in the region, what happens in Iran matters. Sadly, its enormous capacity for innovation and a positive influence on the politics of the region is currently impeded by its international isolation.

One of the key factors enabling the development and continuation of Iran's cultural tradition is the practice of what is called in Islamic thought, *ijtihad*. *Ijtihad* is the interpretation of the sacred texts, to make them applicable to contemporary circumstances. Instead of an interpretation of the Koran and the *hadith*, in which a moral and religious framework developed nearly 1400 years ago is preserved intact and in aspic, *ijtihad* involves constantly rereading the texts to uncover underlying principles that may then be applied to situations that were never conceived of 1400 years ago. It is *ijtihad*, for example, that permits an understanding of the contemporary position of women in Islamic societies. Where it is stated that a woman's testimony in court should count for half of the testimony of a man, this is ordinarily taken to mean that this inequitable situation should be maintained in a contemporary setting Islamic judicial system. However, the practice of *ijtihad* reveals that the principle being established in the text is not a principle of gender inequality: rather, it is establishing, for the first time in the Arab communities in which Islam arose, that women have a right to testify in court. *Ijtihad* therefore identifies an underlying principle (women's rights should be increased, not restricted) that may then be applied in a contemporary setting. The sacred text, far from being restrictive and condemning women to an unequal position, is revealed through *ijtihad* as the basis for continuing efforts towards gender equality. For the Sunnis, however, who are most of the Muslim world, the gates of *ijtihad* have long been closed. No further interpretation of the sacred texts is permitted. Historically, then, it is in Shia Islam that this form of reasoning, which does not depend on the authority of existing bodies of legal thought, continues to be practised most widely. The only country in which a Shia majority has dominated the political landscape is Iran.

If we are looking for rich examples of how democratic politics, rooted in specific regional cultural, social and religious traditions, might be in operation in the region today, we should, therefore, perhaps, look no further than Iran. But something seems to have gone horribly wrong. For, instead of openness, social and political innovation, challenges to religious orthodoxy, the extension of women's rights and the practice of modern democracy, we find in Iran a tyrannical regime dominated by authoritarian and reactionary mullahs, who have consolidated their power with the judicial murder of thousands of citizens, a regime that continues to harass and imprison writers, journalists and human rights campaigners, where women are violently compelled to observe highly restrictive dress codes, whose president is alleged to have called for the elimination of the State of Israel and who defies the international community by insisting on his right to develop nuclear weapons. What is really confusing about this state of affairs is that it is not a simple case of a tyrannical regime stamping out the culture of democracy and openness. The 25 years of democratic politics, the elected parliament, the elected president and the vigorous political debates – all these have happened at the same time as the tyrannical theocratic regime. Indeed, it is the tyrannical theocratic regime that created these very democratic institutions. How can Iran be both things at the same time? How can it be archetypal rogue state, human rights abuser and founding member of the Axis of Evil on the one hand, and heartland of Islamic innovation and democratic politics in the region on the other? Finding a solution to this particular conundrum will be a long and complex task. The present global political situation makes it almost impossible. It is perhaps one of the region's most unfortunate ironies that, as the United States launches its latest and most sustained campaign for democracy in the Middle East, it should find itself completely unable to engage constructively with Iran. Instead, it is reduced to badgering reluctant allies, like Hosni Mubarak, into minimal liberalization measures or trying to introduce a democratic system into Iraq by sheer force of arms. How much easier and pleasant it would be if Iran were part of the conversation, instead of being America's number one regional enemy.

Middle East politics rarely produces surprise election results. Even where there are elections, results are nearly always predictable, mainly because, in so many instances, they are prepared in advance, often with shockingly little regard for plausibility. There have only been two real shock results in recent times. Three, if the Hamas victory in Palestine in January 2006 is allowed to count (they were at least expected to do very well and their opponents very badly). Both of the two really astonishing election shocks have been in Iran. First, there was the landslide victory of Mohammed Khatami in the presidential election of 1997, and then the success of Mahmoud Ahmadinejad in 2005. Given the paradox of Iranian politics and the strange coexistence of tyranny and openness, these two results might be understood as indicating ways in which apparently rigid political structures only partially contain considerable political volatility. This might help us understand the dynamics in contemporary Iranian politics and the precise place that democracy and democratic thought might occupy in Iran's political future. Before turning to these two elections and what they might tell us about Iranian democracy, it is worth spending a little time setting the political context. In particular, with this combination of rigidity and volatility in mind, it is important to understand the paradoxical effects of the Iranian Revolution's most original and unusual political concept, *velayet-e faqih* – the Guardianship of the Supreme Jurisconsult (as it is usually, but somewhat awkwardly translated), devised by and eventually for Ayatollah Ruhollah Khomeini, the leader of the Iranian Revolution.

Velayet-e faqih: innovation and institution

The concept of *velayet-e faqih* started to emerge in Khomeini's thought as far back as the 1960s, while he was in exile, teaching in the Iraqi holy city of Najaf. As part of a five-volume work of jurisprudence relating to the law of sale, for example, Khomeini proposed that a jurist (scholar of religious law), appropriately qualified, might act as a guardian over the wealth of those who are unable to manage it for themselves. He went on to derive from this the more general proposition that Islam constitutes a complete system of financial and political regulations for the conduct of life. This being the case, who else but a suitably qualified jurist to 'undertake government and direct an Islamic state'?[1] By the 1970s this proposition had taken on an even more explicitly political form. In *Islamic Government* Khomeini argued decisively against monarchy and dynastic succession (a statement of direct opposition to the rule of the Shah) and proposed instead that a properly Islamic form of government would be one in which the jurists governed. Since legislative power is God's alone, and neither the Prophet nor the imams[2] are here to guide the people in the right application of the law, only the best-qualified jurist possesses the credentials to govern in accordance with the law.

It is essential to recognize that the concept of *velayet-e faqih* constitutes a radical innovation, even within the framework of Shia thought, which is itself much more open to innovation than the Sunni schools. After all, it is only on the basis of extensive interpretation that the concept of *velayet-e faqih* comes into being. It is, as most analysts and critics of the concept tend to agree, something of a stretch. Without the possibility of the continued practice of *ijtihad*, it would have been impossible to introduce this new idea. Indeed, it is *ijtihad* itself that gives the jurist – the scholar who practises it – the grounds for his authority over others, because it is the scholar who is entrusted with the task of *ijtihad*. Most previous Shia thought keeps the religious hierarchy out of the political domain. Until the political activism promoted by thinkers like Khomeini in the second half of the twentieth century, Shia attitudes to the political were broadly quietist. This reflected enduring political realities – the Shia did not exercise political power even, for most of the Islamic era, in Iran where there is a substantial Shia majority. For Shia clerics, keeping quiet and getting on with spiritual matters without engaging in political struggle was preferable to getting involved. As long as they kept their religion out of politics, there was a reasonable chance, particularly under the relatively relaxed religious regulations of the Ottoman Empire, of being left alone. In the event that this became impossible, there was always the option of resorting to *takiye*, the traditional Shia dispensation to dissimulate. You could pretend not to be a Shia if there was a threat to your life or livelihood. So the idea of a militant, activist clergy was already a departure from tradition, derived from an innovative extension of juridical authority into the political arena.

While this may seem like an arcane theological or philosophical point, it is important to recognize that it is evidence, a product if you like, of a rich and disputatious tradition of religious scholarship in Iran.[3] Not only is this a long tradition, it is one that continues to this day, as we shall see shortly. Two unusual but significant features of this culture, particularly that in which Khomeini and other prominent Iranian scholars and clerics immersed themselves in Qom in the middle of the twentieth century, are the exploration of philosophical questions and the study of mystical Sufi thought that it permitted. One might not expect either the study of philosophy or mysticism to lead to political activism, and the study of both simultaneously might be expected to lead instead to an absolute and final repudiation of the world of practical political realities, but in Iran it appears to have had the opposite effect. Philosophy offers an image of the individual human as capable of great knowledge and wisdom, while mysticism can generate a sense of the individual's capacity to transcend his own limitations.

This offers a way of understanding how someone might develop the view that all human affairs might be best ordered under the supervision of a philosophically enlightened, self-transcending and utterly pure and disinterested individual. European culture has thrown up its own version of this powerful fantasy for intellectuals, in the form of Plato's proposal for a republic to be ruled over by a philosopher king. Plato never sought to put this proposal into practice, offering his republic as an ideal or utopian vision (which has struck many readers as decidedly dystopian). Khomeini, by contrast, attempted to put his conception into practice, and it is perhaps not fanciful to suppose that at least one element of the Iranian Revolution was an attempt to actualize a highly refined philosophical ideal, within the sphere of real life government and politics, initiated by someone whose whole cast of thought and view of the world was strangely aloof from such worldly considerations. That such unworldly aspirations should translate so rapidly into such unphilosophical blood-letting is a tragic irony from which few major revolutions have been immune. The strengths and weaknesses of the intellectual and political opposition to the current Iranian political establishment and the principle of *velayet-e faqih* are similarly characterized by their participation in this kind of scholarly debate. Some of the leading intellectual figures in what was to become the reformist movement after 1997 are very much part of this tradition of a highly philosophical approach to religious scholarship.

This culture of ongoing debate and accumulating scholarship (most of it elaborate textual commentary) is only possible on the understanding that the gates of *ijtihad* remain open. It is this condition that makes a whole infrastructure of religious scholarship and education possible. Without it, there is no clergy to imagine themselves becoming militant and engaging in political struggle. *Ijtihad*, and the flexibility for innovation that it permits, is thus the necessary precondition of the emergence of the concept of the *velayet-e faqih* and the decisive entry of Iran's Shia religious leadership into the political domain. The energies driving Shia political Islam are therefore energies naturally directed towards innovation and change. They are energies that we might reasonably suppose to be consistent with the development of democracy.

And herein lies the paradox of post-revolutionary Iranian politics. For it was the innovative concept and practice of *velayet-e faqih* that subsequently became institutionalized within the constitutional and political structures of the Islamic Republic as the role of the supreme leader, and became the basis for some of the strongest institutional resistance to subsequent change and innovation. The first constitution of the Islamic Republic, drafted after the referendum that established the republic itself, did not specify the powers of the supreme leader, but instead conferred substantial executive powers upon an elected president. Sharia was not made the basis of the law. The constitution also, incidentally, contained substantial provisions for civil and human rights. In many respects, as Ali Ansari points out, it resembled not only Iran's own earlier constitution of 1906, but also that of the French republic.[4]

The role of the supreme leader, to whom gradually many of the powers initially assigned to the president were to pass, grew out of experimental practice, and was almost entirely dependent on the charismatic figure of Ayatollah Khomeini. It began in ambiguity.[5] The section of the 1979 constitution that dealt with *velayet-e faqih* was drafted by Khomeini's deputy Ayatollah Montazeri, who took the view that it envisaged the supervision of the government by the leader, not a clerical monopoly on power. Critics of this provision feared that a clerical monopoly was precisely what it was likely to produce, and they have, in many respects, been proven correct. Because of Khomeini's personal authority and charisma, however, the idea was carried forward. Once inscribed in the constitution, it provided the basis for Khomeini to continue to extend his power by the charismatic and patrimonial use of his personal authority.[6]

In retrospect, it is pretty clear that the role was *sui generis*. Without the popular authority Khomeini commanded as leader of the revolution, it is unlikely that political and constitutional power would have leaked away from the formal institutions of government in the way they did. Alongside this leakage of power away from the elected president, prime minister (a position that was abolished in 1989) and cabinet there developed a parallel set of institutions, formal and informal, associated with and responsible only to the supreme leader. By the time the former president, Ali Khamenei, was appointed to replace Khomeini after the latter's death in 1989, there was an entire structure – political, religious and, perhaps crucially, intelligence and military – working for the leader's office rather than for the government. As Khomeini's successor, Khamenei would govern by using the machinery of *velayet-e faqih* built up over ten years, in the absence of the charismatic personal authority enjoyed by Khomeini. The ambiguity introduced into the system by the inclusion of *velayet-e faqih* in the constitution has developed, over the period since 1979, into a powerful and decidedly unambiguous cluster of unaccountable religio-political authority, which has been one of the most substantial checks on political reform in Iran in recent years. It is through the institutions of the leader, and often through their control over the means of violence, that the conservative establishment has effectively defended itself against successive reforming challenges. The irony of the situation is that what was initially an assertion of the innovative potential of *ijtihad* has turned into perhaps the most effective imaginable mechanism for its practical repudiation. The radical idea that someone might have the authority to interpret the law and thus set the political agenda has turned into the reality that one person and one person alone possesses such authority, and that his authority will be used to prevent any change in the political agenda. Perhaps the key question facing us, therefore, in an analysis of the prospects for democracy in Iran is this: how can democracy properly develop while the concept and practice of *velayet-e faqih* persists? It is to this question that some of the most interesting advocates of reform are now starting to turn, and for many of them, as we shall see, the answer is decisive. While there is no incompatibility between Islam and democracy, democracy and *velayet-e faqih* are, at least now, inimical.[7]

Consolidation and failed reform

Following the death of Ayatollah Khomeini in 1989, the Islamic Republic of Iran entered a phase of post-revolutionary consolidation. This may well have taken place even had Khomeini not died at this point, since the Iraq War had not only left the country in need of serious economic repair, but had also, over a period of eight years, encouraged the development of authoritarian structures in which military and security forces acquired significant political power. President Khamenei was elevated to the rank of ayatollah (some of the religious establishment objected to this highly politicized honour) and installed as supreme leader to replace Khomeini. The speaker of the *Majlis*, Hashemi Rafsanjani, was elected president and the constitution was amended, abolishing the post of prime minister (held at this point by Mir Hussein Mussavi). In retrospect, this process of consolidation around Rafsanjani, who was establishing himself as the dominant figure in the regime, may be seen as a swing away from a leftist radical orientation towards a centrist conservative position.

However, from a Western perspective, it seemed to be a moment at which some kind of rapprochement with the Islamic Republic might have been possible, for Rafsanjani's aspirations for economic (if not political) reform looked like they might compel him to lead Iran back to the global environment of international trade and finance. Iran's restraint during the 1990–1 war to expel Iraq from Kuwait was widely interpreted as reflecting Iran's acquiescence in the regional status quo and a willingness not to contest increasing American involvement in regional security. The United States government, however, did not share this interpretation and chose instead to continue to take at face value the regime's revolutionary rhetoric. For much of the 1990s the relationship between Rafsanjani and Khamenei was characterized by Rafsanjani taking actions that might encourage an engagement with the West, while Khamenei said things that seemed designed to prevent it. Many analysts took the view that the West, notably the United States government, was wrong not to regard Khamenei's words as strictly for domestic consumption. By the same token, the Iranian government may have been guilty of overestimating the international community's capacity to read such diplomatic sophistication.

By the mid-1990s the policy of 'dual containment' devised by Martin Indyk to keep Iran and Iraq in positions from which they were unable to challenge American hegemony in the Gulf had come to dominate US thinking on both countries and the prospects for a decisive improvement in relations diminished, despite a brief period of optimism associated with Madeleine Albright's public apology for the American role in the 1953 overthrow of the elected Mossadeq nationalist prime minister. Meanwhile, Rafsanjani's economic reforms were making only very limited progress and political power in Iran was consolidating further around a conservative establishment consensus between the clerical authorities and the bazaar. Some radicals and leftists who had participated in government before 1989 increasingly came to see the political sphere as crucial, and started to advocate civil society freedoms and democratic reform as key policy platforms.

Rafsanjani's second term as president expired in 1997. More than 200 candidates initially sought to run in the election to choose his successor, but the Guardian Council gradually reduced this to just four and two of these were eliminated in the first round of voting. The final round of the 1997 presidential election therefore pitted the *Majlis* speaker, Ali Akbar Nateq Nuri against a comparatively little known former minister of culture, Mohammed Khatami, drafted in by reformists who had failed to persuade Mir Hussein Mussavi to stand. As minister for culture and Islamic guidance, Mohammed Khatami had pursued liberal policies designed to foster new intellectual and cultural openness, but had resigned in 1992 in the face of conservative opposition to his work. Nateq Nuri was more or less the anointed successor, enjoying the public support of Ali Khamenei and the conservative establishment, including the Revolutionary Guards. He was expected to win a comfortable victory. Khatami enjoyed the support of the younger generation, particularly students and particularly in Tehran. He was backed by many of the former leftists who now saw increased public freedom as a prerequisite for necessary political reform, and also by technocrats associated with Rafsanjani, who had formed a proto-party under the name of the 'Servants of Construction' during Rafsanjani's presidency.

In the second round runoff Khatami won a landslide victory, taking 69 per cent of the total vote. His triumph looked like it had the potential to inaugurate a period of renewed change after the blockage of the Rafsanjani years. Khatami enjoyed considerable international goodwill, appearing to Western eyes as a quiet and rather bookish figure, quite unlike the popular image of a fanatical ayatollah that the stern features and charismatic populism of Khomeini had imprinted in so many Western imaginations. For Western observers, Khatami may have been a mullah, but he seemed conversant with Western philosophy and reputedly had been much influenced in his thought by the work of Immanuel Kant, the foremost systematic philosopher of the European Enlightenment. Quite why Western observers viewed an interest in

Kant as a positive sign is a little mysterious, given that Western political leaders are rarely admired for their interest in such matters. Perhaps it made Khatami seem appealingly otherworldly. His support within Iran, however, was ultimately much more important, and to begin with, really very substantial.

A whole generation had grown up knowing nothing but revolution, war and a rather stifling isolation. The rhetoric of the revolution simply did not resonate with this younger generation, many of whom, particularly students, had developed fervent desires for freedom of the kind enjoyed in the West. Millions of Iranians were ready to embrace change, and the fact of such an overwhelming election result in favour of 'reform' – whatever that might turn out to be – was an exhilarating experience that generated an enormous wave of new expectations in Iran, in the region more generally and in the West. But this surprise election and the optimism it generated never fulfilled its promise. Although a pro-Khatami majority gained control of the *Majlis* under the banner of the Islamic Iran Participation Front and the leadership of the president's brother, Mohammed Reza Khatami, and Khatami himself was comfortably elected for a second term in 2001, it had already become clear that he was facing substantial internal political opposition. The presidency enjoys only limited powers, because of the way in which executive authority had gradually leaked into the office and institutions of the leader, and without the full support of Khamenei, who had already had eight years working both with and against Rafsanjani in which to consolidate his grip, a reformist Iranian president would enjoy only limited room for manoeuvre. The story of Khatami's reform project, which seemed to be brought decisively to a standstill with the second election shock that brought the current president Mahmoud Ahmadinejad to power in June 2005, is an increasingly dispiriting narrative of disappointment and failure, in which the parallel institutions of the supreme leader, often acting through secretive and unaccountable security forces, gradually asserted control over the limited new political space opened up by Khatami's victory. Reformers both religious and secular who had associated themselves with Khatami and the reformist project would find their newspapers and websites censored and closed, and in many cases would find themselves tried and imprisoned, and in some of the worst cases, assassinated by agents of the regime.

The presidential election of 2005, which was held over two rounds on 17 and 24 June, illustrates both the weakness of the reform movement and the enduring strengths of the parallel establishment, and teaches important lessons about the future course of Iranian democratic politics, depending on how the unexpected events of 17 June are interpreted. Khatami, whose term of office was in any case at an end, had effectively been discredited by 2005, with many of his supporters having deserted him, weary of his failure to impose himself and his agenda on the political situation. The reformers had lost control of the *Majlis* in the parliamentary elections of 2004, mainly because the Guardian Council, a largely clerical body tasked with the approval of all election candidates, had disqualified nearly all the leading reformists, including numerous sitting MPs and Khatami's own brother. Part of the reason for this decline in popular support was a loss of faith in Khatami: the gentle student of philosophy had lost out against the hard men of the regime, and his supporters figured that they would need a tougher political fighter in their corner if they were ever to prevail. But it was also indicative of a new trend in which the idea of the religious regime reforming from within had lost currency. Perhaps there could be no compromise between the continued participation of the religious leadership in government and the project of long-term political reform. It was in this context that arguments about the legitimacy or otherwise of the concept of *velayet-e faqih* and its incompatibility with democratic politics began to be heard in Iran with increasing frequency.

The 2005 election: what happened?

The reformists therefore entered the presidential election of 2005 in bad shape. Much of the build up to the election was dominated by the eventually rather tedious and predictable saga of Rafsanjani's candidacy. It had turned out that, unlike the American constitution, the Iranian constitution prohibits a president from serving more than two consecutive terms, but permits him to take office for a third term so long as someone else has been president in between. So would Rafsanjani stand? It was widely believed that he would, but he delayed announcing definitively until very late in the day. Many observers attributed this apparent procrastination to the fact that he wanted to avoid running a prolonged campaign because if he did all kinds of allegations about his and his family's allegedly corrupt acquisition of wealth would eventually surface. In the West there were many analysts who expected Rafsanjani to stand and who imagined that he might represent the best hope for the continuation of the reform agenda. After all, Rafsanjani had appeared to be a cautious reformer of a sort in his previous terms of office, he had created the Servants of Construction, which looked like a techno/democratic move; he had supported the election of Khatami in 1997 and he could prove now, as a wily old-timer, just the ticket for smuggling a reform agenda past the watchful glare of the conservatives. But in reality most Iranians regarded Rafsanjani as a conservative and a fairly unsavoury one at that. Young and more radical supporters of reform viewed him with particular contempt. In their eyes he was neither acceptable nor electable. 'A stick would win against Rafsanjani,' commented one reform-minded Iranian blogger. So, whatever Rafsanjani chose to do, the reformist camp would have to put up its own candidate. An attempt to persuade former leftist prime minister Mir Hussein Mussavi to stand failed (as it had in 1997) and the choice eventually fell on Mustapha Moin. Moin was not a cleric and had served as minister of higher education under Khatami, before resigning in 1999 as a protest against the violent suppression of student political activity by security forces.

Seven candidates were eventually approved. Initially, the Guardian Council refused to accept Moin's nomination but Ayatollah Khamenei intervened to insist that his name go forward. Former *Majlis* speaker, Mehdi Karrubi, another former leftist with reform-ist leanings and a man considered capable of building bridges between the reformists and conservative clerics within the establishment, also stood. Among the conservative candidates the most prominent were Mohsen Qalibaf and Ali Larijani, both of them men in their late forties, Qalibaf a former police chief and Republican Guards general, Larijani a former head of Iranian radio and television and Khamenei's adviser on national security. They represented a new generation of conservatives, as did the relatively unknown mayor of Tehran, Mahmoud Ahmadinejad, who was the third distinctively conservative candidate to contest the first round. One further candidate, a lesser-known reformist called Mohsen Mehralizadeh, also stood, after having initially been excluded, like Moin, by the Guardian Council and reinstated by Khamenei.

From a reformer's point of view, the good news was that there were three conservative candidates who could very well split their natural vote and make way for Moin to enter the second round. Rafsanjani was the front runner and it was assumed almost universally that he would enter the second round, probably as the candidate with the largest vote. This meant that voters in the runoff might face a choice between Rafsanjani (a tarnished not-quite reformer whom nobody liked) and Moin (an untarnished reformer whom nobody knew), but it still looked likely that Rafsanjani would win in the end because he continued to lead in the published opinion polls. However, the situation was compli-cated by the fact that Mehralizadeh and Karrubi (as well as Rafsan-jani) could take votes away from Moin, and by the boycott campaign led by disillusioned reformists who had abandoned any expectations that an election could bring about genuine change. They argued that participation in the election would legitimize a process that was actually not democratic at all. With the reformists split between the boycott and participation, and with the pos-sibility of their initial vote being distributed among three (or even four) candidates in the first round, Moin might not even make the runoff. Instead, the final round might be a straight fight between Rafsanjani and one of the conservatives, most probably Qalibaf who had the strongest opinion poll showing of the three conservatives. In the last few weeks of the campaign Moin seemed to be gaining ground and the reformist camp grew confident that he would win second place, after Rafsanjani, and that they could then concentrate on winning the runoff. If Rafsanjani was really so widely hated that a stick might win against him, then surely Moin had a chance.

The results that came in were a shock. All through the night of 17 June and the following morning there had been feverish speculation all over Tehran. Everyone recognized that opinion polls were very difficult to interpret. It was assumed though that Rafsanjani would be way ahead of the field. Moin had been improving but had apparently not achieved a real breakthrough. As polling was coming to a close, Karrubi seemed to have had access to data suggesting he was in second place. A newspaper published a report that Rafsanjani and one other were through to the second round, but did not name the other. Rumours started to circulate that Ahmadinejad had pulled off a major surprise by coming in third. It started to sound like a disaster for the reformists, with Moin back in fourth place and Rafsanjani facing Karrubi in a runoff. But the results, announced by the Guardian Council rather than, as had been anticipated, the interior ministry, showed Rafsanjani first with 21 per cent, followed astonishingly by Ahmadinejad with 19 per cent. Karrubi had 17 per cent, Moin and Qalibaf each won 14 per cent, Larijani 6 per cent and Mehralizadeh 4 per cent. Both Moin and Karrubi immediately cried foul, alleging fraud and manipulation by the Guardian Council and the Revolutionary Guard. In the second round, held a week later, Ahmadinejad swept to victory by 62 per cent to 36 per cent of the vote. Moin, Karrubi and Mehralizadeh all endorsed Rafsanjani and urged their supporters to vote for him, but clearly many did not. The percentage of votes for the three reformists and Rafsanjani combined in round one was 56 per cent. Over a third of these failed to transfer across to Rafsanjani, despite the reformist leaders' urgings. Rafsanjani had proved the depth of his unpopularity. A stick had won.

Ahmadinejad: how did he win?

No one seemed to have seen him coming. If a conservative was to make the second round, it would have been Qalibaf. But in any case, Rafsanjani was supposed to win. Once again, as in 1997, the Iranian electorate had demonstrated a high degree of volatility and had delivered a shock to the political system. Alternatively, the political system might have delivered a shock to the electorate in the form of a conspiracy to fix the result. Defeated candidate Mustapha Moin seemed to be alleging such a conspiracy in his angry response to the first round result:

> We must take seriously the danger of fascism and the disappearance of the role of the people and the danger of the elimination of republicanism under any name or organization. I warn that moves of this kind have henceforth brought into question not just the structure of free and fair elections but also their soundness. We must believe that this structural deviation is far more harmful than the danger of offences, cheating and problems in elections. I warn that this organized military and supervisory interference in the elections had consequences beyond the violation of the rights of people who voted for me and the likes of me. I declare that this is a threat to the people's choice and free elections, and, even more, a threat to Iran's national interests and to the elevation of the system of the Islamic Republic.[8]

This statement seems to go further than an allegation of fraud or vote rigging: what has happened, he says, is 'more harmful than the danger of offences, cheating and problems in elections'. It is a systemic disorder, a threat to national interests, a 'structural deviation'. It is, in effect, Moin seems to be saying, a *coup d'état*. He will not come straight out and say it, but the implication is hard to avoid. Assume for a moment that the organizers of this putative '*coup d'état*' knew all along what many reformers had repeatedly claimed and what the result of the 24 June runoff decisively showed, namely that Rafsanjani could not win. He had enough support and money to run a campaign that would see him through to a final round, but the core 'we hate Rafsanjani and would rather vote for a stick' constituency constituted an absolute majority of the electorate. If this is the case, the planners of a '*coup d'état*' might reason, what matters is who comes second in the first round because, whoever they are, they will become president.

Conspiracy theories about stolen elections are often hard-luck stories losers tell to make up for missed opportunities. Iran's political structure, with its parallel institutions, is bound to give rise to such theories. After all, when there is a large unaccountable network of individuals and organizations working in the shadows on a daily basis, and with a proven record of undermining and obstructing the work of elected governments, it is far from unreasonable to imagine that they might be meddling in the conduct of elections. All the more so when they have openly done so only months earlier, when the Guardian Council sought to veto the two main reformist candidates. The theory of a much wider conspiracy, hatched among these shadowy institutions, derives its credibility from real instances of interference, even if the theory of total conspiracy remains somewhat fantastical.

But other realities can perhaps explain the Ahmadinejad's surprise victory. In the first place, organized and improvised fraud and intimidation may well have taken place, and may perhaps have been quite extensive. In particular, it seems quite likely that there was a concerted attempt to direct naturally conservative voters towards Ahmadinejad. This looks like a vote-maximization strategy designed to prevent a three-way split in the conservative vote. The reformists will have sought to do something similar to avoid the kind of split in their own vote that would deny Moin a place in the final round. But without the Revolutionary Guards to implement such a strategy, the reformists will have been at a distinct disadvantage. Taking account of the possibility of a marginal but by no means negligible intervention of this kind, the underlying electoral arithmetic, when examined for a moment or two, makes Ahmadinejad's victory a great deal less improbable than at first it seems, particularly when the depth of Rafsanjani's unpopularity is taken into account. The three broadly pro-reform candidates gathered between them 35 per cent of the vote in round one; the three broadly conservative candidates won 39 per cent of the same vote. It is therefore far from surprising that one of the three conservatives should have gone through to the second round. The reformist percentage in round one includes Karrubi's vote, much of which did not transfer to Rafsanjani in round two despite reformist urgings that they should do so, probably because many of those who voted for Karrubi were not committed supporters of reform. The 2004 *Majlis* elections had suggested that the core reformist vote was more like 25 per cent than 35 per cent.

It is easy enough to understand why this might be the case. In the first place, the reformists had been in power (or something that at least looked like power) for eight years. And for most Iranians, particularly those outside the major cities where the social and cultural liberalizations enjoyed by some of the Tehrani middle classes, for example, will not have taken place, the impact of the reformist agenda on their daily lives will have been very limited and in some cases even negative. Part of the response to the reformist agenda seems to have been a traditionalist backlash against what many conservative Iranians may have viewed as the introduction of alien and inappropriate values and behaviours. The idea of a corrupt and decadent reformist cosmopolitanism infecting the purity of the republic is a classic popular reaction to the promotion of liberal values. So there is clearly a constituency out there in Iran ready to respond positively to someone presenting himself as the polar opposite of the liberal, cosmopolitan reformer, especially if that person, like Ahmadinejad, offers an image distinctly different from that presented by the familiar elderly mullah. That the conservatives were able so effectively to mobilize this vote on behalf of a single candidate is also due in part to the long-term failure on the part of the reformists to build a mass political constituency of their own.

It is this more than anything else that looks like the most vital lesson to be learnt from the presidential election of 2005. The reformists did far too little to consolidate the mass popular support with which Khatami secured his first landslide victory in 1997. Not only did they fail to reach out to ordinary people, lingering for too long in the rarefied air of policy debate and philosophical thought, they proved incapable of even protecting their own. They failed to prevent militant gangs terrorizing students on the university campuses of Tehran and other cities in 1999. They failed to prevent politically motivated court cases brought against prominent pro-reform politicians like Abdullah Nuri and Gholamhossein Karbaschi. They were powerless to prevent a series of assassinations of journalists and intellectuals associated with reform. They did little to resist the systematic attacks on the press and media, thus abandoning the defence of the very political space they were committed to expanding and using as the basis for promoting their own agenda. Of course, they faced powerful opponents in the parallel institutions, opponents who were not afraid to demonstrate their ruthlessness in mobilizing violence and intimidation. But, in the final analysis, they failed. In a sharp and critical analysis of this failure – essentially a failure to fight back effectively against an assault launched from within the parallel institutions – Mehrdad Mashayekhi identifies six related failures, among which one, in particular, seems to have the broadest and most profound ramifications, not simply in Iran, but for supporters of democracy across the region:

> The reformist movement's relation to the popular forces was elitist and instrumentalist. While the leadership was capable of mobilizing millions on election-day, it refrained from more permanent types of political mobilization (political parties or social movements). Thus the Islamic Participation Front (IPF), the largest reformist grouping in Iran, now reportedly has only a few hundred members. In their reliance on negotiations 'from above' and bypassing grassroots, the reformists increasingly distanced themselves from the 20 million people who enthusiastically supported them in 1997.[9]

Reading Habermas in Tehran

This brings us to a crucial issue facing democratic politicians across the region, the problem of political space. Where and how do people gather to talk, plan and collaborate in ways that might bring about social and political change? Among Iran's leading intellectuals like the philosopher Abdol-Karim Soroush and the reformist theologian Mohsen Kadivar, the name of the contemporary German philosopher Jürgen Habermas is frequently invoked (along with other Western champions of the principles of liberalism, Richard Rorty and Karl Popper). One of Habermas's most influential contributions to social and political thought has been his theorization of what he called 'the public sphere'. In his now famous early work, *The Structural Transformation of the Bourgeois Public Sphere*,[10] Habermas gives a detailed historical account of how the middle classes of Europe managed to create, in tacit opposition to the monopoly of public space enjoyed by the rulers of the *ancien régime*, a series of public spaces, and within them, modes of public discourse, that were gradually to lead to liberal democracy not just as an ideological position but as an underlying way of life. From the coffee house, the gentleman's club, the scientific association and the literary salon grew the reform campaign, the political party, the parliamentary coalition and the establishment of democratic government as a normative experience. The emphasis Habermas places on the seemingly trivial and non-political origins of this kind of sociality almost certainly springs from his own immediate historical situation, growing up in the aftermath of the Second World War and contemplating the destruction wrought upon Europe by Nazi tyranny. The ideas of Habermas, who has spoken publicly in Iran at the invitation of pro-reform intellectuals, offer a valuable way of thinking about social and cultural activities that might be the necessary preconditions of an enduring democratic politics. Without them, suggests Habermas, it is all too easy for authoritarian governments to maintain an effective monopoly of public space – literally they control access to public buildings and police the streets; and metaphorically they set the terms of political debate and prohibit alternative voices.

The evidence of Iranian attempts to create new public spaces has recently led to two successful publications outside Iran – the collection of texts and images from the Iranian 'blogosphere', *We Are Iran*, and Azar Nafisi's moving memoir, *Reading Lolita in*

Tehran.[11] Both tell of personal efforts to bring people together in spite of and often in direct conflict with the regime's own efforts to keep people apart by maintaining its own control of public space, both actual and virtual, real and discursive. Both the reading group of female students run by Nafisi at her Tehran home and the proliferation of Iranian blogs, in Persian and in English over the last three years are evidence of the potency of this kind of public communication, even where the publics in question are relatively modest in scale. Reading foreign literature is a minority pursuit worldwide, not just in Iran, and internet access, especially of the permanent kind that would permit sustained blogging, remains out of reach of the vast majority of Iranians. Even so, the act of reading Habermas in Tehran would be one way of opening up the Iranian experience into a wider consideration of what might be necessary, in the Middle East more widely, in order for a democratic politics to take root and flourish in native soil. As we have already seen, there are ample supplies of fertilizer for such culture in Iran. The disputatious culture of Shia scholarship, its inventiveness and engagement with new ideas, has nurtured not only the authoritarian militancy that produced *velayet-e faqih*, but also underpins the questioning, sceptical and erudite scholarship of the regime's intellectual critics, men like Soroush and Kadivar. The point of reading Habermas in Tehran is that reading philosophy is not enough. As Habermas's great predecessor in German political philosophy, Karl Marx famously said, 'Philsophers have only interpreted the world. The point is to change it.'[12] Reading Habermas is only a good idea if you are subsequently able and willing to do something about creating, sustaining and extending the public sphere. In Iran, and in much of the Middle East, the first problem you will encounter in trying to do just that will be that the public sphere, as currently in operation, looks like and sounds like a mosque.

Learning from Iran

This is the first of five issues that emerge from the Iranian situation and that might, with care and consideration for cultural diversity, usefully be applied to other situations in the region. After the problem of the mosque come the intimately related issues of political parties, coalitions, the religious–secular split and the ownership of and access to mass media.

It is no accident that the political movements that have enjoyed recent electoral successes in the region (the Muslim Brotherhood in Egypt, the Shia coalition in Iraq, Hamas in Palestine) have organized, recruited, discussed and planned their political campaigns in a public space the government cannot close down – the mosque. The mosque is so much more than just a place of prayer: it is at the centre of networks of social support; it is a place of education, an advice bureau, even an employment agency. It is where men gather to talk, and where their talk is legitimated and protected from the eyes and ears of the authorities (not always but often). Across the region governments are fearful of the mosque for this reason, but have limited powers to control it. But at least, reason the guardians of national security, we can make sure that we restrict this kind of seditious talk and activity to the mosque. This is a terrible mistake, even from the perspective of a guardian of national security, let alone for an advocate of gradual and peaceful political change. What it guarantees is that everyone who wants to take collective social and political action to improve their lives and the lives of their fellow citizens eventually gravitates towards the mosque, with the inevitable consequence that the only political movements that emerge with a viable popular reform programme are those based around the mosque.

The refusal to permit the opening up of public space outside the mosque is one of the most significant contributions regional governments have made to the growth of Islamist political movements. Let public spaces proliferate, let citizens believe, and believe correctly, that they can gather where they like – in Starbucks if need be – and talk politics, form groups, publish newsletters, initiate campaigns, lobby, argue, canvass and plot – and alternative politics, perhaps more congenial even to the guardians of national security, are much more likely to emerge. To many in the region, and in Europe for that matter, Starbucks looks

like just one of the latest instances of the spread of American cultural and economic power. It may be better to look at it as a much
delayed reciprocation of an ancient gift. For it was the Islamic world
that made the West the gift of the coffee house, the very place in
which Habermas's public sphere had its origins, when European
visitors to Istanbul brought a strange new and sociable stimulant
back to the capital cities of the *ancien régime*.[13] So, issue number
one: reclaim Starbucks and break the monopoly of the mosque and,
in the particular case of Iran, try to convert a long tradition of
enlightened scholarly debate into a wider culture of political
openness.

If Mehrdad Mashayekhi is right, and the pro-reform Islamic
Participation Front in Iran numbered only a few hundred people
by the time of the 2005 election, then it represents a particularly
striking example of a more widespread problem: the tendency
across the region for democratic political parties to take the form of
small elite groups. The problems associated with the formation of
political parties in the Middle East are considerable and complex.
One of them is the personalization of political life, which encourages short-term formations around powerful or charismatic
individuals, often perpetuating networks of clientelism and patronage as their only way of reaching out beyond the core group.
Another is the formation of groups around very narrow sets of
ideological and political interests or aspirations, often abstractly
intellectual in form and quite often Western in origin (this is a
phenomenon readily observed in leftist and Marxist groups across
the region, though factionalism on the far left is a more or less
universal phenomenon). Such groups, even when they form parties
and compete in national politics, also have a strong tendency to
talk to themselves rather than address themselves outwards. This is
intimately related to the problem of public space. The absence of
non-religious public space makes the task of building a mass
participation political or social movement very difficult, while
when you have the mosque at your disposal, this is really very easy
because the space comes ready made. Taken together, these problems with political parties, both in Iran and in the region more

widely, lead to a third crucial lesson that democrats across the region will be reflecting upon – the imperative of building coalitions.

Coalition building involves recognizing that the initial group, possessed and animated by a specific vision, often as articulated by one or two appealing individuals capable of building a group of close allies, is not ultimately enough. Limited coteries of like-minded political idealists need a broader movement within which to promote and develop their ideas into political action. Although it is exciting and personally fulfilling to sit together in seminar rooms or living rooms or even coffee houses and find oneself in thrilling accord with friends and colleagues who share exactly your reading habits, intellectual tastes and political values, the real political task is to move beyond that zone of comfort and engage in the daily labour of promoting the adoption of at least some of your ideas within a wider community. American neo-conservatives, for example, needed the wider community, not to mention the formidable institutional machinery of the Republican Party, to be able to turn their ideals into political action. A political party like the Republican Party is in fact a coalition. Probably all the major successful political parties in the West are coalitions in which people with widely diverging views and values on a range of issues can come together around a broadly defined set of common objectives. The British Labour Party was formed and developed as a coalition between inheritors of a liberal and non-conformist tradition, urban socialist intellectuals, and organized labour in the form of the trade union movement. Its more recent success under Tony Blair has been founded upon the ability to forge a new coalition, between what is left of the now largely post-unionized working class, an aspirant middle class in search of security and prosperity, urban professionals, and young people of the post baby-boom generation. More pertinently, perhaps, in the Middle East context, Kadima in Israel, if it survives the departure of its founder Ariel Sharon, is pure coalition, while both Hamas and the Muslim Brotherhood actually represent electoral alliances whose members and activists span a broad swathe of political opinion. Ideological purity and warm intellectual fellow feeling will get you only so far in practical politics. Building a viable coalition requires a major effort of persuasion. The experience of building a coalition by means of persuasion, by preaching to the unconverted, is a vital experience for any party that wants to secure the long-term support of an electoral constituency: the arts of persuasion in each case are effectively the same.

There's a religious–secular debate in Iran among the reformers. The failure of Khatami, the liberal face of religious politics, has led many to conclude that it is the sheer fact of religion in politics that constitutes the problem. It has strengthened the conviction that the key issue in Iranian politics is the removal of religion altogether from the political sphere, articulated in some quarters, not all of them strictly secular, as a separation of religion from the state. Given the miserable record of government by clerics in Iran, it is not surprising that this issue is felt so keenly here. Others, like, for example, Mohsen Kadivar, focus instead on the principle of *velayet-e faqih*, arguing that while this is clearly incompatible now with democratic politics and should be abolished, there is no inherent incompatibility between Islam and democracy. If coalition building is to be a priority these long-term issues of the relationship between religion and politics will probably have to be set aside. Secular and religiously-minded reformers will need to work together. This is a lesson for Khatami and his associates – who perhaps did not do enough to embrace their secularist colleagues – and for the secularists themselves – who may have to grit their teeth and face the fact that, for the time being, religion is going to play a major role in Iranian public life. If a coalition between such forces is to succeed, it seems most unlikely that it will do so by adopting a stance in which the issue of secularism versus religion remains live. The issue itself needs to be removed from the field. It needs to become a 'final status' issue. Politics across the region can often look as though they are polarized on a secularist–Islamist axis, and many institutional structures and habits of minds (in both groups) contribute to the perpetuation of this schism, as does much analysis emanating from the West.

But it may be neither necessary nor useful to maintain this

polarization, or even the axis on which it arranges itself. If the crucial political task ahead is to build broad-based and lasting coalitions around specific policy ideas and programmes for action, there is no reason to limit contributions to this task to either secularists or religious movements. A coalition that is prepared to embrace both and to reject the split might be more viable. The Turkish social and political movement that Recep Teyyip Erdogan put together under the banner of Justice and Development may turn out to be the start of such politics in the region. Although Justice and Development is still regarded, in both Turkey and beyond, as the acceptable face of Islamism, it also draws support from well beyond the community of the devout; it still wears religious clothes, but it is beginning to operate across the religious– secular divide. It is notable that groups that began as religious in orientation seem to find it easier to do this than those that began from a secular foundation. Many of the region's secularists are proving less flexible and pragmatic than the so-called Islamists (who some secularists accuse of tactical dissimulation). Democracy in the region may, however, depend on them changing the habits of a lifetime. Their supporters in the West might do well to stop seeing them and encouraging them to see themselves as the defenders of liberal secularism against the rising tide of Islamism.

One of the defeated candidates at the presidential election, Mehdi Karrubi, launched an unusual initiative at the end of 2005 – a satellite TV station. This is an expanding and increasingly important field in the region.[14] The politics and economics of globalization, as well as technological advances, are altering the regional mediascape. The internet is part of it and its potential political significance is nowhere more vividly illustrated than in the close attention the governments of the region pay to blogs and other sites of debate and discussion online. Iran has been no exception in this regard, with sites blocked, bloggers detained and lurid fantasies circulated about a 'spider's web' of internet subversion operated by the CIA making use of Iranian dissident bloggers both inside and outside the country.[15] But as Hossein Derakhshan, incongruously dubbed 'godfather of the Iranian blogosphere' by the

Los Angeles Times,[16] points out, blogs are a limited form of communication. His critique of the reformists for their failure to use mass media echoes Mashayekhi's arguments about their wider failure to engage a broad constituency:

> The reform movement can't reach beyond a certain population. They only have newspapers and Internet, with an approximate reach of five to seven millions. While the regime has a monopoly on TV and radio, the reformists can't even reach the majority of the middle class, especially the youth, who are not into reading anymore, let alone the lower-class in rural areas. On the other hand, satellite TVs which has a much wider reach than print and Internet, are promoting exactly the opposite message of the reform, which has proved it only benefits the regime, especially during the elections, by creating an atmosphere of apathy. Until the reformists change this balance, they are doomed to loose [sic] the elections. They have to invest time and money in satellite TV channels etc. and try to decrease the widespread apathy, especially among the youth.[17]

Other opponents of the regime recognized the potency of satellite television, as Derakhshan noted in 2004, in the context of a discussion about why so many Iranians viewed President Bush so favourably:

> A dozen of LA-based satellite TV channels are still widely available in almost every house in both rural or urban areas. They are mostly founded and run by pro-monarchy Iranians who left Iran after the revolution and have been totally disconnected from the reality of today's Iran. Almost all of those that have political content – many have no talk shows or news programs – strongly support Bush and promote the idea that should Bush be re-elected he would bring down the Islamic regime and 'liberate it'. It's obviously a catching idea among less-educated and the youth who have a hard time dealing with the regime's strict control over their social lives.[18]

Karrubi's attempt to set up a satellite TV station looks like a response to precisely this problem. He is moving tentatively, however. His initial plan had been to broadcast Saba TV from Dubai, but when his representative arrived in Dubai, with the tapes of the first broadcast with him ready to go on air, Iranian officials intercepted him and, following some kind of behind-the-scenes compromise involving Karrubi himself, the planned launch was postponed. This postponement appears to have become a ban, though it is unclear how far the Iranian government can go to enforce it. The channel's production manager, Behrouz Afkhami, a film director and former member of the *Majlis*, challenged Ali Larijani (Khamenei's security adviser and failed conservative presidential candidate) to explain what right he had to control all broadcasting in Persian, inside and outside the country. Since it is thought that Iranian viewers are currently receiving more than 20 Persian-language opposition channels illegally, it seems unlikely that the regime could long hold out against an opposition determined to resist threats and inducements. Obviously, this is much more difficult in practice for an internal opposition group than it is for exiles more or less comfortably resident in California. In this context, Dubai becomes an interesting political location, especially for Iranians, many of whom have settled there over the centuries, and which is now, with its economics-driven investment in Dubai Media City, perhaps offering the kind of freedoms for regional politicians and intellectuals that Beirut once offered as the publishing capital of the region. A satellite station that allowed a domestic rather than an exiled opposition to speak directly to the Iranian viewer/citizen would clearly represent a much greater threat to the regime than the LA-based stations, the blogs and the intellectuals with their philosophy books (even though each of these makes its distinctive contribution). The key point is that it would radically transform the virtual public sphere, laying foundations for a new political mobilization, for participation politics and coalition building.

Some of the key themes of this book emerge directly from the Iranian experience. The Iranian experience is unique, but it is also instructive. We have already commented on the importance of thinking specifically about the social, political and cultural conditions of each individual country before pronouncing on how best democratic politics might be conducted there, and the same caution needs to be exercised here: just because Iran is closer, and perhaps more like, the other countries in the region than Washington is, that is no reason to assume automatically that what works in Iran will work in Egypt or Kuwait. However, as future chapters will show, some of the lessons of the Iranian experience, translated from their native Persian into the various Arabics of the region, may prove to be viable exports.

Three lessons in particular may bear constant repetition and will echo through the chapters to follow. Broad coalitions rather than narrow factions are the more likely agents of change. Secular and religious groups and individuals have more to gain from working together than they have from perpetuating the idea of a secular–religious struggle for ascendancy. Access to and effective use of mass media that are opening up spaces for debate will be a crucial site for the negotiation of change and the development of a new politics in the region.

Chapter 3

Palestine: Democracy under Occupation

T he last major election to be held during the period in which this book was written was perhaps the most significant.[1] It certainly had one of the most surprising results and generated the greatest media attention. This was because the elections on 25 January 2006 for Palestine's Legislative Council were won by an electoral list called Change and Reform, and because that list effectively represented Hamas. Change and Reform won 74 seats in the 132-member parliament, which gave it an overall majority and the right to form a government. The prime minister, Ahmed Qurei, and his government resigned at once. Hamas formed a government, nominating Ismail Haniya as prime minister on 16 February, and has sought to govern despite intense financial difficulties, exacerbated by US-led efforts to deny financial assistance.

The Hamas victory has focused global attention on one of the major themes of this book, confronting policy makers in the West with the uncomfortable fact that the politics of change in the Middle East may be led by people and movements the West views with suspicion or even hostility. If President Mubarak's refusal to engage constructively with the Muslim Brotherhood prevents change in Egypt, and American efforts to isolate Iran are an impediment to continued political innovation there, the question of how the West will respond, in the medium term, to Hamas's success, may determine the extent to which the West may be able to play a constructive role in regional political change. If the West simply rejects Hamas and refuses to recognize that it represents a politically significant element in regional politics, then it will find it increasingly difficult to exercise any positive influence on political change. If, however, Western policy makers are prepared to make the effort needed to see Hamas as it is – as more than an expression of militant Islamism – then the West can hope to keep a stake in the process.

Hamas's victory exceeded expectations. It was widely known that the ruling party, Fatah, which had enjoyed a majority in the Legislative Council since 1996, had become deeply unpopular. The peace process, to which it had nailed its colours, had failed to deliver further gains to the Palestinians since 1996, the economy was in ruins and the post-Arafat government was deeply tainted by allegations of corruption. Hamas, by contrast, had continued to oppose the peace process, had made significant gains at local level, winning popular support through the provision of welfare services and projecting an image of honesty and integrity. Opinion polls (and the results of local elections) had suggested that Hamas would do very well at legislative elections, perhaps winning as much as 40 per cent of the vote. Most polls, however, continued to suggest that Fatah, despite suffering a major setback, would still win, although it would be deprived of a majority.

During 2005 Hamas leaders had repeatedly alleged that Fatah leader and Palestinian president Mahmoud Abbas was afraid to call elections because he knew that Hamas would make significant gains at the expense of Fatah. No one, however, quite expected the scale of the Hamas victory. Talk in the months leading up to the election had focused on how many seats Hamas might win, and whether or not Hamas might be prepared to take ministerial positions in a Fatah-led government, in recognition of the support it had gained. Conversations in the summer of 2005 with senior Hamas leaders, including the now imprisoned West Bank spokesman for Hamas, Sheikh Hasan Yousef, who featured prominently on the Change and Reform list, suggested that the movement (for it is not a political party) remained uncertain about how to handle such questions. 'We will be clever about how much we want to participate,' he said, 'We do not propose ourselves as a political alternative. We will wait to see what the people want.'[2] His Hamas colleague, Ramallah medical equipment supplier Ziad Dayyeh, regarded as one of the ideologists of the movement, and an elected local councillor for El Bireh, hints at a reason for this reluctance on the part of Hamas to commit itself too far to the present political institutions: 'Some people in Hamas are wary of risking being seen as corrupt like the others,'[3] he said, implying that there is such widespread popular revulsion at political corruption that anyone who takes a political post is liable to be tarred instantly with the same brush as the current crop of crooks and thieves. Hamas then seems to have been surprised by the scale of its victory, apparently unprepared for the possibility that Fatah would simply be defeated, give up its right to govern and leave the field open for Hamas to take power. Hamas leaders would have to confront the question of what to do about government rather sooner than they had anticipated.

All of a sudden Hamas has been catapulted from the relative security of opposition and local government into a global spotlight. Since January 2006 much of the attention given to Hamas under this spotlight has centred on the questions of whether or not Hamas will recognize Israel, and whether the international donor community, particularly the United States, will continue to contribute financially to the Palestinian Authority once it is led by a government that includes members of Hamas, formally designated as a terrorist organization. Less attention has been paid to the implications of the Hamas victory for the broader question of political change in the Middle East. Some commentators were swift to jump on this result and portray it as a hilarious boomerang in the face of the American president and his plans for promoting democracy in the Middle East. 'How do you like it now, Mr President?' was the tone of much of this comment.

Scott Carpenter, deputy assistant secretary of state and the man responsible for the administration's Middle East Partnership Initiative (MEPI), which distributes US funding to democracy projects in the region, was far from dismayed, however, just a week after the election. He agrees that the election is of enormous significance simply because it shows that a democratic election in the region can allow the people to vote out a lousy government, and that, as far as he is concerned, is democratic. He also reports that everything he has heard from observers confirms that this has been one of the freest and fairest elections they have seen, a claim that Fiona Shukri, just back from witnessing the election, corroborated at the National Democratic Institute. Carpenter, whose current mission partly entails supplying training to nascent democratic movements, expresses ready admiration for the organizational capabilities of the Hamas election machine. He recounts a story of how Hamas drove supporters to polling stations and meticulously inspected registers to make sure that everyone entitled to vote could do so, even if their names turned out to be misspelt. 'I'd like to know where they got their training.' For a moment the possibility that the State Department might actually hire Hamas on a consultancy basis under the MEPI programme drifts into view. Carpenter is open to optimistic versions of the Palestinian future under a Hamas government, keen to point out that both the president and Condoleezza Rice have been very measured in their responses. He is also very clear, though, that the United States government is under a legal obligation not to fund designated terrorist organizations and that this will present a real difficulty. Part of the difficulty is probably that the US administration would prefer to be funding Hamas (and keeping an eye on it) than making the movement dependent on other, particularly Iranian, sources of finance.[4]

Hamas, it should be recalled, did not campaign on a manifesto that called for the destruction of the State of Israel (although this remains an element in the movement's charter). Hamas leaders have consistently indicated that they are willing to observe a more or less indefinite 'calm' as regards Israel and they have implicitly accepted that a two-state solution might be acceptable. The issues of recognizing Israel and renouncing the armed struggle, which were the preconditions Israel set for negotiating with the Palestinians, will still be hard to grapple with. While they are clearly of cardinal importance for Israel–Palestine relations, they fall outside the remit of this chapter, which is to explore the implications of the Hamas victory – or, rather the Change and Reform victory – for the wider region and its prospects for change. In this context the victory for Change and Reform is significant because it represents a unique instance of regime change by ballot box in the Arab Middle East; because it creates a situation in which a so-called Islamist movement will be seriously, if not severely, tested by the task of government; and because Palestine is central to any consideration of the prospects for negotiated change in the region.

Palestine
The problem of Palestine is one of the most serious obstacles to the development of democratic political life in the Middle East. It is often because of Palestine that American calls for democracy generate hostility rather than enthusiasm. Democracy, after all, is a matter of political self-determination and respect for the rule of law. These are not easy values to promote while you are at the same time lending moral, political, financial and military support to an illegal military occupation. To insist on self-determination as an absolute value (democracy) while denying self-determination to a whole people (the Palestinians) is widely regarded in the region as either a profound self-contradiction or the most naked hypocrisy. Either way, it is a poor advertisement for democracy. If this is how democrats behave then what possible moral or political value is there to be found in democracy? Democracy starts to look like a euphemism for doing what America says.

For democrats in the region this is a calamity, and hands a massive political advantage to their opponents, for there are not many people left in the region who really want to do what America wants. American support for Israel's illegal occupation of Palestine is a millstone round the neck of the advocates of democracy in the Arab world. The weight of the millstone is felt most acutely in Palestine where, perhaps paradoxically, the movement for a genuinely democratic politics is one of the strongest in the Arab world. This means that long-term success for the democratic movements in Palestine would be of enormous political significance throughout the region. However, such success is most unlikely until and unless the Israeli occupation comes to an end. In this respect America's continued and apparently unconditional support for Israel (routinely hailed in the United States as the only democracy in the region) actively blocks the emergence of the next most likely democracy – Palestine.

How is it that Palestine – a country that does not even officially exist and whose people are ultimately under the authority of an occupying power – has some of the most democratic politics in the region? A range of explanations are traditionally offered for this. There is a significant urban middle class, which historians of democracy often identify as the basic constituency necessary for the development of democracy. Palestinians are highly educated, which is another important factor according to historians, even though many of the doctors, lawyers, writers and technocrats in fact live and work in the diaspora. They are unusually cosmopolitan, even by Arab standards, and have therefore had ample opportunity to sample the best and worst of other political systems, democratic and non-democratic. Many Palestinians also point to a long but largely unacknowledged history of local democratic politics, under Ottoman and British rule, as providing a social basis for participation and consultation.[5] As in other parts of the Arab world, the practice of *shura* is part of the culture.

One other factor, again perhaps a paradox of a kind, is that for nearly the whole period in which the modern Palestinian nation has been taking shape there has been no such thing as a Palestinian state. This bears a little thinking about. A succession of colonizing powers, starting with the Ottomans, followed by the British and ending up with the Israelis, each of them distinctive in their own way, have shared, through much of the twentieth century, a common basic attitude towards the Palestinians: 'We really wish they didn't exist and so we may as well just let them get on with it and hope they go away.' Although the Israelis, through their direct occupation since 1967, have had to engage more actively than the Ottomans or British did in controlling the Palestinian population in the Occupied Territories, they have never shown much inclination to intervene in what we might call the Palestinians' internal or domestic political arrangements (apart from the myriad ways in which military occupation interferes with and even prohibits such arrangements). While the Palestinians have suffered an occupation that has drastically constrained their personal and social freedom and their prospects for economic and human development, they may also be said to have enjoyed (if that is the right word) a certain lack of government. With a self-appointed political leadership operating in exile (Amman, Beirut, Tunis) for much of its lifetime, the Palestinians in Palestine have been left to get on with it in ways that would be unimaginable in say Egypt or Syria, where the government traditionally seeks to intervene at every level of social and economic life.

The present state of democratic politics in Palestine clearly owes much to this rather odd history, in which, more or less by accident, Palestinian people have got used to doing things for themselves. A more recent factor is the peace process. The political institutions within which the struggle for Palestinian democracy is being waged are the direct result of the peace process. This has proved to be a mixed blessing. On the one hand, the Oslo accords (of 1993 and 1995) established a legal framework for democratic political institutions. But on the other hand, these institutions were compromised at birth by the fact that Israel and the United States played such a major role in their conception. This has proved compromising on two counts: first, the Palestinian groups that opposed the Oslo accords initially decided they wanted nothing to do with these new 'democratic' institutions; and second, the institutional framework has been vulnerable to manipulation by Israel and the United States, both of which have been ambivalent at best about the actual practice of democracy by the Palestinians.

The institutions the Oslo accords created are therefore far from ideal; they are tarnished by association with a widely discredited process and subject to all kinds of external (and internal) disruption. However, they are the institutions that exist and they are better in many respects than comparable ones elsewhere in the region. They create a genuine framework within which a democratic culture can continue to develop, and the Palestinians have already struggled hard to improve and strengthen them, often in the face of violent attempts to undermine or destroy them altogether. They also offer an interesting test case for the relationship between the kinds of democratic institutions that can be imposed from outside and the kinds of democratic practices that develop on the ground.

As we shall see however, the best hope for democracy in Palestine today may well rest with those who rejected outright the democratic structures bequeathed to them by the deal done between the exiled leadership and the occupying power. In many respects, the defeat of Fatah at the legislative elections of 25 January 2005 represented a definitive and democratic rejection of an untenable deal concluded by an unaccountable regime. One reason the deal was untenable was because the regime that did it was unaccountable. Now that regime has been called to account, and a new government, with a strong democratic mandate, will have to decide how to live within the structures bequeathed by that deal, structures that have unexpectedly delivered power into its hands. It may also have to decide how to work out an alternative deal. Although the prospect of such a new deal might seem remote at the beginning of 2006, it is worth bearing in mind that any deal done with Hamas, with its record and its mandate, is far more likely to stick than a deal done by an unelected exile leadership behind the backs of its own negotiating team. Thus, the question of the occupation, and how to resist it now it is in government, will always hover above the Hamas leadership (and the rest of this chapter), even as they try to focus on other issues, like the everyday problems of living in Palestine under occupation.

Who are Hamas?
Yamama Shalaldeh is a recently elected member of the municipal council in the Palestinian village of Sair, near Hebron. She is 25 years old and is, in many ways, typical of educated Arab women of her generation – frank, direct, ambitious. She is dressed trendily in

a blue and red denim tracksuit and wears a dark patterned scarf wrapped around her hair, in keeping with social custom but doing nothing to cover her individuality. She is clearly completely at ease with the experience of defying conventional expectations. Sair is a socially conservative town and when word got out that she was thinking of going to university in Cyprus to study architecture, there was, she says, much disapproving talk around town: Yamama would never be the same again; she would come back wearing mini skirts. She staunchly resisted pressure not to go and, while she was in Cyprus, she had what she describes as a sort of revelatory experience. She found a shrine dedicated to a Muslim woman, a woman who had, it seems, been one of the companions of the Prophet Mohammed. That a woman had clearly played a key role in the early days of Islam and that she had travelled independently to Cyprus suddenly made Yamama intensely aware that present-day values and social traditions were distorting the true role of women in Muslim society. She offers this as a partial explanation for her decision to stand for election to the municipal council. She wanted to start working to correct and counteract the stereotypes of Muslim women, in her own society as much as in the West, and to show that a Muslim woman such as herself has equal rights in and responsibilities towards the well-being of her community. As part of her preparation for the election campaign she researched widely on the past involvement of women in the politics and governance of Muslim societies, so that she would be able to answer questions with authority and confidence, and help potential voters in the town overcome their own social conservatism and recognize what she might have to offer them as their elected representative.[6]

Yamama Shalaldeh is just one among no doubt thousands of progressive, committed Palestinian women, active in social and political life, who could, if only the occupation were to come to an end, play a truly historic role in the development of democracy in the Arab world. Indeed, she is precisely the kind of figure that Western supporters of democracy in the region fervently want to see emerging. She is pragmatic, open-minded and talks persuasively about the urgent need for transparency, accountability and good governance. She avoids sloganeering and focuses her conversation on day-to-day practicalities like how to get council employees to come to work on time, how best to collect water and electricity fees, how to improve services and how best to use the web to communicate with the townspeople she serves. If there is anyone who looks like they represent the new generation in Palestinian politics, it is Yamama Shalaldeh. Although she is not a member, Yamama Shalaldeh was happy to stand for election on a list presented by Hamas.

Hamas is a significant social and political movement, with deep roots in Palestinian culture and legitimate aspirations to social and political leadership. As the results of January's elections show, it enjoys substantial grass-roots support among Palestinians in the West Bank and Gaza, has proved to be an effective and democratic force on the ground, and has acted responsibly and capably in local government. Its success also owed much to the contempt in which many ordinary Palestinians held Fatah, and some have gone so far as to dismiss Hamas's support as a 'protest vote'. Like similar claims about the Muslim Brotherhood in Egypt, this line of argument feels a little desperate, as though throwing out a government were 'merely' protest. The similarity with the Muslim Brotherhood does not, however, end there.

Ziad Dayyeh explains this aspect of Hamas's history and emphasizes that the resistance to occupation is almost a temporary diversion from the movement's real work. Hamas's emergence as a social and political force is not a novelty. The kind of work Yamama Shalaldeh describes in Sair is entirely consistent with what Hamas has always stood for. Although its formation as the Islamic Resistance Movement dates from the first few days of the first *intifada* in 1987, it is in fact an incarnation of the Muslim Brotherhood. As the Muslim Brotherhood in Palestine, established in 1943, it fought alongside leftist and nationalist forces in the war of 1948. Members of the Muslim Brotherhood were among the founders of Fatah in 1958–59, but by 1960 the mainstream of the Muslim Brotherhood had consolidated its position outside Fatah. While

Fatah began to develop a strategy of armed resistance to Israeli occupation, the Muslim Brotherhood chose not to follow this path. Khaled Hroub, the most authoritative historian of Hamas, notes that this was the point at which 'the Brotherhood withdrew from the political-national effort to liberate the homeland'.[7]

Hamas's origins thus lie with those who initially rejected the armed struggle in favour of grass-roots social, educational and religious activity. After the defeat of 1948, the Muslim Brotherhood in Gaza fell under Egyptian influence while the Brotherhood on the West Bank became integrated into Jordanian society and politics. In Jordan, the Palestinian Muslim Brotherhood took part in parliamentary elections and, after electoral victories in 1954, 1956 and 1962, won seats representing Hebron and Nablus. The Palestinian Muslim Brotherhood came to be accepted in Jordan as part of the 'loyal opposition': while other political parties, notably those of the left, were illegal and operated underground, the conservative social and political values of the Muslim Brotherhood meant that neither the king nor his governments viewed them as a political threat. So, the Muslim Brotherhood in Palestine, which currently takes the form of Hamas, is a socially and politically conservative organization that for more than 30 years refrained from participating in the struggle for national liberation, was acceptable to a conservative monarchy in Jordan, and concentrated on providing social services and religious education.

The movement's trajectory towards resistance had its origins in the situation in Gaza in the late 1970s. In 1978 the movement's main institutional structure, the Mujamma al-Islamiya (Islamic Centre), registered with the Israeli authorities as a charitable society not despite but because the Israeli government knew it harboured aspirations of a social and political nature. At first, Islamists associated with the Mujamma (who included future Hamas leaders like Abd al-Aziz al-Rantisi, Mahmoud Zahar and Sheikh Yassin) were seen as a useful counter to the then dominant leftist and nationalist forces that dominated political life in Gaza. With funding to build mosques flowing in from Israel, Saudi Arabia and Kuwait, the Mujamma gradually established a strong social base in the communities of Gaza, and started to encourage its supporters to engage actively in professional associations (for lawyers, doctors and engineers) where they competed with the Palestine Liberation Organization (PLO) and other leftist organizations. The Mujamma then built further social support by calling strikes in protest at aspects of Israeli rule. It also secured control of both the management and the student union of the Islamic University of Gaza. The similarity between this strategy of mobilization in Gaza and the strategy pursued by the Muslim Brotherhood in Egypt (which won control of professional associations in the 1980s) is far from coincidental. They are, after all, the same movement. A similar strategy was developing in the West Bank, where activism in the universities, in particular, brought the predecessors of Hamas into direct political confrontation with Fatah and the left-wing nationalists. Once again, the fact that the Brotherhood seemed to be focusing on an internal struggle with the Palestinian nationalist mainstream and the left encouraged Israel to adopt a relaxed and supportive attitude towards it.

But, by the time the *intifada* erupted in 1987, the social and political activism developed from the Mujamma had penetrated deep into Palestinian society. With the PLO uncertain about how to respond to a popular uprising, the future Hamas leaders were among those in the community able to play a role in guiding the movement politically. Even so, the formation of Hamas in February 1988 did not concern the Israeli authorities unduly, for they still regarded the Islamists of the Mujamma as potential interlocutors who might supplant the unacceptable PLO as the legitimate representative of the Palestinian people (or at least the Palestinians in occupied Palestine). In this respect the Israelis were absolutely right. In the short term, however, they were about to be proven wrong. In April 1989 members of Hamas kidnapped and killed two Israeli soldiers and all contacts were suspended, Hamas was proscribed and membership became a punishable offence.[8] Gradually, Hamas and the PLO changed places in Israeli perceptions: the PLO became the acceptable face of Palestinian nationalism and was rewarded with a place at the negotiating table, while Hamas became the illegitimate terrorist organization with which no negotiation would ever be possible.

Hamas fully intends to return to its original mission. When the occupation is over, says Ziad Dayyeh, Hamas will simply transfer people currently engaged in political work back to other tasks. These other activities (the movement's core business, if you like) have continued alongside the various strands of political resistance since its entry into the national liberation struggle in 1987, and Ziad sees no conflict between these two tracks: 'the two lines must continue ... we are sharing with other parties in building our future.'[9] Hamas, then, needs to be understood as a dual phenomenon. Both its historical origins and its present political identity are as a popular social movement committed to religious values and traditions of social cohesion and conservation. It supports strong families, integrated local communities and comprehensive social services, provided locally by local people, all within a framework shaped by Islam. The decision to enter the national liberation struggle clearly came after a period of careful preparation through the 1980s and may be regarded as the natural consequence of the social, economic and cultural devastation wrought upon the Palestinians of the West Bank and Gaza following the war of 1967 and stemming from Israel's occupation of those territories. The formation of Hamas as a resistance movement in the context of the 1987 *intifada* was a response to the conditions in which the community the Muslim Brotherhood sought to serve had found itself. Taking the path of resistance was an attempt to preserve the social structures and values to which the Muslim Brotherhood had been committed since its foundation.

It is generally assumed in the West that the popularity of Hamas reflects the extent to which 'radicalized Muslims' have come to identify with a movement that persists with armed struggle, that displays an obdurate refusal even to imagine negotiations with 'the Zionist entity' and that glorifies martyrdom. In this vision the Palestinian population is militant, fanatical and thinks only of the struggle with Israel. The reality is somewhat different. Popular support for Hamas derives from its contribution to the fabric of everyday life, and from the fact that many Palestinians share the values of the movement – social cohesion, solidarity, religion. It is also very clear that public anger over the corruption that characterized the Palestinian Authority under Fatah worked in favour of Hamas. While Fatah members of the Palestinian Authority (PA) administration (many of whom are from the exiled cadres) are seen to have grown wealthy and to live lives far removed from those of ordinary Palestinians, Hamas's leaders have always lived in the communities from which they derive their support, and are widely regarded as 'honest' and 'pure' by comparison with the corrupt politicians. Hamas benefits from not being seen as a 'political' movement in the narrow sense, while other Palestinian factions, such as Fatah, are widely seen as purely 'political' in the worst sense – interested in power for the sake of personal advantage, and far more expert at political rhetoric than at social action. Surveys of Palestinian public opinion in the years leading up to the 2006 election regularly showed corruption to be the single most pressing issue for the majority of Palestinian voters.

As Hamas enters government and the discredited representatives of the corrupt Fatah government opt for opposition, what are the prospects for the secular forces in Palestinian politics? Will opposition – that blessed state of purity that few ruling parties ever live to savour – release energies of democratic reform within Fatah? The passage into opposition of a former government represents a moment of opportunity, since the only way back to power is by winning back the trust of the electorate. For the first time, perhaps, that will now be the task facing Fatah.

Young Fatah

Fatah's opponents used routinely to refer to the Palestinian Authority in terms normally used for one-party states: they call it 'the regime'. It certainly behaved rather like Arab 'regimes' we know from elsewhere: it employed a plethora of armed security organizations; it was intolerant of dissent; it sustained only minimal standards of accountability for public expenditure, offered poor public services to its citizens and spent a disproportionate percentage of its income on security and defence. As Fatah goes into opposition, only Mahmoud Abbas remains in office – he was elected president in January 2005 and his position is formally unaffected by the legislative council elections, although he has threatened to resign if a Hamas government pursues policies he considers unacceptable. What is interesting about Abbas's position is that, as prime minister, he had tried and failed to push through reform within Fatah.[10] His supporters among pro-reform members of Fatah always used to claim that Mahmoud Abbas had effectively been blocked in his efforts by Arafat and by Arafat's cronies. Initially, there was some expectation that with Arafat gone and Abbas elected as president, he would be able to move ahead with reform. He did not. But now the cronies are gone too and perhaps this gives Mahmoud Abbas what is perhaps his third chance to reform Fatah from within. Many more Fatah members than ever before are likely to accept the necessity of such reform.

Ahmed Ghneim is 'Young Fatah'. Although he was personally close to Yasser Arafat, he is one of a younger generation of Fatah leaders who rose to prominence through the second *intifada* and who recognizes the need for a genuine commitment to democracy within Fatah. Perhaps the most prominent individual of this generation is Marwan Barghouti, who initially announced his candidature for the presidency after Arafat's death, only to withdraw it to give Mahmoud Abbas a clear run. Polls taken after he had announced his candidacy suggest he could have won. He would, however, have found it difficult to campaign. Marwan Barghouti is currently in an Israeli jail serving five life sentences for murder arising from his alleged leadership of the second *intifada*. Since the terminology of 'Old Fatah' and 'Young Fatah' is now fairly well-established, Ahmed Ghneim needs to qualify the precise meanings of the designations. Sitting upstairs in a downtown Ramallah café owned by a Fatah member – a place where people are happy to sit and smoke, and talk and talk all night – he explains that 'Young' is not strictly speaking about age. Abu Mazen (Mahmoud Abbas), for instance, is an older man, but he counts as 'Young Fatah'. Later in the evening an elderly gentleman in a blue shirt gets up from a nearby table and makes his way to the stairs. Ahmed Ghneim calls out a word of greeting to him and then turns back to me and says, 'He is Old Fatah, in both senses, but he's a good man.'[11]

For Ahmed Ghneim, 'Young Fatah' is to do with a commitment to reform of the administration and to democratic politics, including turning Fatah into a democratic organization. He genuinely believes that Abu Mazen remains committed to reform, though he was speaking before Fatah's January election defeat. Under the pressure of the impending election, the struggle within Fatah broke out into the open in December 2005 when 'Young Fatah' announced the formation of a breakaway group that intended to fight the legislative elections as a separate list. Ahmed Ghneim emerged as one of the key spokesman for this initiative, called al-Mustaqbal (The Future), which named Marwan Barghouti at the head of its electoral list. After two weeks of behind the scenes negotiation, a unified Fatah list was agreed, with Barghouti, once again, at its head. This appears to have been a muscle-flexing exercise on the part of the reformers, and their almost inevitable withdrawal a move that had been calculated in advance to act as a marker of the reformers' loyalty to the movement. Their task now will be to ensure that loyalty to the movement means radical change.

Given that Abu Mazen's record on administrative reform has been pretty feeble to date, it is unclear exactly how to take the suggestion that he is bona fide 'Young Fatah'. Even with the advantage of his personal democratic mandate he proved incapable of moving against those members of his administration whom many Palestinians saw as no better than crooks and thieves. In some circles, passing conversational references to the now ex-prime minister Ahmed Qurei used to elicit enthusiastic utterances like 'the bastard!' and political independents like Abduljawad Saleh are thunderous in their denunciation of the cronyism and gangster-like behaviour of many government figures. Perhaps it is simply not appropriate for Ahmed Ghneim to join in such full-throated condemnation of his organization, even though he is perfectly willing, when he feels he needs to, to confront government ministers. His personal affection for Arafat may also shape his thinking. He speaks at some length about the last message he delivered for the late president ten days before his death – to the Chinese government – and about how Arafat wanted to make sure that he was carrying enough copies, naming each of the key people in Beijing who should be on the distribution list. He was called back early from Beijing, but by the time he got to Ramallah Arafat was already in Paris. The personal influence of Arafat, even among those whose task it may be to dismantle the political system to which the old man devoted so much of his manipulative energy, is a powerful factor and one that may make the task of reform within Fatah difficult to accomplish. 'Young Fatah' may find it hard to kill 'Old Fatah' so long as it looks on 'Old Fatah' as a father figure.

That relationship may now be at an end, terminated by the election defeat of 2006. The reformers in Fatah – all of whom it should be noted owe their prominence to their role in the *intifada* and their status as 'internal' rather than 'exile' leaders – may offer the best chance not only for reform within Fatah but also for engaging constructively with Hamas. Relations between Hamas and men like Marwan Barghouti and Ahmed Ghneim are clearly cooperative. Khalil Shikaki has commented on this convergence, noting that 'young guard militants also sought an alliance with the Islamists, while siding with refugees and the inner city poor against the wealthy and the urban commercial class.'[12] The story of leftists and Islamists finding common cause in their prison cells is not unique to Palestine; it is clearly increasingly important, for example, in the development of anti-government activism in Egypt. Ahmed Ghneim affirms that Hamas supporters constitute a significant and real sector of Palestinian society who need and deserve representation at every political level, with whom, like it or not, the secular forces of Fatah (and others) must engage in political dialogue and competition. Lindsey Hilsum, reporting for Channel 4 Television on her interview in prison with Marwan Barghouti, explained the connections between Barghouti and Hamas, and Hamas's decision to take the democratic route to power:

> One of Barghouti's closest associates in prison is Sheikh Abdel Nasser Issa, from the new generation of Hamas leaders. It was the Hamas prisoners who persuaded the leadership outside to participate in the elections; Barghouti's influence is believed to have been essential. 'Hamas is part of the Palestinian people and they have the right to participate,' he said. 'I welcome this historic decision from Hamas, because it means they are ready to work according to the rules of democracy.'
>
> Many Israelis are not convinced. Hamas has a ceasefire now – again partly because of Barghouti's influence – but its official position is that it has the right to use any means to destroy Israel. Yet even Israeli politicians understand that Barghouti has a greater chance of influencing Hamas to accept a two-state solution than any other Palestinian leader.[13]

This adds a fascinating new complication to the already dynamic and intricate relations between Fatah, Hamas and the Israeli government. The emergent reformist Fatah leadership may indeed encourage Hamas along the path to a two-state solution. If this were to lead to a negotiated peace settlement it would remove the context in which Hamas undertook its task of national resistance, and allow the movement to do just what Ziad Dayyeh seems most fervently to desire – return to its old job as an everyday working branch of the Muslim Brotherhood. Such an outcome would do wonders for Palestinian democracy too, creating conditions of possibility (an end to occupation) and viable democratic movements ready to make use of them (the Muslim Brotherhood and a reformed Fatah).

The Third Way?

It was between the Fatah regime and the Islamist challenge presented by Hamas that various other political movements, loosely known as 'The Third Way' emerged in the late 1990s in Palestine. Although they are under-resourced and performed disappointingly at January's legislative elections (rather like secular democratic parties in Egypt, though for rather different reasons), they represent a significant current in Palestinian politics and the natural home for some of its most dedicated advocates of democracy and negotiated change. Perhaps its most prominent representative is Mustapha Barghouti, founder of Al Mubadara, the Palestinian National Initiative, and the man who finished second to Abu Mazen in January 2005's presidential election, with over 19 per cent of the vote. Al Mubadara formed the basis of the Independent Palestine list that contested the 2006 legislative elections, winning just under 3 per cent of the vote and securing two seats in the Legislative Council. The gap between Barghouti's personal vote and the showing of the Independent Palestine list a year later is only partly accounted for by the presence of other similar lists on the ballot: it must also have been the result of a two-party squeeze, in which intense competition between the two leading parties concentrated voter attention on the main race at the expense of those not expected to be competing for power.

Other figures associated with this tendency in Palestinian politics include Hanan Ashrawi, who rose to international prominence through her leading role in the Palestinian delegation to the Madrid peace talks in 1991, Haider Abdel Shafi, who chaired the Madrid delegation, and a range of other intellectuals, civil society activists and campaigners for worker rights. They are largely activists from within the Occupied Territories, rather than members of the PLO leadership that returned from exile after concluding the Oslo agreement with Israel. Hanan Ashrawi campaigned for another Third Way list, actually called Third Way, at the legislative elections of 2006. This list also won two seats with a slightly smaller share of the vote than that obtained by Independent Palestine.

Mustapha Barghouti is among those who believe that the exiled PLO leadership under Arafat effectively sold out the Palestinian national cause at Oslo, by agreeing – without even speaking to the official Palestinian delegation – to terms offered by Israel that could only ever lead to catastrophe and national humiliation. The PLO under Arafat first made intolerable concessions to Israel, negotiating incompetently from a position of weakness, and then sought to take maximum advantage from the ensuing 'statelet' that was granted under the terms of Oslo, to establish an authoritarian regime that tolerated no opposition. It then responded in a deeply confused manner to the failure of the Camp David talks in 2000 (for which it somehow allowed itself to take the blame) and the outbreak of the second *intifada*. Having caved into Israel on nearly every point at Oslo, the PA/PLO under Arafat then sought to re-establish its nationalist credentials by initiating new campaigns of military violence. Mustapha Barghouti describes this as 'swinging between madness and capitulation'.[14] So not only does the Third Way interpose itself between Fatah and Hamas, but it also seeks a political strategy that avoids the crazy alternation of madness and capitulation.

Although Barghouti spent much of his political career in the Palestinian People's Party (the communist party) and therefore looks very much like a man of the left, he comes across as a genuine 'Third Way' politician – articulate, pragmatic and smooth. His critics, including those who continue to identify with the left, suggest he has lost touch with grass-roots reality (though Barghouti actually talks a lot about the time he spends out and about talking to ordinary people), and that he is now far too concerned with establishing a media-friendly profile. He was a regular and effective commentator for CNN on Palestinian politics during the days of Yasser Arafat's death and funeral. Like Hanan Ashrawi, who is much admired in the West, some see him as the kind of politician who will play well with foreign visitors and appear persuasive on television, but who no longer plays so well at home.

While some refer to prominent Ramallah figures such as Barghouti and Ashrawi disparagingly as 'the Bold and the

Beautiful', there is clearly important political work to be done by a responsible secular opposition, and part of that work will inevitably involve building and sustaining good relations with opinion formers and policy makers outside Palestine. Like it or not, perceptions are a big part of politics ('Third Way' politicians have always known this). The Palestinians achieved real progress in their efforts to shape international opinion during the 1990s – largely as a result of the overwhelmingly positive impression created by Ashrawi and Haider Abdel Shafi and other members of the Madrid delegation. In doing so they started to counteract the strong pro-Israel sentiment in the American media, offering an alternative vision that started to look positively attractive when ranged against the surly intransigence displayed by their leading Israeli antagonist, Yitzhak Shamir.

What some see as a big negative may yet be a vital asset. In an article published in *Al-Ahram* shortly before his death in 2003, Edward Said bemoaned the fact that during the second *intifada* the Palestinians had largely failed to get articulate and persuasive spokesmen and women onto American television to counter the constant drip-drip of 'suicide bomber' propaganda now more or less routinely and thoughtlessly delivered to American viewers. In another article for the same newspaper, Said also welcomed the formation of Al Mubadara as a genuinely democratic coalition, untarnished by either corruption or collaboration, and offering the first genuine alternative to the otherwise dispiriting (to Said) choice between the Fatah autocracy and the reckless militancy and social conservatism with which he identified Hamas.

Perhaps the current Third Way politicians have missed their moment. Maybe a new generation of democratic reformers is needed. One of the problems is that 'Third Way' leaders cannot agree among themselves, especially when it comes to leading electoral lists. Barghouti says he is tired of sitting around with academics talking about the 'Third Way' and not being able to agree a coherent political strategy. Abduljawad Saleh, who seems to share much Third Way thinking even if he appears unimpressed by the current Third Way leadership, certainly hopes and believes that a grass-roots alternative represents the way ahead. He contemplated a bid for the presidency after Arafat's death, but ran into serious obstruction and intimidation from 'the regime'. He supports moves among a younger generation of activists to create an alternative, but is tired of the direct political struggle and wants to devote his time and energies to writing. Mustapha Barghouti is 58. 'Third Way' poliicians are often a little younger, at least in their Western incarnations. Perhaps there is a generational change under way in Palestinian politics. If so, that would certainly favour Yamama Shalaldeh.

Mustapha Barghouti certainly believes that, despite the fact that he lost so decisively, genuinely contested presidential and parliamentary elections are extremely important. The elections were important not just in Palestine, but elsewhere in the Arab world. Along with several other Palestinian advocates of democratic reform, he thinks that it was particularly important in Egypt, where people saw that the Palestinians were able to hold a contested presidential election despite being under occupation, and decided that there was no reason why they should not be able to do so too. This is an important context for Barghouti, and he is very clear that he sees the development of a still small opposition in Egypt and developments in Lebanon as parts of a broader move towards Arab democracy to which he – and Palestinians generally – are also contributing. In emphasizing the importance of working at the grass roots he makes the very important point that such activities are not just about gathering support for one party or another, but that they are also about getting people used to the possibilities of democratic politics, when all they have known until now is authoritarian rule and, in the particular case of the Palestinians, foreign occupation. He says that when he is out in Palestinian villages trying to explain the work of Al Mubadara, it is often widely assumed at first that this educated and official looking man is actually a member of the government, perhaps the vice president. Creating the social conditions for a pluralist politics, in which it is understood that there is an opposition and not simply a government handing down decrees, is an important task, he believes, for real democrats whose interests lie beyond achieving power for themselves.

Pluralism and unity

The enormous challenge facing people trying to conduct democratic politics while under occupation is how to preserve pluralism when national unity is essential. The conflict between ideas of national unity and ideas of political pluralism is one of the most serious issues facing many Arab countries as they grapple with the process of negotiating change. It is at its most acute under occupation – as Ahmed Ghneim insists, when you are engaged in resistance you simply cannot operate two strategies on the ground – but it clearly remains problematic in several countries. As we shall see, a great deal of symbolic legitimacy derives from figures who can present themselves as unifiers. This is part of the enduring appeal of monarchy, for instance. At the same time, arguments about the primacy of national unity, and the claim that pluralist politics must come second, if at all, for fear of the disunity they may create, are among the most familiar apologies for authoritarian rule in this region and elsewhere.

One of the valuable lessons of the Palestinian democratic experience is that national unity was almost certainly undermined rather than enhanced by the unchallenged rule of Fatah, and that the free expression of dissent and opposition may turn out to have made a positive rather than a negative contribution to Palestinian national unity. Unity for its own sake (we stay together because we are together) is not, ultimately a genuine political value. Consensus, which is valued highly in the region from the Gulf's monarchies to the cells of Hamas, is valuable when it is a consensus arrived at through the articulation of a plurality of views, not when it is the beginning and the end of the debate. Even though some Palestinians look at their internal divisions with dismay, and bemoan their leaders' failure to get things together, to get things done, it remains the case that the political space opened up by pluralism, such as currently operating in Palestine, with all its faults, is an important prerequisite of political change. One of the concerns about the future of that space, under the political leadership of a Hamas government, is that Hamas has not yet demonstrated a great deal of skill in the maintenance of such pluralist debate. Hamas leaders appear practised in the arts of compromise and coalition-building – and these are important – but some of them seem to prefer talking to people they agree with rather than engaging in debate with those they do not. Their new responsibilities will place new demands on these leaders. Maintaining Palestinian pluralism will be one of them. Their political opponents will also have a big role to play in keeping that space open and alive. That alone is a positive state of affairs.

Chapter 4

Syria and Lebanon: Party Problems

Without elections there is no democracy. But elections alone are not enough. The election in which the ruling party or the president obtains over 99 per cent of the vote is still a feature of the politics of the Middle East, and the object of much satirical comment across the region. Such elections are widely held to be evidence, not of democracy, but of its absence. In the absence of democracy, there is a pretend democracy, in which the practices and institutions of democratic politics take the form of mere decoration. Between the institutions of the pretend democracy (with its elections, committees and assemblies) and the lives of the citizens, with real needs and aspirations, there sits a vast chasm. The machinery of the 'democratic' institutions spins endlessly, driven by its own internal logic, but completely unconnected to the realities of everyday life. It is like a car with no transmission. The engine turns over but the wheels of the vehicle do not move.

In a genuinely functioning democracy there are mechanisms that mediate between the engine and the wheels, between the citizens and the institutions of power. These mechanisms take the form of political parties, which organize and coordinate the needs and aspirations of the citizens. They constitute the continuity of citizens' participation in the work of government. The citizen is not simply called upon to say yes or no to the government and its policies at an election every four or five years. Instead, the citizen has the opportunity to join with other citizens in proposing and developing policies, and giving shape to governments. Political participation is thus both effective (it helps make policy) and continuous (it exists on a daily basis not just at elections). The intermediate political organization that is the political party has traditionally – in Western democracies at least – filled the gap between the citizen and the government. For many analysts of the politics of the Middle East, the relative absence of effective political parties (or, in some instances, of any political parties at all) appears to be a substantial obstacle to the development of sustainable democratic institutions.

What is wrong with political parties in the region? Why have they largely failed, so far, to contribute to the development of lasting democratic institutions and political cultures? We have already noted that even where they exist attitudes towards them are profoundly ambivalent, and participation in them very low. Even in Morocco, where the political parties have a substantial history and have engaged in genuine competitive elections, it still took an act of stage management to secure the '*alternance*' of power from one party to another. Even here, where political parties of a democratic type appear to be at their healthiest, it still seemed necessary for the king to assist the parties in bridging that gap between citizens and government. Two intimately related historical factors may help explain the ambivalence, or even hostility, with which parties in the region are viewed.

On the one hand, there is a powerful ideological attachment to the idea of unity. This might be attributed to regional features of very long duration, such as the Arabic language and the claims of the Islamic *umma*. But it may also be considered in relation to more recent developments, most particularly the experience of colonialism (and subsequent forms of post-colonial hegemony). The colonial situation requires a unified political movement dedicated to liberation. The multiplication of political parties constitutes a victory for the divide-and-rule policies of the colonial power. Later, the ideas of a parliamentary democracy and a multiparty system continue to bear the stigma of the colonial period: only a unified national movement can stand up against the continued exercise of Western power in the post-colonial situation. This impulse to unity in the face of an antagonistic power – whether in place as occupier or in retreat but still present as former colonizer – is exacerbated by an entirely rational concern about the possibilities of division. In many instances across the region the creation of nation-states as the primary post-colonial political structures cut against the grain of existing structures of social and political affiliation, such as tribe and family. In the post-colonial nations of the region the development of national identity required that divisions based on these preceding structures should be minimized. The formation of political parties in such a context would almost certainly tend to emphasize rather than minimize these potentially divisive forces.

At the same time, there is also a set of conflicting pressures around ethnic and sectarian identities. In many instances, colonial interventions tended to emphasize the existence of sectarian and ethnic division. This was often simply because colonial powers counted things and people in a systematic way and needed categories into which to place them. After the end of colonial rule one way of emphasizing postcolonial national unity would be to seek to deny or de-emphasize the significance of sectarian or ethnic identity. This can take benevolent or sinister forms, leading either to a kind of multicultural ecumenism, or to attempts to deny the existence of certain types of people (such as the designation of Kurds as 'mountain Turks', for instance). In either case there will be good reasons to avoid the kind of political system that might produce and sustain ethnic or sectarian difference. The risk of political parties emerging as representatives of sectarian or ethnic identities was one to be avoided. However, the experience of colonialism also contributed, not only passively or accidentally (such as through census-taking), to the politicization of certain ethnic or sectarian identities. In many countries colonial powers forged alliances with particular ethnic or sectarian groups, thus leaving behind a legacy of political antagonism based on sect or ethnicity that might not otherwise have taken shape. A general regional ambivalence towards a competitive multiparty politics needs to be understood in this context.

The experience of political parties in the region might, then, be characterized in terms of a tension between two equally problematic formations – the unity of the one-party state and the factionalism of a multipartyism shaped by sectarian and ethnic identities. The anxieties quite reasonably provoked by this situation may also be understood in relation to language, at least in the Arab parts of the region. The Arabic word for party – *hizb* – carries with it a very strong sense of exclusivity. In this sense, to be a member of a *hizb* is to stand apart from one's fellow citizens. It is a claim to be right, to have a particular and exclusive access to the truth. Those who are not members of the *hizb* are, by definition, in error. Membership of a *hizb* is therefore incompatible with proper participation in public debate and political activity, since the purpose of such debate and activity ought to be the attainment of consensus by means of communication and compromise. All too often, in public debate and political activism, the role of the *hizb* has been to insist upon its own views and to decry those of its competitors. Public dissatisfaction with political parties, in the West as much as anywhere, often stems from this perception of the party as a rigid bearer of ideology, bent on antagonism rather than cooperation, unresponsive to the demands of dialogue. In the contemporary Middle East, perceptions of political parties have additionally been shaped by negative historical experiences, characterized by extreme examples of both the drive to unity (the one-party state) and the factionalism inherent in the idea of the *hizb* (Lebanon). The politics of Syria and Lebanon are not only deeply intertwined, but they also offer two related but perhaps polar examples of the functioning of political parties in the region. Syria and Lebanon, both deeply marked by the experiences of colonialism and postcolonial conflict, thus stand as twin warnings to the rest of the region, both often understood as warnings about the perils of political parties. On the one hand the Scylla of the one-party state; on the other the Charybdis of extreme factionalism.

It is small wonder then that Ammar Abdulhamid speaks with such passion as he declares, 'I hate parties'. Ammar Abdulhamid is a Syrian writer turned political activist, currently living and working in Washington, DC, with a fellowship at the Brookings Institute and a role in the developing Syrian opposition. He is *persona non grata* with the Damascus regime of President Bashar al-Asad as a result of having published criticism of the regime both inside Syria and abroad. Travel restrictions and a sequence of interrogations in Damascus about his activities in Washington, including a personal 'interview' with President Asad's brother-in-law Assef Shawkat, left him convinced that he and his family would be wise to leave Syria. He is only just coming to terms with the idea that he has become part of something called the 'opposition', and his idiosyncratic and personal writing (regularly available to a global readership by means of his blog – *Amarji: A Heretic's Blog*)[1] suggests a distinctive individual voice rather than a party man.

But he is part of the opposition now, like it or not, and grappling with the practical realities of collaborating with other people, helping to organize collective activity and articulating a united front against a common antagonist. The previous weekend had seen a gathering just outside Washington of a broad spectrum of the Syrian opposition, including activists from inside Syria as well as the exile community. Ammar is still fielding calls from journalists asking him to remind them of the names of the colleagues with whom he had shared a press conference earlier in the day. His office at the Brookings Institute has a temporary feel to it: only a few books in a small pile break up the barren stretches of empty shelves. The reluctant political activist looks rather like a man in need of the kind of practical and organizational support that a political party can provide. So what is wrong with parties? Are Ammar's feelings simply an expression of a more personal antipathy towards political parties? Do they point to something particular to the Syrian situation, to the situation of an opponent of an authoritarian regime? Or might they instead be related to broader difficulties with the function and performance of political parties in the Middle East? The answer in each case appears to be yes. There are so many problems with political parties.

Political parties represent politics at its most political. For many people that is simply too much politics. A political party is an organization specifically for politicians. It is – self-evidently and self-avowedly – a vehicle for obtaining political power. As people seeking power, politicians are automatically suspect. They must, we imagine, be up to no good. If they are prepared to be so open about seeking power, then they must want power for its own sake. They will put their own interests and those of the party first, and those of their constituents and fellow citizens second, or third, or last. Politicians and the parties they create to promote themselves do not have our interests at heart. They are prone to corruption. They tend to emphasize ideology, where the ordinary person is looking for practical solutions. No one really likes political parties any more.

If this is true in the democracies of the West, where the supposed 'end of ideology' has been accompanied by a steady decline in party membership, increasing scepticism about the motives and competencies of politicians and diminishing participation in elections at every level, can it also be true in the Middle East, where few citizens have enjoyed the luxury of growing tired of their democratically elected leaders? In the absence of competitive elections in which power may be acquired through the ballot box, why would political parties look like a bad idea? Might they not in fact retain some of the potential they seem, at least for the time being, to have lost in the West? Might not the active and systematic development of political parties, organizing and campaigning for political change, be a vital contributory factor to the construction of the democratic politics in which such parties might compete peacefully for power? It is certainly hard to imagine how a pluralist democratic politics could take shape without the formation of parties. The formation of enduring political parties, based on factors that transcend tribal, confessional or other patrimonial of clientelist affiliations, is widely held by professionals in the democracy development business to be an essential step towards lasting democratic politics. One might therefore expect someone like Ammar Abdulhamid to be immune from the 'post-political' malaise and anti-party ennui that afflicts the jaded voters of the Western democracies. Perhaps, then, his feelings about parties have their origins elsewhere, in factors particular to his own political situation, but also of wider relevance to the region. That this is indeed the case will soon become apparent.

The Washington meeting of the Syrian National Council in which Ammar Abdulhamid participated was potentially a highly significant moment in the development of an opposition coalition prepared to work collectively to change the Syrian government. Not only was the meeting significant in itself, but it also came at a time when the Syrian government was facing increasing international pressure in the wake of the Mehlis report on the assassination of the former Lebanese prime minister Rafiq Hariri, and when the United States government appeared to be moving towards a more enthusiastic embrace of the Syrian opposition as a possible agent of 'regime change'. Although the primary focus of this chapter is on the question of political parties, the intimate and uncomfortable political relations between Syria and Lebanon play such an important part in shaping the political environment in which Syrian democracy is becoming a live issue, that a brief overview of the present state of Syria–Lebanon relations will be important to an understanding of contemporary politics in both countries

In both countries the ways in which political parties function differ significantly from the ways in which they are expected to function in democratic political systems: in Syria this is because one party has a monopoly on power and in Lebanon it is because parties share power rather than compete to form the government themselves. Both these models have implications for the way in which one might think about the development of political parties elsewhere in the region.

Syria and Lebanon

Syria never fully accepted the legitimacy of the expanded Lebanese Republic the French colonial authorities created in 1920. This problem, exacerbated by the fact that many Arab Muslim citizens of Lebanon have historically felt a far stronger historical and cultural affinity with the Arab Muslims of the rest of a notional 'Greater Syria' than with their Maronite Christian fellow citizens from Mount Lebanon, has indelibly marked Lebanon's own politics. The Lebanese 'national pact' of 1943 – an unwritten but fundamental agreement regulating inter-communal relations in the multi-confessional Lebanese Republic – sought to contain this difficulty on the basis of a reciprocal agreement that the Maronite Christians would cease to seek integration or permanent affiliation with a French political entity while the Muslims would renounce their aspirations to be part of 'Greater Syria'. Nonetheless, Syria has continued to play a leading role in Lebanon's domestic politics, and its army and security forces effectively held at least parts of the country as a result of its intervention in the civil war from 1975. Successive Lebanese governments were unable to function without Syrian consent. Syria armed and funded the Shia militia of Hizballah, both as an arm in the struggle against Israeli occupation of South Lebanon and as a key political backer for continued Syrian hegemony.

In 1992, after the ostensible end of the Lebanese civil war in 1990, the Sunni Arab businessman Rafiq Hariri emerged as the dominant figure in Lebanese politics, enjoying support from Saudi Arabia, and up to a point Syria too, for an ambitious programme of economic regeneration, most visible in the reconstruction (some would say antisocial gentrification) of downtown Beirut. Hariri resigned as prime minister (for the second time) in October 2004, having become increasingly frustrated by the restraints imposed on Lebanese action by the continued Syrian presence. Syria's inter-vention to support the unconstitutional extension of Emile Lahoud's presidential term of office beyond its four-year limit was the final straw. Then, on 15 February 2005, as Rafiq Hariri was travelling in a convoy of cars towards Beirut's corniche, he was killed in a massive car bomb explosion. Six months later the site of the assassination remained cordoned off, the twisted wreckage of cars still on the street, some, but by no means all of them covered up with grey tarpaulin. The temporary shrine to the 'Martyr' Hariri was still in place next door to the new mosque Hariri had planned and financed. The walls of the surrounding buildings were covered with anti-Syrian graffiti – 'Back to Syria, Bashar, you whore!'

This assassination, which many Lebanese immediately blamed on the ubiquitous Syrian secret services, triggered a sequence of massive political demonstrations demanding the resignation of President Lahoud and of the government, and the withdrawal of Syrian troops from Lebanon. These demonstrations had captured the attention of the global media, which rapidly dubbed the protests 'the Cedar Revolution' (after the tree that is Lebanon's national symbol and that sits at the centre of the national flag, which was the dominant image of the demonstrations) and hailed the largely young and educated protestors as potential agents of democratic political transformation in Lebanon. Counter demonstrations organized by Hizballah, in support of Syria, had drawn even bigger crowds to the streets of Beirut. But the weight of popular opinion and international pressure led to the unexpectedly hasty withdrawal of Syrian forces from Lebanon and the electoral victory of the political coalition that claimed to represent the will of the demonstrators. Hariri's son Saad headed an electoral list named for his father and comprising a broad range of Lebanese political parties and leaders, both Muslim and Christian, united in opposition to Syrian domination.

Despite this victory Saad Hariri remained in exile, fearful of what fate might await him if he returned to the country where his father had been murdered. But other political leaders famous for their opposition to the Syrian role in Lebanon returned to the political scene. Samir Geagea, the controversial commander of the Lebanese Forces and the only senior militia leader ever to be convicted and jailed for actions taken during the civil war, was released from prison and General Michel Aoun, the former army chief who had once tried to establish a rival anti-Syrian government with Iraqi support, returned from exile to take part in the elections. Meanwhile, a United Nations investigation into the murder, conducted by the German Detlev Mehlis, moved predictably enough towards convincing claims of Syrian responsibility at the highest level, including indications of the involvement of Assef Shawkat. With the flight into Parisian exile and subsequent denunciation of the government by Vice President Abdul-Halim Khaddam, who claimed in an interview on Al-Arabiya on 30 December 2005 that President Asad had personally threatened Hariri on several occasions in the months before his murder, implying that Asad was the prime mover of the assassination, it looked like the Syrian regime might be falling apart.

The stability and direction of the Syrian regime had been the subject of intense speculation ever since the death of President Hafiz al-Asad in 2000 and the elevation of his son Bashar to the presidency. Bashar al-Asad was widely believed to be a 'modernizer' and 'reformer', whatever these terms meant in a Syrian context. Much was made of his supposedly progressive interest in computers and of the fact that he had trained in London as an ophthalmologist. This apparently meant that, unlike his father – a ruthless and battle-hardened military strongman – he would be able to lead his country towards a kinder, gentler future – more moderate, more British and with better eye hospitals. To do so he would have to be tough enough to face down the 'old guard' of varying loyalties that had grown up around his father. But he would, some analysts expected, introduce more liberal economic policies, gradually bring younger and less hardline officials into senior positions and, eventually, effect an orderly transition from dictatorship to some kind of democratic opening. Some of the early signs were indeed promising. For a brief period, now generally referred to as the 'Damascus Spring' (it lasted from June 2000 for just over a year), a number of prominent intellectuals in Damascus started to constitute the beginnings of a politically active civil society. Salons or forums (muntadat) held in the houses of men like the lawyer Michel Kilo, the MPs Riad Seif and Maamoun Homsi, the economist Aref Dalila and others became a space for the articulation of specific political demands addressed to the regime – for the end of the state of emergency, the release of political prisoners and the repeal of article eight of the constitution that makes the Ba'ath Party the leading institution of the state.

The intentions of the various participants seem to have been to stimulate and nurture genuine political debate and to engage members of the Ba'ath Party, and the government political apparatus too, in the process. It was most definitely not an explicit or coordinated attempt to bring about the fall of the regime, or even to constitute a political opposition. Although some political prisoners were released the regime eventually responded negatively, enforcing the closure of all but one of the *muntadat* (only the Atassi Forum survived until it too was closed in 2005), and key participants (including Kilo, Seif, Homsi and Dalila) were arrested, tried, convicted and sentenced to prison. However, as the Syrian regime came under increasing pressure from the international community after the Hariri assassination and the Mehlis report, five of those imprisoned after the Damascus Spring were released (on 16 January), which enabled them to participate, at least indirectly, in the moves to formalize a new opposition coalition. It is clear that the new movement, whatever form it takes, will work actively towards ending the Asad–Ba'ath regime rather seek to engage it in a dialogue about the possibility of reform.

The 'Damascus Declaration', issued by a broad spectrum of opposition leaders in October 2005, now seems to have become the agreed basis for the new movement. This statement calls specifically for a process of national democratic change, and therefore identifies its signatories, who include leaders of the Muslim Brotherhood as well as secular and liberal figures, as a self-proclaimed democratic alternative to the present regime. The Washington meeting of the Syrian National Council, which included telephone communication with Riad Seif and representatives of the Atassi Forum from Damascus, was significant for its consolidation of the new cooperation between religious and secular opponents of the regime, as well as for the participation both of exiles and current residents of Syria. Subsequent developments point to a continued commitment to this broad partnership. The fact that one of the most sophisticated and plural gatherings of democratic activists on the current political scene should be rejecting the formation of political parties – at least as part of their current strategy – is worth taking seriously.

In this situation, it seems, the reasons are clear. The prerequisite for success, in the participants' eyes, appears to be the breadth of their support. All political, religious, personal or ideological differences must be set aside in the interests of securing a coalition that presents a united and representative challenge to the regime. With the 'Damascus Declaration' the only (and appropriately general) formal understanding of the nature of Syrian political arrangements after the departure of the present regime (they will be democratic and Islam will occupy a privileged place in legal matters), and with all other post-regime questions effectively postponed until the day the regime is defeated, the maintenance of non-partisan cooperation is the order of the day. Ammar Abdulhamid comes across as disarmingly generous in the language he uses to characterize his fellow members of the opposition. His choice not to discuss political differences or express criticism of underlying political or ideological positions comes across as sincere rather than merely pragmatic. It is probably both, for the political party as an obstacle to the effective mobilization of opposition to an authoritarian and repressive regime has a potent recent history, right here in Washington.

During the 1990s Ahmed Chalabi tried to turn the Iraqi National Congress (INC), which began as a broad coalition encompassing almost the full range of opposition to the rule of Saddam Hussein, into his own political party. In doing so he generated suspicion and intensified rivalries among the various groups and individuals who had participated in the initial formation of the INC. His behaviour was widely regarded as an attempt to make his own play for power. It is clear that those involved in the creation of the Syrian National Council wish to avoid repeating this.

It is perhaps for this reason that Farid Ghadry – sometimes referred to as 'the Ahmed Chalabi of Syria' – did not receive an invitation to attend the Syrian National Council. It may be no coincidence that Ghadry – another exile based in Washington –

had earlier established the Syrian Reform Party, with himself as its leader, thus perhaps revealing a significant difference between his approach and that of the Syrian National Council. Part of this difference seems to be over the extent to which the opposition coalition ought to include all shades of opinion within the anti-regime ranks. While the Syrian National Council appears open to the Muslim Brotherhood's participation in a broad-based move-ment, Ghadry, who views the Muslim Brotherhood with some suspicion, seems to believe that this would be a mistake. Although the Brotherhood's public political leadership – men like Ali Sadreddin Bayanouni – may look like viable partners, Ghadry believes that standing behind the public leadership are unaccep-table elements with which a democratic opposition should not entertain relations. The combination of Ghadry's position on the Brotherhood, the fact that he speaks positively, as did Chalabi, of US-backed intervention in support of democracy, and suspicions that he sees himself as the natural leader of a movement he wants to construct as a political party, seem to have contributed to the Syrian National Council decision not to invite him to participate. Ghadry himself, talking about his plans a week or so after the conference, continues to speak of the Syrian opposition in general as 'we', and shares the general view of the importance of maintain-ing a broad coalition. Even Khaddam will count as a member of the opposition until such time as the regime is defeated, at which point it seems he will be answerable to the Syrian people as a whole for his conduct as a member of the Asad–Ba'ath regime.

To form a party at this stage is to announce oneself as a contender for power. To hold back from doing so is to insist on the primacy of the task of opposition. Herein lies a dilemma. The absence of any credible alternative is a great political advantage for any unpopular regime. Even a desperately unpopular democratic government can win re-election if the opposition fails to persuade the electorate that it could form an alternative. The British gov-ernment of Prime Minister John Major, for example, won the 1992 general election more or less in spite of itself. Where the government is an autocracy, and has been in power for over 40 years, as is the case with Syria's regime, it takes real courage and imagination at a collective level to imagine the possibility of an alternative. That is even before summoning up the further courage and imagination required actually to begin the task of throwing out the regime, especially a regime as vindictive and violent as the Syrian Ba'ath. Since the regime itself came to power by means of cunning party organization and carefully organized violent action, it requires a leap of faith and imagination to see how something as loose, disorganized and potentially unstable as an opposition coalition like the Syrians are creating might achieve its overthrow. Surely only a similarly ruthless, dedicated and highly organized group could do so – a political party, in short, with guns.

The problem for the Syrian opposition is a problem that recurs, in different forms, across the region, and not only in situations where the overthrow of a non-democratic regime is the aim of political development. Even in countries where there is something more closely resembling a pluralist polity than there is in Syria, there is acute tension between the inclusiveness of the coalition and the potential effectiveness of the party. The dilemma facing the Syrian opposition is one of the main reasons for the existence of this tension, but there are others, too, of a historical and cultural nature. The prospects for the successful development of democratic politics may depend to a considerable extent on how these historical issues are understood and how, if at all, this tension or problem around political parties is eventually resolved. It is important not to generalize too readily from any specific situation. The resolution of the tension around political parties may take diverse forms in the region's differing political ecologies. The principal objections to political parties as agents of democratic change may be broadly grouped under four main headings – the party as the vehicle for dictatorship; the party as reinforcement of social cleavage; the party as ineffectual elite in-group; and the party as faction and obstacle to national consensus. In both Syria and Lebanon, understanding the situation of 2006 requires a consideration of the history that has brought us here.

Syria: the one party state

For many people in the Arab Middle East, the idea of a political party may be fatally contaminated by association with some of the most negative and debilitating features of the region's political life since the Second World War. In particular, they may associate the idea of the party with the reality of the party dictatorship, which has taken a variety of forms across the region over the last 60 years. While there is obviously overlap between the various types in this category, they could be categorized roughly as follows: the liberation movement that takes exclusive power (Algeria, People's Democratic Republic of Yemen, pre-unification), the neo-fascist apparatus (Iraq, Syria), the establishment bureaucracy with military backing (Egypt, Republic of Yemen, post-unification). There is also, clearly, within these types, ample scope for the emergence of personalization around the dictator (Hafiz al-Asad, Saddam Hussein, Muammar Qadhafi), which to some extent diminishes the sense that it is the party as such rather than the dictator that determines the political situation. In all cases though, the image of the party as machine, as the apparatus by means of which power is taken (often violently and never democratically), consolidated and enforced, constitutes a powerful warning against the use of the political party as an agent of democratic political change. The party is the obstacle, the machine that must be destroyed if the organic life of democratic politics is to flourish in its place. The fact that such a machine could have been brought into being as a result of a high-minded and idealistic political vision is a familiar irony that only intensifies the general scepticism about the desirability of political parties.

The Syrian Ba'ath Party was initially the creation of two middle-class Damascus intellectuals, Michel Aflaq and Salah al-Din Bitar. At the end of the Second World War the strongest new rising current in Arab politics was pan-Arab nationalism. This new form of nationalism saw all the Arab people as a single nation. The boundaries between the various Arab states of the region were artificial. They had been produced by Ottoman or European imperialism rather than by the will of the Arab people, who recognized among themselves a profound collective identity, founded not simply in language, but also in religious experience. For, although Aflaq himself was a Christian, Ba'athist ideology contained more than a dash of Islam, at least in its identification of the time of the Prophet as a moment of ideal and transparent political and social community, and a state of grace from which, divided and oppressed by foreigners, the Arabs had fallen. The name of the party, Ba'ath, means rebirth, and the programme of the party was organized around the idea that the Arab people could be led into a restoration of former unity and glory. This rather romantic vision had been fused, in the thought of Aflaq and Bitar, with radical political ideas from Europe, encountered while studying at the Sorbonne in Paris.

Socialism was at the heart of the European legacy that the two Ba'athists brought back to Syria, and it was a socialism that was to be developed in a specifically Arab national context: it would not be part of a wider international movement such as that once promised by communism, with which Ba'athists maintained at best uneasy relations. Although there was this crucial European component in the Ba'athist political fusion, political realities also determined that Ba'athism, like other variants of Arab nationalism at the time, should be a fiercely anti-colonial movement. This, then, was the ideological formation of Ba'athism and, although it was to spawn Ba'athist movements and parties in other parts of the Arab world, most particularly in Iraq, where a Ba'ath Party achieved long-term political power, it was in Syria, first and foremost, that the ideology was developed. Although these basic ideas – Arab nationalism, socialism and anti-colonialism – continued to exercise a powerful hold on political sentiments throughout the Arab world, the strange idealism of Ba'athism itself very rapidly succumbed to the logic of the machine that it inadvertently created. There was, from the outset, a profound gulf between the misty and romantic ideology promulgated by Aflaq and Bitar, and the political action to which it lent inspiration. For the founders of the Ba'ath, it was always imagined as

more than a party ... a state of mind, an atmosphere, a faith,
a doctrine, a culture, a civilization with its own worth ...
awakening of instinct, of intelligence and of consciousness,
reflecting a desire for one's own recognition, for affirmation
in the eyes of others, and for the recovery by the Arabs of
their national existence in the world.[2]

The sheer generality of such a vision may have effectively
condemned the Ba'ath to becoming both much more and much less
than a party. On the one hand, it aspired to be a transnational
nation, a cultural movement of popular unification, while at the
same time it stood somewhat aloof from the actual practice of
politics, permitting the gradual capture of its name and rhetoric by
men who were willing to act first and ask questions later.

A small group of lower-middle-class intellectuals, captivated by
aspects of European 'socialism' and enraged at the appalling decline
into which their culture and civilization has fallen, create an
ideology that resonates sufficiently with a population seeking
political change that it acquires a rank and file. But there is a huge
gap between highfalutin ideology and ordinary people's grievances
and aspirations, which continue to find expression in action
undertaken in the name of the party but with only tenuous
reference to its misty ideological origins. In this model of the party,
then, ideology becomes the preserve of an elite leadership – and
ends up as little more than slogans – while the responsibility of the
rank and file cadres becomes action divorced from thought.

Patrick Seale suggests that this is precisely how and why the
younger generation of Ba'athist military officers, including the
future president Hafiz al-Asad, came to take over the Ba'ath after
Aflaq and Bitar's temporary dissolution of the party as part of the
ill-fated union with Nasser's Egypt.

Rural raw-knuckled men like Asad ... had never much
admired the middle class Damascene theorists. Now, as the
young officers pondered their plight, they persuaded
themselves that 'Aflaq and Bitar had secretly welcomed the
party's demise because it served to silence criticism welling

up from more radical forces below. From this resentment the seed was sown of the great Ba'th schism which was to lead in 1966 to the bloody ousting of 'Aflaq and his friends, the triumph of Asad's group and the long-running, violent, irreconcilable and, to outsiders, largely incomprehensible quarrel which ever since has separated the Syrian Ba'th from its cousin in Iraq where 'Aflaq eventually took refuge.[3]

The military committee Hafiz al-Asad, Salah Jadid, Muhammad Umran and three other officers formed in Cairo in 1960 was essentially a Ba'athist conspiracy nurtured within a party that had already effectively ceased to exist. The Ba'ath was well on the way to becoming much less than a party, as a means to becoming much more. The conspirators returned to Damascus to recruit to their organization within the military. A new party, in effect, what some analysts (Itamar Rabinovich for example) have called the neo-Ba'ath, was now under development. This was not a mass revolutionary movement in which supporters and members gathered around a publicly articulated set of demands; it was a structure that mimicked the organizational values of the military within which it was incubated – hierarchical, based around discrete units with specific tasks and in which obedience to the leadership and loyalty to the in-group are the primary social values. These values would be replicated once the neo-Ba'ath was in power.

Once it had seized power in March 1963, the Ba'ath Party would, in effect, continue to create itself, using patronage, violence and indoctrination to build the mass movement it never was. The revolutionary mass movement would be called into being only after the 'revolution'. The neo-Ba'ath would, however, behave in power as though it were the leadership cell of a revolutionary opposition movement, inculcating and reinforcing discipline, orthodoxy, paranoia and secrecy in all its members. Just two months after seizing power, the Syrian neo-Ba'ath purged from the ranks of its government all the Nasserite elements it had initially appointed and, one month later, in June 1963, it consolidated its exclusive grip on power by eliminating the remaining independent officers from positions of authority. In order to gain total control of the government of a single Arab state a movement that had set out to be the rebirth of pan-Arab unity had reduced itself to a tiny, secretive military gang. The vision would never recover, blundering onward as a kind of living dead, until the Iraqi invasion of Kuwait in 1990 finally soured the dream of unity for even its most tenacious adherents. Of the 'neo-Ba'ath' that had come to power in Damascus, even Asad's controversially 'sympathetic' biographer writes: 'They were a fraction of what was itself a minority, a military splinter group of a semi-defunct party without a popular base. The experience of those early years affected their attitudes for years to come: even when the party grew strong and secure, it never rid itself of habits of wariness and repression.'[4]

This has made the task of government very difficult. The neo-Ba'athist regime had no social base in the networks of trade, family and patronage through which Syrian society had traditionally understood itself and organized its interactions. Who were these rapidly promoted young officers and doctors who suddenly held all the key offices of state in the mid-1960s? What strings did they have to pull other than the strings they would have to manufacture themselves, the strings of the state-party apparatus set up, effectively, as an alternative to society? The various attempts made by the regime to embed its power in actual social reality will probably be seen as contributing to the gradual weakening of its position. To give just one example, the consolidation of power through the promotion of members of the Alawite minority (of which Asad, Jadid and Umran were themselves members) fails on two counts: on the one hand it aims to narrow still further the political base of the regime, while at the same time it produces further sources of division, both within society at large and within the regime itself.

So, instead of the development of a mass participation party in which the rank-and-file membership might exercise some influence over the direction of the party and its politics, the Ba'ath Party developed first into a clandestine vanguard organization whose only real objective became maintaining its own power. It created a mass movement only after obtaining power, and did so to create networks of political dependency that would service the machine and prolong indefinitely its grip on power. Raymond Hinnebusch sees the apparatus of the Ba'ath Party as a socially pervasive 'corporate' entity created to maintain control from the top while also creating a social base for the regime through the social advancement, through membership and loyalty, for members of its core client groups – a 'middle-lower class populist alliance'.[5] Of course a full analysis of the nature of the Syrian regime would emphasize a range of other factors in its self-perpetuation – corruption, sectarian privilege, the emergence of competing or balancing centres of power in military, economic and security formations – and this would reveal that the party, as such, was not solely responsible for the persistence and persistent nastiness of the regime. The Ba'ath Party would be understood as one key way of obtaining influence (if you are going up), or maintaining control (if you are looking down). Nonetheless, as in Iraq, the Ba'athist character of the regime seen as a totality persists. Even if a real Ba'athist would try to claim that this particular regime bore no relation to the founding ideals of the Ba'ath, just as a real communist will have claimed that the Soviet Union had nothing to do with communism as such, the fact remains that for anyone else, Syria is a Ba'athist one-party state, just as the Soviet Union was, to all intents and purposes, communism incarnate. The Party is dead, long live the Party.

  This conception of a political party continues to exercise a baleful influence over thought in the region, fuelling paranoia on all sides. Clearly, such parties tend towards paranoia: they are constantly on the lookout for enemies without and within, forever anxious that they may have been penetrated by their political opponents, their plans betrayed and their lives endangered. At the same time, rulers throughout the region fear the emergence of political parties because they imagine them (or cultivate the fear of them) as secretive cells working illegally to overthrow the existing political order. That a political party such as the Ba'ath, founded in a moment of political pluralism, should have transformed so rapidly into a violent machine for the appropriation of exclusive power still resonates through the region as a warning against political parties. Even if this particular historical lesson is often rather opportunistically deployed by leaders reluctant to cede or share power, or even permit processes of political change, it remains a significant factor and an obstacle to the development of what we might want to call 'normal' party politics in the region. Similar and similarly dispiriting lessons can and have been drawn from the experience of other one-party state parties in the region. Not only have these parties been rabidly anti-democratic in their conduct, but they have, in the process, established in the minds of many the idea that democracy and political parties simply do not mix, at least not here. They have also given support to the even more fatalistic argument that democracy and the Middle East do not mix, that there is some deep-rooted addiction to authoritarian rule among, particularly, the Arab people of the regime. This is actually a reworking of a familiar Western fantasy of Oriental despotism (of which more in the next chapter) according to which the Arabs actively enjoy their own submission to the whims of a cruel and violent autocrat.

It would be wrong, though, to confuse historical precedent with historical inevitability. That the Syrian Ba'ath turned nasty is insufficient basis for concluding that Arab political parties are all doomed, or even for supposing that nationalist and socialist parties in Arab countries have no future other than sterile dictatorship or oblivion (the fates of such parties in Syria and Iraq at the time of writing). The Syrian Ba'ath arose and developed in particular historical circumstances, and those are not the circumstances in which political parties will be created and work today and in the future. In any case it is not the social and cultural context in which the Ba'ath arose that determined the path it would take so much as the historical oddity of the Ba'ath's repudiation of its own social and cultural context. By failing to embed itself in existing social structures, other than those of the military, it condemned itself to a life as an alien force within the Syrian body politic. Its affirmations of Arab identity failed to gain traction in the particularity of Syrian political, social and economic life, proving to be more airy abstraction than cultural grounding. Any or all of its key ideological affiliations (to nation, to socialism or even to Islam) could then have formed – and still could today – the basis for a genuine party with real members and a genuine engagement with social forces.

The fact that this did not happen in the case of Syria may also be seen in the light of external pressures: both the rivalry with Iraq and the effective state of war with Israel provided justification (whether specious or genuine is hardly material at this point) for a militarization of the state that encouraged an effective coalescence of party with armed forces at the expense of any possibility of independent civilian political organization, either within or beyond the Ba'ath. Part of the task of understanding the indigenous factors either encouraging or inhibiting democracy in the Middle East is to recognize that the interplay of internal and external factors is as much part of the environment as social and cultural traditions and practices. This will be increasingly evident in the case of Lebanon, to which we now turn.

Lebanon: the multi-party state

If the warning from Syria is about what happens when there is only one political party, the lesson from Lebanon might be about the perils of too many. Lebanese politics are notoriously complicated. There is a multiplicity of political actors. Their alliances with one another seem to shift with bewildering speed. Motivations are difficult for the outsider to assess. Lebanon is constantly cited as the country whose politics defy explanation. Many Lebanese revel in this fact, while deploring much of what it produces. The idea that Lebanon's political classes, those from whom leadership of its political parties has been largely drawn, have somehow betrayed Lebanon's image of itself and its potential, is widely held.

The country appears to have suffered a devastating and inexplicable political collapse. Lebanon was once considered to be the most democratic of all Middle Eastern countries. Beirut was the centre of Arab intellectual and literary culture, outshining Cairo, which laboured under various forms of political repression, and had become the favoured location for writers and publishers interested in debate, critique and experiment. Today it features, at least in the Western imagination, as the absolute epitome of destructive sectarian conflict, a zone without even the semblance of normal politics – violent, impossible, insoluble. The confessional or communitarian divisions nascent even in the 'liberal' Lebanon of fond memory turned out to be the canker that fuelled its degeneration. Lebanon today, so the story goes, is divided beyond repair.

From this story of a dreadful fall from the fresh bright morning of democracy to the nightmare of civil war, it would be very easy to draw another pessimistic account of the prospects of democracy in the Middle East. Such an account would no doubt emphasize the inevitability of political parties forming around confessional or communal lines. It would speak about the inability of political leaders to transcend their communal affiliations. It would identify the political institutions as under-developed or pre-modern in character, insufficiently robust to contain the latent antipathies that must, surely, lie at the root of communal or confessional politics. Although the complexity of Lebanon's confessional structure is perhaps unique – with no fewer than 18 groups awarded recognition in the allocation of political positions – other societies in the region have similarly divided communities. Give them the poison of political parties and a bloodbath along Lebanese lines would inevitably ensue. If the Syrian experience of political parties is bad news, then the news from Lebanon is frankly apocalyptic. But this view is open to challenge.

The Republic of Lebanon's political system was effectively bequeathed to it by an earlier political formation, the autonomous Ottoman province of Mount Lebanon, which functioned from 1861 until its abolition by the Ottomans in 1915. The Ottoman governor was assisted in his duties by a 12-member administrative council, the members of which were chosen as representatives of the different communities living on the Mount, by means of a process of consultation and appointment among the respective communities. Thus, the council comprised two Maronite Christians, two Druze, two Greek Orthodox, two Greek Catholics, two Sunni Muslims and two Shia. This system, which it may be noted involved a 50–50 division of representation between Christians and Muslims, made use of longstanding practices of formal consultation within the communities and benefited from traditional accommodation between the two most powerful groups on the Mount, namely the feudal leaders of the Maronite and Druze communities. With the formation of the republic under a French mandate in 1920 – a state that extended well beyond the Mount to include the coast, including Beirut, the Bekaa and the south – the demographic composition of the polity changed and the traditional influence of Maronite and Druze feudalism diminished. Since the overall population of the new country contained a far greater proportion of Sunni and Shia, continued Maronite hegemony in the new state would not be possible. The 1926 constitution established terms for the allocation of representation within the republic that still exist in a form modified but not radically altered by the 1989 Charter of Lebanese National Reconciliation (the Taif Accord). The Taif Accord also gave written expression to the principles contained within the unwritten 1943 National Pact.

This means that the positions of president, prime minister and speaker of the National Assembly shall be a Christian, a Sunni and a Shia respectively, that seats in the National Assembly are to be allocated on confessional lines, with half going to Christians and half to Muslims (with subdivisions of these according to specific sect), and that public sector jobs are also allocated with a view to confessional balance. Taif brought to an end a previous allocation of parliamentary seats that favoured the Christians by a ratio of 6:5, in a move that was supposed to reflect demographic change. The demographic shift away from the Christians towards the Muslims actually means that the Muslims are now in a substantial majority and that the Shia are particularly under represented, since they are now thought to constitute around 40 per cent of the total population. There has been no census, however, since 1932.

This is not the only factor that makes calculations about the fairness of political representation very difficult. The electoral system also generates further confusion. Members of parliament are elected from lists in multi-member constituencies, in which seats are allocated on a confessional basis within constituencies in order to maintain the overall national balance. In practice, this means that decisions about where, for instance, the Sunni or the Armenian Orthodox seats are located at any given parliamentary election will influence the extent to which any particular group may or may not be effectively represented. Gerrymandering of constituencies to skew the balance is fairly widely practised. Even so, it is fairly clear that the present system under represents Muslims generally and the Shia in particular.

This leads some people, including naturally many Shia, to argue that the confessional political system is undemocratic (or at least insufficiently representative in that it prevents the expression of majority opinion) and that it should therefore be abolished and replaced with a system that allows a majority to take power. It is fairly clear, however, that no such majority exists and, further, that placing power in the hands of one major confessional group (of which the Shia would obviously be the most likely given their numbers) would create a completely untenable situation and lead directly to the resumption of sectarian conflict. The confessional system is thus a mechanism for avoiding conflict and for protecting the rights of distinct communities, minorities and political traditions. It constitutes a democracy in which power is shared rather than a democracy in which power is contested. This is why Lebanese politics, including its political parties, have to be understood in a framework that differs substantially from the familiar one of a party system designed to promote competition and achieve majority rule. The purpose of the political party in Lebanon is not, as it is in many other democratic systems, to obtain power and thus become the government. The party seeks instead to become the organization through which a distinct community secures its own representation in national government. In many cases Lebanese political parties also, as we shall observe, see this

responsibility of representation as existing alongside other responsibilities like providing services, access and sometimes security to
the communities they represent.

The distinction between a democracy that produces a temporary
winner-takes-all outcome and one that produces a permanent
sharing of power between groups is very important. It is not,
however, a distinction that is as clear cut as it sounds. For an
American (or for that matter a British) observer, the distinction
will seem much clearer than it would to a German, let alone an
Austrian or New Zealander. For democratic systems differ from
one another in significant ways with regard to the ways in which
representation is managed. While the United States and the United
Kingdom both practise versions of majoritarian democracy, many
other states operate variations on the theme of proportional
representation. The typical virtue of a majoritarian system is that it
produces a clear winner (even if that takes a while, as in the
unusual case of the 2000 presidential election in the United States).
The demerit of the majoritarian system is that it tends to award
power in a disproportionate way, almost always reducing levels of
representation for minority groups or parties, and sometimes,
although exceptionally, producing results in which the party or
candidate with the majority or largest percentage of the vote does
not actually win. The 2000 presidential election was one example
of this; another was the 1951 general election in the UK when the
Labour Party not only won more votes than the Conservative Party,
but even secured its largest ever share of the popular vote but was
still defeated because of the way the votes were distributed in
single-member constituencies. The chief virtue of a proportional
system, aside from its proportionality or perceived fairness, is that
it encourages some cooperation between parties, usually resulting
in the formation of coalition governments. This has been the case
in Germany, for example, ever since the restoration of democracy
after the Second World War. With this perspective in mind, the
idea that the purpose of democratic representation might be to
maintain and facilitate power sharing rather than a constant
competition for power does not seem so unusual. Indeed, there are

plenty of examples, both historic and contemporary, in which considerations of communal representation are also written into election systems in order to preserve the rights of minorities (New Zealand is one such example, while others are often devised in immediate post-conflict situations as in Burundi in 2005 and New Caledonia in 1998).

Political parties in Lebanon take various forms and fall into various categories that permit an understanding of how they work and what they are doing in the Lebanese political system, given that none of them are doing what political parties in a majoritarian democratic system would be doing – seeking to become the government. Many Lebanese parties fall into more than one of the categories under which they are introduced below (elite, confessional, ideological, military). Many might even be said to move between them, such is the volatility of the situation. They also move between alliances with one another, some of which, like for example the present agreement between Michel Aoun's Free Patriotic Movement (radically anti-Syrian Christian ex-militia) and Hizballah (pro-Syrian Shia militia), look bizarre to the outsider but make sense within the complex mutual balancing and manoeuvring between parties that is characteristic of the situation. In recent years tactical alliance making has almost always been played out in relation to the question of Syria. Despite Syria's departure in 2005, Syria remains integral to Lebanese politics, and important actors on the Lebanese scene remain committed to their relationships with Damascus.

Another factor that needs to be borne in mind throughout this consideration of Lebanese political parties is that, despite their diversity, their profusion and the relative freedom in which they operate when compared with many other countries in the region, they are not the dominant players in the political system. Less than a quarter of the members of the 2000 parliament were members of political parties, and even in the parliament elected in 2005, where perhaps just over half the members represent parties, many of the most important groups within parliament are either electoral lists or blocs, or alliances formed within parliament itself. This is why the political scientist and MP Farid el Khazen can convincingly claim that 'Lebanon does not have a party system'.[6]

Thus, with certain exceptions, Lebanese political parties conform to the pattern already observed in Egypt, and that will also be seen in Jordan, in which there is very little grass-roots involvement in political parties. For Farid el Khazen this means that 'they are performing functions similar to those performed by parties in authoritarian regimes'.[7] If they are not the government (as are the Syrian Ba'ath and the Egyptian NDP) they are not trying to be the government, either because that is expressly forbidden (Syria), practically impossible (Egypt) or very unlikely given the leading role of the monarch in government (Jordan).[8] One might go so far as to say that one crucial reason for Lebanese political parties behaving as though they were under an authoritarian regime has been that, in effect, that is exactly where they have been, with the regime in question being Syria. What will happen and what the political parties will do once the effects of this authoritarian regime start to wear off is one of the many questions that Lebanese politicians and analysts currently find so absorbing.[9] The brief survey of Lebanese parties that follows does not claim to be comprehensive in its coverage, merely to illustrate some of the salient features with reference to specific examples of party formation and characteristics.

Among the first parties to be established in the mandate period (1920–43) were parties based around the personalities of leading Maronite landowners. These included the National Bloc (Emile Eddé) and the Constitutional Bloc (Bechara el-Khoury). Emile Eddé was a Francophile Lebanese nationalist who served as prime minister (1929–30) and president (1936–41), and as president again in 1943 after independence. On his death in 1949, he was succeeded as head of the National Bloc by his son Raymond Eddé, who played a prominent role in Lebanese politics, campaigning against both the Israeli and Syrian presences in the country, before going into exile in Paris in 1976 after an unsuccessful presidential bid and three attempts on his life. The National Bloc is currently led by Carlos Eddé, Raymond's nephew. It does not participate in government and has had no parliamentary representation since 1972, but continues to function, nonetheless.

A second important party from the mandate period might be classified as an ideological rather than an elite party. The Kata'ib (Phalange) was founded in 1936 in emulation of Spain's Phalangists. Its ideology was ultra-nationalist (Lebanese, rather than Arab), and it was not a major player in the mandate era, only becoming a significant force during the civil war when it became one of the most prominent Maronite militias. Despite having a clear ideological stance, emerging after 1958 as a powerful force for the articulation of Christian interests in Lebanon, it was also, like the National Bloc, inextricably bound up with the fortunes of one family – the Gemayels. Its founder was Pierre Gemayel, his son Bashir set up its military wing in 1976 and became president in 1982 (after the Israeli invasion). His assassination is believed to have provoked the massacre of Palestinian refugees in the camps of Sabra and Shatila by Phalangist militia. Bashir's brother Amin took over as leader of the Kata'ib and as president of Lebanon. He went into exile in 1988, returning to Lebanon in 2000 to attempt to relaunch the Kata'ib, which is now effectively split into two parties, one led by Amin Gemayel, the other by Karim Pakradouni. Pakradouni's Kata'ib aligned with the pro-Syrian president Emile Lahoud, while the Amin Gemayel group became part of the anti-Syrian opposition, and has members of parliament elected under the banner of the Qornet Shehwan Gathering (a group of anti-Syrian and mainly Christian politicians). Amin's son, Pierre Jr, was elected to parliament as a member for Metn in both 2000 and 2005, and in 2005 he was appointed minister for industry in the government of Fouad Siniora. Bashir's son, Nadim, is active as a member of the Lebanese Forces.

In the cases of both the National Bloc and the Kata'ib a typical weakness in Lebanese parties is obvious – the way in which leadership stays in the family. In many cases a political party, especially if initially formed around an elite family such as the Eddé, is really a fairly small group of individuals loyal to the powerful founder and leader. On his death there may be competition for the leadership of the party from within this group and, with members lacking political constituencies of their own, such power struggles can often be indecisive, leading to the selection of a son or other family member as a figure who carries some of the authority of the previous leader and around whom the rivals within the party can unite. Often this means that the new leader suffers from practical political weaknesses: either they may be unsuited to political leadership, or, as in many recent cases, they have little experience of living in Lebanon. Carlos Eddé, for example, grew up in Brazil.

This phenomenon is not unique to the Christian parties, elite or ideological: it can also be observed as a development within parties initially of a confessional/ideological origin. Typical here is the Progressive Socialist Party (PSP), which was one of a wave of parties to be formed after independence that espoused ideological positions and affiliations with broader international political movements. Founded in 1949 by the Druze[10] leader Kamal Jumblatt and five others, the PSP claimed a secular and non-sectarian status, and a commitment to socialist principles such as national insurance and worker rights. Like most other Lebanese parties it transformed into a militia during the civil war of 1975–90, securing control of the Druze area of the Shouf in a struggle with Mount Lebanon's other major community, the Maronites, for whom the Lebanese Forces were the leading militia. Kamal Jumblatt was assassinated in 1977 and was succeeded as leader of the PSP by his son Walid, who continues to lead the party today. It is, in effect, a party to serve Druze interests and dominated by the Jumblatt family. Jumblatt is famous for what his critics claim is opportunistic flexibility, but which is probably best understood in terms of constant attention to preserving the interests of the Druze. He supported Syria's continued presence in Lebanon until 2000, but has since been a leading figure in the 'opposition', and took the PSP into coalition with other major opposition groups in the elections of 2005.

Other ideological parties have their origins in the heyday of Arab nationalism and socialist activism. These include the Lebanese wing of the Ba'ath Party, which had three members in the 2000 parliament, and the Lebanese Communist Party, which has never entered parliament and has spent much of its life as an illegal party. These ideological parties are long past the high point of their powers, such as they were. The Communist Party, however, has given rise to a significant secular leftist group – Democratic Left – with one seat in the present parliament, but whose influence lies more in its articulation of anti-Syrian positions from a left perspective, particularly by some its leading figures, such as George Hawi and Samir Kassir, both of whom were assassinated, probably by pro-Syrian agents, in June 2005.

Nearly all political parties transformed into militias during the civil war period. Indeed, some owe their existence to this period, and emerged first as militias, only becoming political parties after the end of the war. These include the Lebanese Forces and the Free Patriotic Movement among Christian groups as well as Hizballah. Amal, as we shall see, came into being as a political movement before being established as a military force, but may be included under this heading too. The Taif Accord was supposed to lead to the disarmament of all militias. Refusal to do this is one of the factors that led to the prosecution of Lebanese Forces leader Samir Geagea in 1994. Hizballah, however, has been permitted an effective exemption from this requirement on the basis of its status as a national resistance movement against Israeli occupation. Its special status in this respect, following Israel's withdrawal from Lebanon in 2000, is now a source of intense political controversy, with politicians who united in the opposition coalition against Syrian rule demanding that Hizballah complete its transformation into a mainstream political party by disarming. All of the parties formed as militia are confessional in nature, although Hizballah has made some attempt to broaden its membership and its appeal beyond its traditional Shia supporters. Few observers are convinced that this makes Hizballah non-confessional.

Although nearly all parties formed militias during the war, the most significant militia parties today are perhaps the four that were effectively forged during the war – the Lebanese Forces; the Free Patriotic Movement; Hizballah and Amal.

The Lebanese Forces was the militia created by Maronite Christian parties and initially dominated by Bashir Gemayel's Phalange (the military wing of the Kata'ib Party). Following the deaths of Pierre and Bashir Gemayel in 1982, Samir Geagea and Elie Hobeika gradually secured control. Hobeika signed an agreement with Damascus in 1985 that other Christian leaders, including Geagea, repudiated, and was forced to flee the country, leaving Geagea to rebuild the Lebanese Forces. In 1993 the militia was disbanded and transformed into the Lebanese Forces Party. The party was soon banned, however, and Geagea was arrested in 1994 for allegedly maintaining a militia in the form of a political party, as well as for killings carried out during the war. He was sentenced to several terms of life imprisonment. The Lebanese Forces retained significant popular support, however, particularly in East Beirut, and Geagea's release and pardon in July 2005 were enthusiastically celebrated. The Lebanese Forces formed a significant element in the opposition to Syrian occupation that took to the streets following the Hariri assassination, and now has five members of parliament as part of the Rafiq Hariri martyr list, as well as one cabinet position (tourism minister Joseph Sarkis).

The Free Patriotic Movement was created by General Michel Aoun, who had previously been commander of the Lebanese armed forces and in 1988 had attempted to establish a rival government opposing Syrian control (and backed by Iraq). This led to bitter conflict in East Beirut between Aoun and Geagea's Lebanese Forces, and Aoun's eventual surrender and departure into exile in 1990. Aoun returned to Lebanon in May 2005 and entered the political scene immediately, with the FPM, along with its allies, winning 21 seats in the national assembly.

These two former Christian militias are more than matched in political strength by the two political parties that have developed out of the Shia militias – Amal and Hizballah.

The issue of Hizballah (Party of God) will be addressed again in the closing section of the chapter, as it is one of the most difficult questions facing the country and also raises key issues for our wider concern with political parties in the region. Hizballah is in an exceptional situation, and in the eyes of many it is effectively running a state within a state. Not only is it the only militia not to have disarmed, it is also the only Lebanese political party that can genuinely claim a mass following. Like other Islamist movements – Algeria's FIS, Egypt's Muslim Brotherhood and Hamas in Palestine – Hizballah has been extremely successful in providing welfare services to its constituencies, and it has also demonstrated a high level of organizational capacity, far in excess of most other parties. Hizballah participated in the May 2005 elections in an alliance with Amal, in a list called Resistance Development and Liberation, which secured a total of 35 seats. Hizballah has two cabinet ministers, and a third minister has the party's support. Its origins are as a militia in the 1980s, drawing together a number of militant Islamist groups involved in the kidnapping of Westerners and forging a national resistance movement dedicated to forcing Israel out of south Lebanon. Hizballah's claim to have achieved this objective – something no other movement can claim – is its rhetorical basis for retaining its exceptional status.

Amal (Hope) was the other leading member of the Justice Development and Liberation bloc at the 2005 parliamentary elections. It began as a Shia social and religious movement, inspired by the teaching of Musa al-Sadr, and with an explicit political orientation towards the cause of the 'deprived'. The party's leader, Nabih Berri, has retained his position as speaker of the National Assembly (which makes him formally the most senior Shia leader in the country). Amal is a long-term rival as well as coalition partner for Hizballah and although, like Hizballah, it offers services to a mass membership, these usually take the form of employment and access rather than the provision of health, welfare and education, such as is offered by Hizballah. This means that the social cohesion of Amal as a mass movement is weaker than that of Hizballah. Also, Amal has disarmed. Although currently allied to Hizballah for electoral purposes (an arrangement imposed by Syria), Amal has much to lose from the continued rise of Hizballah, not least its claim, embodied in the figure of Nabih Berri, to political leadership of the Shia community.

When Lebanon's political parties are viewed in the context of the civil war alone, it is easy to see why they might be regarded as not only responsible for the war, but also as the cause of it. A political system in which every political party mobilizes for the exclusive benefit of its own sectarian community sounds precisely like a recipe for civil war. However, it is important to recognize that, while the parties – with few exceptions – chose war as the pursuit of politics by other means after 1975, they did not do so solely, or even primarily, out of domestic political considerations. The real causes of the Lebanese civil war arguably lie outside Lebanon, or rather, in the way external powers and political struggles entered Lebanon. The complex entanglements of the PLO, Israel, the United States, Syria and Iran in Lebanese politics from the 1970s onwards have been covered extensively elsewhere.[11] Without suggesting that Lebanon's political parties and their militia were innocent of what happened, or that they were merely pawns in the grander strategies of the real agents of war, it seems reasonable to recognize that there is no intrinsic or causal relationship between a political system in which political parties are organized along confessional lines and the outbreak of civil war. Farid el Khazen identifies two main lines of argument over the causes of the Lebanese civil war:

> One [approach] attributes the breakdown to causes inherent in Lebanese society and the political system. According to this reading, Lebanon has lived on borrowed time and was bound to fail because it was divided along confessional lines. However, it does not tell us why other divided societies with unstable political systems have not failed and become the scene of protracted armed conflict. Nor does it explain why homogeneous societies were also the scene of internal conflict. More important it does not explain the timing and nature of the breakdown.[12]

A second approach, which is taken by el Khazen and which this analysis broadly shares, 'recognizes that the prewar confessional system, despite its shortcomings, was able to function relatively well.'[13] After 1975 the political system failed and the political parties were unable, in the face of enormous destructive forces, to continue their traditional work of balancing power between their respective communities. The legacy of this failure remains a problem: not only does it leave political parties discredited because of this failure, but within certain communities it also awards political credibility to those who built their reputations on successful military campaigns rather than democratic politics. That Hizballah, Samir Geagea and Michel Aoun are among the major political powers in Lebanon in 2006 illustrates this tendency and gives some people great cause for concern. The extent to which Aoun, Geagea and, perhaps crucially, Hizballah can move beyond their wartime legacies will determine how far Lebanon can reconstruct and develop its democratic institutions.

In Lebanon's confessional power-sharing democracy, political parties perform a range of functions: they represent minorities; they promote the interests of a local leader; they mobilize to secure electoral success; they espouse and promote ideologies; they organize, defend and support communities; they provide social and individual services; and they engage in armed struggle. Those that broadly accept Taif and the continuation of the confessional system all seek to pursue their own objectives with a view to the long-term preservation of a system that permits them to do so. That is, they respect the limits of power sharing because they believe it is the best available mechanism for avoiding the kind of conflict that would follow from the introduction of a majoritarian system, in which a zero-sum power struggle would be launched. As long as everyone is a minority, everyone retains an interest in such a system. The moment anyone starts to think they could be a majority, the system comes under intense stress. Herein lies a pressing problem. Hizballah may now believe that Lebanon's Shia are fast approaching a national majority and so seek radical change in the present informal constitutional arrangements to reflect this and enhance its own power.

It has been suggested in earlier chapters that the democratic future of both Egypt and Palestine will include important roles for the Muslim Brotherhood and Hamas. The commitments of these two Islamist organizations to democratic principles are widely questioned, for they are linked, to varying degrees, with the spectre of Islamist political violence and many secular citizens of the region fear they will deprive them of basic freedoms if they are allowed to win power. It has also been argued, in Chapter 2 on Iran, that the Shia sect of Islam has a unique contribution to make in the field of politics, offering prospects of innovation around the role of religion in politics and in the development of religious thought itself. The presence in Lebanon of a well-organized Shia Islamist movement, engaged in the political process, contributing positively to social development among its constituents, offers the hope that Hizballah, too, could be a genuine participant in the negotiation of political change in Lebanon. In short, it has been claimed already that the so-called terrorists may turn out to be the most convincing democrats: can this be the case with Hizballah, too, perhaps the most famous so-called 'terrorists' of all? This prospect raises issues very similar to those expressed in Egypt and Palestine over the rise of the Muslim Brotherhood and Hamas.

Hizballah first came together as a coherent movement in the Bekaa valley in the early 1980s. Iran had sent units of its Revolutionary Guards to Baalbek in 1982, and Shia Islamists were already active in the area. Young, poor and angry Shia men, for whom the Iranian revolution of 1979 had been a vivid inspiration, showing that the historically oppressed Shia could indeed rise up against their oppressors, were ready to commit to a similar cause in Lebanon, especially when the Israeli invasion of 1982 gave the struggle another urgent and ideologically intense rationale. This created a space in which Hizballah could organize and, once the Israelis had withdrawn from Beirut, start to extend its operations to the capital. In October 1983 the car bombing of the US Marine Corps headquarters in Beirut, which killed 243 marines, was claimed by a group calling itself Islamic Jihad. The following month a car bomb at the Israeli headquarters in Tyre was claimed by Hizballah. Gradually, through the 1980s, Hizballah effectively became established as the principal organization behind the continuation of this campaign of bombings, the kidnapping of Westerners as hostages in Lebanon and other attacks on Israeli and Western targets. In 1985, Hizballah announced itself formally, publishing a manifesto in the form of an 'Open Letter to the Downtrodden of Lebanon and the World', in which it proclaimed its belief in Ayatollah Khomeini's principle of velayet-e faqih, its rejection of the state of Israel, its opposition to the colonial and Western powers, and its repudiation of Lebanon's 'rotten sectarian system'.

By this time Iran and Syria were working together to find a replacement for the now expelled PLO as the spearhead of the anti-Israeli resistance in Lebanon, and Hizballah presented itself as the leading candidate, despite Syria's understandable reservations about collaboration with an Islamist movement (Syria had violently suppressed an uprising led by the Muslim Brotherhood in Homs as recently as 1982). Thus Hizballah, whatever its inspiration and rhetorical commitment to a revolution modelled on Iran, really found its feet and its long-term purpose as a movement of national liberation in the struggle against Israel. This specific project rather than the more nebulous objective of an Islamic state, became its *jihad*, its *raison d'être*.

One possibility, then, in assessing the future development of the party, is that Hizballah has never really aimed to replace the Lebanese government with an Islamic republic, despite the importance attached to the inspiration of Iran and the recognition of Ayatollah Khomeini's status by virtue of velayet-e faqih. By making the war against Israel in southern Lebanon its principal objective from 1985, Hizballah ensured that it would have to compromise: this struggle was a national struggle, waged on behalf of all Lebanese, including Sunnis and Christians. A narrowly sectarian bid for national supremacy would not be consistent with the political objective of expelling Israel from Lebanon. As Judith Palmer Harik suggests, 'the campaign begun against Israel in southern Lebanon in 1985 would not be jeopardized by raising undue apprehensions about the party's radical ideology and ultimate goal for Lebanon.'[14]

Nonetheless, Hizballah's links with Iran and its origins in radical Shia politics arouse continued suspicion and anxiety among other Lebanese, who doubt the party's commitment to the multi-confessional state. Hizballah has not formally renounced its ambition to establish an Islamic republic, but it has adopted an essentially pragmatic position in which that ultimate goal is postponed, in theory, until Hizballah has succeeded in persuading other Lebanese that this would be the best option. Rodger Shanahan cites the party's secretary-general Hassan Nasrallah to this effect: 'We prefer to wait until the day that we succeed in convincing our countrymen – by means of dialogue and in an open atmosphere – that the only alternative is the founding of an Islamic state.'[15]

According to Shanahan, then, Hizballah's participation in the post-Taif political system is a pragmatic move, partly forced upon it by its backers in Damascus and Tehran, but also designed to persuade other parties and constituencies that it is prepared to renounce, or at the very least put to one side, its radical agenda. Its participation in parliament and now, after May 2005, in government, is also presumably designed to increase the party's capacity to lobby at the highest level for the interests of its own community of the deprived. Such a strategy remains consistent with the long-term aim of establishing an Islamic republic, however distant that prospect might seem. In the meantime, Hizballah is focusing political energy on practical, even mundane political issues, such as the campaign to have the electoral system revised to incorporate a form of proportional representation that would increase Shia (and therefore presumably Hizballah) representation in government. Hizballah also supports lowering the voting age from 21 to 18, on the basis of a similar self-interested logic: the Shia are both the largest and youngest sector of the Lebanese population.

It is in fact far from clear how much support Hizballah actually commands, since it has contested all recent national elections as part of a joint ticket with Amal. However, the evidence of local elections in which Hizballah and Amal have competed with one another directly, such as in 1998, is revealing. Hizballah scored major victories in the southern suburbs of Beirut and in the Bekaa, while it also mounted a significant challenge in the south of the country, traditionally Amal's stronghold. Rodger Shanahan attributes this success, at least in part, to Amal's credibility with the poor having been damaged by its participation in government; that it 'has come to represent the very system it was set up to oppose'.[16] This is a problem that Hizballah too may one day have to confront. One of the beneficial effects of democracy is that it encourages actors outside the system to enter the system, and once there to engage in mutual legitimation. According to Harik, Hizballah's success at organizing elections means that it has become 'the dominant list-maker in many Shiite areas and is thus capable of attracting the most influential and therefore desirable candidates to its lists'.[17] This means that Hizballah, rather like Hamas, is able to present lists of candidates for election who transcend the ideology of the party and thus attract voters who are voting for effective service providers, advocates and administrators, rather than ideologues. This ought to have a moderating influence on the party, as it will need to be able to retain such support in order to pursue its long-term goals. It also reveals a contradiction at the heart of the long-term goal of establishing an Islamic state: the more power Hizballah acquires through social action and the ballot box the more dependent it becomes on people who have no interest in an Islamic republic at all. Thus, as Hizballah pursues political power in search of this objective, the objective moves further away. The logic of this situation, combined with the demographic realities of Lebanon, surely means that the objective of the Islamic republic must be considered unreachable and that other more realistic goals, achievable by political means, will gradually replace it.

Hizballah's other main activity is the provision of social welfare to its constituencies. This has been an extremely effective, well organized and professional operation, financed to a large extent by sources within Iran. As well as building up a sense of community and winning loyalty on the basis of reciprocation for services rendered, the fact that Hizballah can provide better services in some cases than those on offer from the government can be presented as a demonstration of the practical efficacy of Islamist solutions. If the slogan 'Islam is the Solution' has credibility, it is surely because in a very practical sense that is how it seems. In reality, it may be the case that spending other people's money on your own healthcare is the solution, but for the grateful recipients of Iranian largesse at the hands of the highly respectable professionals of Hizballah, this is not a distinction that is worth making. If Hizballah were genuinely committed to the installation, by persuasion, of an Islamic republic, this kind of demonstration of how it might work, in miniature as it were, would be one very good way of going about the task of convincing the rest of the country. One suspects, however, that the beneficiaries of Hizballah's welfare provision recognize that, at some level, Hizballah is able to do this precisely because it is not the government, and that an attempt to replicate such provision at a national level under a Hizballah government in an Islamic republic would almost certainly fail. This leaves Hizballah committed to social welfare programmes for their own sake, as it were, or for their short-term political value, rather than for any demonstrative value they might have as regards an Islamic republican utopia.

Therefore, just as participation in electoral politics and in government encourages a focus on the here and now, bread and butter issues rather than transcendent religio-political objectives, so does the provision of services. These two activities are likely to consume the energies of the party, particularly as the ideology of the Islamic republic fades in its homeland, Iran. If the reformist, leftist innovative strand in Iranian Shia thought once again becomes an effective player on the Iranian political scene, it is to be expected that enthusiasm for Khomeinist solutions in Lebanon will decline still further.

Another potential contradiction facing Hizballah as it moves deeper into an engagement with the 'rotten sectarian system' its initial manifesto vowed never to work within, is that as it becomes part of the system – especially with ministers in the government –

it risks trading in one of the main sources of its popular appeal. As Farid el Khazen has observed, Hizballah's position as a political party is unique, not just in Lebanon, but in 'contemporary state–party relations'.[18] This is due, in part, to the fact that it continues to be an armed faction, but also – and this is far from unrelated – because its 'success is measured more by the large measure of autonomy it has from government authorities in political and security affairs rather than from the power in exercises in government.'[19]

As long as Hizballah seeks to remain outside the system, it presents itself as a potential force for replacing the system entirely. While it retains its protected status as a military organization, this will probably continue to be the case, since many Lebanese will refuse to trust Hizballah's participation while it retains the weapons and the foreign support that constitute its alternative sources of power. Again, as with Lebanese parties and militia in general, the problem is not the party as such, so much as its dependency on power beyond Lebanon itself. To be properly democratic, a party needs to recognize that it can rely only on support from within its own electorate. This is why foreign financing of political campaigns is frowned upon more widely. Hizballah does enjoy very considerable support within Lebanon, and from Lebanese citizens: it has by far and away the best claim of all of Lebanon's parties to be a mass participation party. While some of this support is the indirect result of external funding, it is also genuine and rooted in Lebanese reality. The question, then, is whether Hizballah will go all the way and abandon its special status to compete equally with other parties. This may be difficult, since from Hizballah's own perspective the 'rotten system' does not allow equal participation. The change that probably needs to be negotiated is not the abolition of the system, though, but rather its adjustment to reflect the weight of the Shia population. A new deal on parliamentary representation might be the basis for Hizballah decisively entering the system.

The purpose of political parties in Lebanon is to balance interests, preserve political rights and provide economic and social resources for the various communities, rather than to secure majority rule. This is democratic. So, for the time being Lebanon is a self-balancing democracy of minority power-sharing rather than a competitive democracy of majoritarian rule. If that looks undemocratic to Westerners, it is too bad. It may not match criteria of modernization, it may not look like what we think a democratic system looks like, but we meddle with it at our peril. Gradual adjustments to correct manifest injustices rather than a complete reinvention of the system seems the likely way forward.

While the Syrian model of the party helps explain why so many people of the region look at political parties with a mixture of horror and disdain, the Lebanese model, often derided, may offer the region a way of thinking about the role of parties that goes beyond the crude zero-sum competition and majoritarianism that characterizes Western party politics in the eyes of many Arab citizens. That the Lebanese political system still exists is perhaps not a condemnation of the country's failure to address its internal conflicts, but rather a hopeful sign that political parties developing along unusual and locally specific lines might have something to offer.

Once again, as was the case with Hamas in Palestine, if the West is to have any genuine contribution to make, it will only be able to do so to the extent that it recognizes Hizballah as a three-dimensional social and political movement with its roots deep in Lebanese life, rather than as a one-dimensional terrorist demon or cat's paw of the Iranian government. This is not to say that Hizballah and Hamas are the same thing, but rather that both have to be understood in the full complexity of their local situations.

Chapter 5

Jordan and Morocco: The Authority of the Legitimate King

C an a king be a democrat? Strictly speaking, the answer would have to be no. Democracy is rule by the people and presupposes sovereignty to lie with the people. A king is a sovereign, rules by himself and, however liberal, progressive or consultative he may be, he can never, by definition, be a democrat. The people do not have the right to change him. For this simple reason eight countries in the region (all of them Arab states) would appear to possess, at the apex of their political systems, an insurmountable obstacle to democratic change, in the form of a king (or its rough equivalent in the form of an emir or a sultan). These kings and the political structures in which they govern do, however, possess resources that have already demonstrated considerable potential for negotiated political change, often guided by principles that, if not strictly democratic, are shaped by powerful considerations of popular legitimacy. The legitimacy enjoyed by these rulers is itself a potential resource for change because it is a legitimacy that derives, not from God, or simply from force or 'tradition', but from a relationship with the ruled in which notions of popular consent play a significant role. One of the enduring questions about the eight Arab monarchies is to what extent this legitimacy based in consent may permit, or even encourage moves towards a genuinely democratic form of government. Can the legitimate monarch become the constitutional monarch as head of state of a democracy (as in the remaining European monarchies), or will some other way of balancing popular participation and representation with royal sovereignty emerge?

The eight Arab states in which government is monarchical will all surface in the analysis that follows. They are Morocco, Jordan, Saudi Arabia, Bahrain (all of which are now led by men who call themselves kings), Kuwait and Qatar (which are ruled by emirs or princes), Oman (led by a sultan) and the United Arab Emirates, where there is a ruling family for each of the seven emirates, but whose president is drawn from the ruling family of the largest emirate, Abu Dhabi. The focus will be mainly on Morocco and Jordan, where the relationship between monarchy and democratic development has perhaps been most interesting in recent years. Bahrain and Qatar are less significant politically than Morocco and Jordan, but both have taken significant steps towards developing their government structures in recent years; Qatar's moves in this direction will also feature in this chapter. Saudi Arabia clearly occupies a special position, one in which prospects for political transformation look decidedly bleaker than in any of the other monarchies. However, it is not the monarchy, as such, that makes Saudi Arabia's political system appear so much more resistant to change than the other Arab monarchies. It is, rather, the particular configuration of elite wealth and mass poverty, deep social divisions and entrenched religious conservatism that obstructs the tentative reform process on which King Abdullah seems to have embarked, and which will make progress extremely slow.

The king as man of the people
Disguised in the simple clothes of an ordinary citizen, the king queued up at an income tax office. He wanted to see how the state bureaucracy, providing services in his name, was performing. He wanted to see and hear for himself, rather than receive second-hand reports that would invariably be designed by courtiers or civil servants to tell him what they thought he wanted to hear. This was not his first experiment in clandestine inspections. He had 'been

undercover before', according to media reports of this latest surprise visit,[1] touring a hospital, for example, where he had been able to hear directly from patients complaining about shortcomings in the service they had been receiving. His father had done the same kind of thing in his own day, too, and the 39 year-old King Abdullah of Jordan, who had succeeded King Hussein in June 1999 – just two years earlier – was clearly keen to build his own reputation for getting close to his people. King Hussein was following a well-established tradition, for it was none other than the great Caliph Harun al-Rashid, celebrated in the pages of *The Thousand and One Nights*, who would often walk at night in the streets of old Baghdad, disguised as an ordinary man, and thus learn the truth about the city and its people.

The device of the king in disguise seems to have a double meaning. It is a way of checking up on people: it brings the king into direct contact with everyday life problems, without the protective screen that is invariably in place when the king appears in public. It probably helps to generate a sense, among public employees, that they are under scrutiny: in this sense the king's secret missions are emblematic of a wider culture of control and accountability. Perhaps even the photographic portraits of the king that adorn the walls of every government office participate in generating a certain atmosphere of work carried out under the watchful gaze of an all-seeing ruler. For such secret missions to be effective, then, they must not remain secret. They need to end with a moment of revelation, in which the king, metaphorically speaking, at least, strips off his disguise and stands in his full splendour before an astonished people, who thereby learn a precious lesson about public service and the responsibilities of leadership. It is crucial, then, to the success of the king in disguise, that the device should be publicly exposed. Only when you know that the king goes around in disguise does it become possible to imagine that every ordinary customer in the queue, no matter how raggedly or modestly attired, might in fact be the king. And that is how the king can truly be everywhere – more potent than his image – an all-seeing, all-knowing everyman. It was probably the king's own office that passed details of his visit to the tax office to the right journalists, thus ensuring that the story of the king in disguise was flashed around the world by the BBC. Here is where its second meaning really kicks in, for in addition to the idea that the king sees everything, is the crucial idea that the king is indeed a kind of everyman. He is just like you and me and unlike all those puffed-up government ministers, all those snooty bureaucrats and self-interested career politicians, he could just sit down right here and share a cup of tea and talk about how it really is. He would understand our ordinary lives, talk to us in our own language. He goes out in disguise so that he can find out what it is like to be one of us, and so that he can complain to the government on our behalf. The king is, literally, a man of the people.

The king is everywhere and the king is one of us. This conception of the relationship between king and people is crucial to an understanding of the meaning of kingship in the Arab Middle East. It is crucial because it concerns questions of leadership, of representation, of legitimacy and authority – all of which are vital to a consideration of the nature and prospects of democracy across the region. This is an ideological conception: it is a story kings and people tell about themselves and the ways they relate to one another. It has it roots, though, like all good stories, or all workable ideologies, in the material of everyday reality. Kings and people do sometimes sit down together as apparent or temporary equals; the king has, historically, in both Arab and European societies, enjoyed a degree of popular credibility that his courtiers and officials have often conspicuously lacked; the king can bring a charismatic presence, often communicated by means of the 'common touch' to formal public occasions and backstairs political transactions. The nature of modernity, with the expansion of the administration and the specialization of government functions has tended to erode, year after year, the level of personal contact between king and people. Most people never meet the king. The king rarely meets ordinary people. But it remains the case that these kinds of stories, these understandings of the role of the king and his relationship with his people, serve as a deep well of social and political legitimacy for a system of government.

Some might wish to explain this away as mere 'opium for the people', and characterize the politics of such kingdoms as situations in which everyone is simply deluded about the nature of political reality. Others might complain that the legitimacy acquired through such stories and the reservoir of feelings that attach to them is a false legitimacy with no place in the rational business of government. But the fact remains, rather surprisingly, that there are eight countries that fall under the scope of this study whose governments are based on legitimacy of this kind, where the relationship between the king (or emir, or sultan) and the people is both imagined and experienced as a real part of political life, and where there is very little evidence to suggest that there is major popular desire for the removal of the monarchies.

Political anachronisms?

In the second half of the twentieth century it was almost an article of faith among Western political analysts that the various monarchies of the Middle East were anachronistic and doomed to die out, and that the political arrangements that would follow would be, more or less by definition, more modern, more progressive and therefore more democratic.[2] After all, democracy itself had been forged in the fire of anti-monarchical revolution. The French had toppled and executed Louis XVI, giving rise to a struggle that lasted most of the nineteenth century between monarchists and republicans and that ended inevitably in the victory of the republican cause. Elsewhere in Europe monarchs either fell or ceded their powers to new constitutional governments, which derived their legitimacy from the sovereignty of the people rather than the person of the sovereign. The United States of America was founded upon a successful revolution against the tyrannical yoke of the British monarchy, and established itself from the outset as a republic based on the sovereignty of the people expressed through democratic means.

The remaining Arab monarchies were thus regarded, in the West at least, as obsolete holdovers of a colonial settlement: the kings of Libya, Egypt and Iraq all owed their positions to the deals they had cut with colonial powers and, with the process of decolonization gathering pace, their days would be numbered. And so it proved to be, with the Free Officers in Egypt bringing the reign of King Farouk to an end in 1952, with King Feisal of Iraq overthrown in 1958 by an avowedly nationalist and republican movement headed by the armed forces and King Idris of Libya ousted in 1969 by the revolutionary nationalism of Colonel Muammar Qadhafi. Those that still held out looked like temporary exceptions. The monarchies of the Arabian Gulf states were, so the story went, recently fabricated polities, without deep social or political roots, and the security of the emirs, kings and sultans who ruled them was entirely dependent upon a new kind of colonialism, in which Western dependence on the region's oil ensured continuing practical and financial support for rulers who would never survive, so it seemed, on their own. With the spectacular fall of the Shah of Iran in 1978, his ultra-monarchical rule the victim of a popular revolution inspired by radical Islamism, the writing was apparently on the wall for the new oil monarchies of the Gulf. It was entirely in keeping with much pro-democratic and progressive analysis of the region that even before the shock of the Iranian Revolution one of the most comprehensive and detailed Western accounts of the region's politics should have carried the confidently predictive title of *Arabia Without Sultans*.[3] But the writing on the wall appears to have been wrong.

Thirty years on, the Shah of Iran remains the last regional monarch to have lost his throne. The kings of Morocco and Jordan continue to rule, and in both instances the sons of long-reigning fathers have relatively recently succeeded, not only without serious contention but also amid expectations that they may give fresh impetus to social and political reforms of a democratic nature. The roles of King Abdullah of Jordan and King Mohammed VI of Morocco in the leadership of such processes will be at the heart of this chapter's account of the contemporary situation. In the Gulf, meanwhile, all six ruling families in the GCC states continue to exercise power. Although each has confronted serious challenges to the continuity of monarchical rule, it hardly seems credible today to suppose, as seemed obvious in the 1970s, that political development and democracy can only begin once the monarchy has been overthrown. The questions that are asked today are about the role of the monarchy in the process of democratic political development. The monarch is a key player in this process, not an obstacle to be removed from it. To understand why and how this is the case certain common cultural and political misunderstandings need to be set aside.

The fantasy of the Oriental despot

At the heart of these misunderstandings is the classic Orientalist fantasy of the exotic, mysterious and absolute Middle Eastern ruler, or despot, perhaps most visible in all kinds of Western popular entertainment from Mozart's comic opera, *The Abduction from the Seraglio*, to any number of films and TV dramas featuring Omar Sharif.[4] Clearly, this fantasy figure has come into being through a process of historical construction in which Christian Europe's most immediate neighbour is perceived as a threat and then painted in colours that are both threatening and alluring (the classic colours of vice), colours designed to highlight the virtues of the Christian European rulers and to lend moral and emotional justification to any Crusade they might choose to launch against the vicious despots of the East. The main components of this fantasy of the Arab or Turkish despot include fabulous wealth and lavish expenditure on ornament (furnishings, jewellery, architecture, gardens), elaborate structures of servants and slaves, a harem (or seraglio) of beautiful and passive women, a taste for gratuitous and arbitrary acts of cruelty, a heady cocktail of barbaric attitudes and unfathomable sophistication, all of which are indulged in a context of absolute political authority in which the despot's subjects live in daily and abject fear.

Of course, this fantasy image of the Arab or Turkish despot is wildly inaccurate, and probably describes European absolutist rulers of the seventeenth and eighteenth centuires far more accurately than it ever described an Arab or a Turkish king or sultan. As we shall see, Arab ideas and practices of monarchical rule are rarely if ever based on a conception of absolute power, which was the ideology of European kingship in the early modern period. Indeed, the often overlooked irony of Mozart's *The Abduction from the Seraglio* is that the cruel and tyrannical Turkish Muslim 'Pasha Selim', who holds the beautiful European Constanze against her will, is in fact not a Turk at all, but actually a Spanish nobleman who had earlier converted to Islam and then risen to political power in the Ottoman Empire. For Mozart, who composed his opera in Vienna in 1782, and his audience for whom the Turkish military threat was still a vivid cultural memory, the fantasy figure of the Oriental despot was, quite literally, made in Europe.

It is clear that aspects of this fantasy figure have become attached in recent years to real life Arab rulers who are not in fact kings at all, but simply authoritarian leaders. The terms in which Saddam Hussein, with his sons and his palaces, were discussed in the months and years leading up to his removal from power by US military invasion in 2003 borrowed substantially from this repertoire of images. But this repertoire of images also continues to furnish commentators of all kinds with ways of talking and thinking about existing Arab monarchs. On the cover of Fred Halliday's *Arabia without Sultans*, for example, (in its 1979 reprint), there is a caricature of a Gulf Arab that might be taken as exemplary of an updated version of this often racist fantasy. No doubt Halliday would deplore the image too, in spite of his strong political objections to the regimes it caricatures. The image, drawn, as it happens by Peter Fluck, who later went on to television fame as one of the co-creators of the UK latex satire show, *Spitting Image*, shows a modern Arab despot emerging from a barrel of oil. He wears the traditional headdress of the Gulf Arab, a stylized moustache under a prominent nose, his sunglasses are flying off his head as the oil splashes from the barrel, and the fingers of his one visible hand are adorned with big bejewelled rings. The hand is raised in a gesture that seems to suggest a cruel and lustful clutching. It is, frankly, the kind of image that used to circulate in the popular media of Nazi Germany, only this time it is an Arab rather than a Jew who is portrayed seizing unearned wealth from an encounter with European modernity.

The witless way in which the contemporary American film-maker Michael Moore associates the Bush administration with the Saudi royal family in his film *Fahrenheit 9/11* rests similarly upon racist stereotype. Moore proceeds on the basis of a conviction that his fellow Americans will automatically recognize the image of the rich Arab ruler who lives a life above and beyond the law. He seeks to damn his own (dynastic) administration by showing it to be hand in glove with fantastically wealthy Arab rulers who have somehow colluded in an act of terrorism. It is Saudi Arabia that most often falls victim to this kind of presentation and not entirely without reason. While it is certainly the case that Saudi Arabia's monarchical system of government is currently presented much more credibly as an obstacle to political change than as an agent for reform, this political reality needs to be dissociated from fantasies that not only damage our capacity to understand the kingdom, but also our capacity to think about the role of kings and other monarchs in the region. The particular conservatism that characterizes Saudi politics is casually translated into a virulent version of the Orientalist fantasy, which is then carelessly spread to cover a range of other monarchical states, from Morocco to Kuwait, in ways that radically distort reality. A typical example of the fantasy at work comes from the back cover blurb for David Holden and Richard Johns's book, *The House of Saud*.[5] Soberly assessed by the *Observer* newspaper as 'a carefully constructed and objective account', by the *Financial Times* as 'meticulous and thorough' and by the *Sunday Times* as 'a penetrating analysis and a major contribution to the literature of the subject', this book is billed somewhat differently, above these words of praise and in capital letters, no less, in the following sensational terms:

THE DESERT RAIDER IBN SAUD TOSSED THE HEAD OF THE TOWN
GOVERNOR FROM A PARAPET DOWN TO HIS FOLLOWERS BELOW ...
THUS WAS THE KINGDOM OF SAUDI ARABIA FOUNDED. TWO-THIRDS
THE SIZE OF INDIA, IT HOLDS A QUARTER OF THE WORLD'S OIL AND
HAS SIX TIMES MORE OVERSEAS ASSETS THAN THE USA. A LAND OF
DESERT UNCHANGED FOR CENTURIES, WITH WEALTH AND POWER TO
MAKE THE WORLD TREMBLE ... THE DOMAIN OF THE HOUSE OF
SAUD.

It is a dense cocktail of popular ingredients – desert, cruelty, wealth, fear, desert, timelessness, desert.

Such thinking is politically dangerous as well as inaccurate (and sometimes racist) because it tends to present the Arab and Muslim king as an unchangeable feature of a fixed cultural and political landscape. If Arab kingdoms are ruled by fantasy despots then there is no hope for political change, short of overthrowing the despot and instituting a whole new kind of political regime.

The reality, thankfully, is rather different, as the various Arab monarchies are all, in their different ways, governed according to principles, traditions and practices that allow the fashioning of new political developments. None of them, not even Saudi Arabia, are as brittle in their resistance to change as some of their republican neighbours. Even in Saudi Arabia, it is possible to imagine a process of political change in which the monarchy would remain. In Syria, by contrast, it is almost impossible to imagine a process of gradual and organic change that would preserve the current leadership. The fall of the regime would appear to be a prerequisite for change. Experience suggests that this would have been the case in Iraq, too, although the American invasion means that we will never know whether a process of change from within could have begun (it seems somehow unlikely).

The monarchies enjoy what we might imagine as a kind of cushion, or room for manoeuvre, in which the current rulers can either initiate or respond to pressure for political change without having to abandon their claims to legitimacy. Perhaps we might think of a government like Syria's as a 'digital' regime – it is either on or it is off – while the monarchies function according to old-fashioned 'analogue' principles, which allow for flexibility – bending, ducking, weaving and, indeed, innovating. Any process of political development that got under way in Syria today would almost immediately undermine, probably fatally, the legitimacy claims of President Asad, rendering him incapable of either controlling or even contributing to the process. He would be swept away, rather as Western commentators in the 1970s imagined would be the fate of the remaining monarchies. That the monarchies have not been swept away, and now look so much more likely to last than several of the republican regimes, is attributable to a range of factors. And these factors, which include skills of adaptability, are also likely to contribute to any processes of democratic development that take shape in these countries.

In thinking about the relationship between democratic development and monarchy in the Middle East it is important not to imagine that monarchy *per se* is necessarily the determining factor. Nor indeed, should we imagine that the effects of monarchy in the countries in question are the same. There are great differences – of culture, history, social organization – between the eight Arab monarchies. Morocco, in the West – a large country in both geography and population, an indigenous citizenry that is almost 50 per cent non-Arab and a history marked by proximity to southern Europe – presents to its rulers, present and future, a wholly different set of political challenges to those faced by, say, Qatar – a tiny principality whose indigenous Arab population forms a small minority of an otherwise mainly immigrant population and whose future viability depends upon the exploitation of oil and gas resources.

Nonetheless, certain aspects of monarchical rule in an Arab social context are held in common between many of the eight monarchies. Indeed, some of those aspects of social and political relations in the Arab monarchies may also be discerned in some of the Arab republics. There are some very obvious ways in which the leaders of several contemporary Arab republics are trying to revive aspects of monarchy in a republican context, often as a means of securing wider public legitimacy among a population for whom modern secular and nationalist regimes have never satisfactorily replaced the social structures of allegiance and belonging offered by more traditional forms of leadership. At its most obvious, this republican imitation of monarchy involves the development of what one might call dynastic republicanism. The case of President Bashar al-Asad of Syria, who succeeded his father in 2000, is so far the first instance of direct dynastic succession in an Arab republic, but there is considerable speculation that the next presidents of Libya and Egypt may be a younger Qadhafi and a younger Mubarak respectively. The fact that these states (Syria, Egypt, Libya) are experiencing uncertainty over the transfer of power from one leader to the next and that they exhibit, in response, this tendency to keep it in the family, might suggest that the non-democratic republican form of government runs against the grain of Arab society and political practice. Indeed, perhaps this might be taken as evidence that the Arab monarchy, in its various forms, offers a political system more conducive to democratic transformation than do the republican structures put in place following the overthrow of monarchs in the immediate post-colonial period.

Symbolic power

One advantage enjoyed to varying degrees by all the rulers of the eight Arab monarchical states, which the republics possess in only very limited ways, is a rich repertoire of symbolic resources for sustaining and enhancing legitimacy. The way in which some of the republics seek to fabricate such symbolic resources is often very revealing, not only about the republics, where there is a legitimacy deficit, but also about the monarchies, where these resources seem to be more meaningful and effective. Lisa Wedeen has written a richly detailed analysis of the rhetoric of public communication in Syria, for example, in which she shows how the pervasive cult of (now former) President Hafiz al-Asad forced Syrian citizens into incessant complicity with preposterous lies and exaggerations about the 'beloved' president. Syrians who routinely repeated bizarre effusions of love for the president and who acquiesced regularly to claims that he was the nation's 'premier pharmacist' did so not because they believed a word of it, but because both the system and often their own lives and livelihoods depended on them acting 'as if' they did. The fact that there was a void at the heart of such expressions only fuelled their proliferation.[6] By comparison, however sceptical we may be about public expressions of loyalty, affection or grief for political leaders (and we have become very sceptical indeed in the West with good enough reason) we have to take seriously much of the popular support enjoyed by the Arab monarchs. The enthusiasm with which the accessions of King Mohammed VI of Morocco and King Abdullah of Jordan were greeted by their respective citizens was by no means fake. Nor was the public grief expressed in Jordan following the death of King Hussein in 1999, nor the public response to the death of Shaikh Zayed, first president of the UAE and the Emir of Abu Dhabi, in 2005. These were not people acting 'as if'. Nor, it must be said, were the people in question simply dupes of royal ideology. The symbolic resources of the monarchies are real and have real political effects. The rulers and their actions embody aspects of how at least some of their citizens imagine themselves to be. How does this work?

When King Abdullah of Jordan decides what to wear when going undercover, the choice is not difficult. He probably already has the necessary clothes in his wardrobe. One aspect of Arab kingship that is not often remarked upon is the relative absence of ostentatious displays of status. Arab kings do not, in the main, wear rich and elaborate robes, nor, indeed, do they ever wear crowns. They are not surrounded by liveried courtiers and servants. The legacy of European feudalism is manifested in the United Kingdom, for example, in elaborate pageantry in which dress is of supreme importance, and in which the monarch is set apart from the panoply of lavishly attired aristocrats by the overwhelming splendour of her ceremonial clothing. In the Arab monarchies – which do not have their origins, like their European counterparts, in the great landowning families and wealth acquired over centuries – the king or sultan is not invested with symbolism of this kind. The symbolic function of ceremonial or formal dress for Arab monarchs works in an opposite direction. The Arab monarch dresses simply, in the traditional clothing shared by his fellow citizens. The symbolic meaning is about inclusiveness.

Rather than a monarch who dazzles with his glamour, marking out the distance between himself and ordinary citizens, we have a monarch who seeks to emphasize his closeness to his people. Even in situations where the royal family is extraordinarily wealthy, as for example in Saudi Arabia or Kuwait, this wealth is not communicated by means of dress. Indeed, tradition would appear to demand a certain modesty of dress, emphasizing the equality of all people in the eyes of God. While members of the Saudi and Kuwaiti royal families may display their wealth in ostentatious ways outside the particular frame of personal appearances in public – and may, indeed, face criticism for such display – they appear in public dressed in much the same way as their fellow citizens. Their legitimacy is symbolized in terms of their embeddedness in the life of their society rather than in terms of their elevation above it. The point here is not that Arab monarchs function without ceremony. On the contrary, for in a culture where personal conduct is often minutely regulated by social convention it is natural that the monarch should be surrounded by elaborate protocols of etiquette and distinction. But these protocols tend to emphasize dignity, respect, grace and hospitality rather than power, superiority, wealth or the subjugation of the citizen. Ceremony associated with the king therefore tends to emphasize commonality, inter-connectedness and collective participation in a web of reciprocity.

The religious dimension of symbolic power is of particular importance in Morocco and Saudi Arabia, where the ruling families make formal and specific claims to very particular religious legitimacy. In Saudi Arabia the king is custodian of the holy places. In Morocco he is the commander of the faithful. In the case of the king of Morocco the connection between this religious claim to legitimacy and the social dimension of Arab kingship, in which the king is, in effect, one of his own people, is particularly strong, and provides the king with significant opportunities to enhance his political authority by symbolic means. Take, for example, the 1993 ceremonies to inaugurate the new King Hassan II mosque in Casablanca. The mosque, named after the king, supported by nearly compulsory public donation as well as by royal funds, was clearly intended as a project that would enhance the king's authority, particularly during a period in which Islamist militancy was a serious concern for the Moroccan government. Neighbouring Algeria was in the toils of a bloody civil war, which had broken out following the cancellation of a general election in which the FIS (Front Islamique de Salut/Islamic Salvation Front) had been on the verge of victory. Although the Islamist movement in Morocco had not achieved anything like the degree of popular support enjoyed by Algeria's FIS, the king and his advisers clearly felt that a vivid reassertion of the king's religious legitimacy would assist them in keeping it that way.

So in 1993, on the occasion of the Prophet's birthday, the new mosque was inaugurated by the king in a ceremony broadcast on national television. The choice of the Prophet's birthday for this event was significant, for, although this is not a major festival in the Islamic calendar, it carries particular resonance in Morocco, where the ruling Alaoui family claims to be descended directly from the Prophet Mohammed. The choice of this day therefore served as a symbolic reminder of family continuity – a rooted connection between past and present. King Hassan's use of this sense of continuity and his symbolic position as king, fellow Muslim and fellow Moroccan is analysed in detail by M. Elaine Combs-Schilling in an article that draws upon anthropological understanding of the relation between religion and political power. She explains how the king's dress – the white robes that many Moroccan men normally wear, especially at formal-traditional events – always serves to make the king visually as well as imaginatively one of his own people. She describes how during the ceremony a series of three white-robed poets all stood up in turn to recite verses in praise of the king and his new mosque, and how, then, to audible astonishment from viewers, a woman, also dressed in the white that symbolically binds together Moroccan male society, stood up to speak. The inclusion of a female poet in this ceremony was simultaneously a break with social tradition – women do not speak in public in the mosque in front of men – and the establishment of a new tradition, namely that women are to be included as part of what Combs-Schilling calls 'the white-robed body of the nation'.

This move, clearly carefully orchestrated by the king, came in the wake of significant political agitation for improvements in women's rights and, in particular, a petition calling for reform of the *moudawwana*, Morocco's conservative and restrictive body of personal status and family law, which will be discussed in more detail below. Because the king's legitimacy is experienced as intimately connected to his membership of his people, his symbolic resources can very readily be deployed to redefine who 'his own people' are. If it had been conventionally understood that 'people' could be represented by a gathering of men only, the king's organization of the mosque ceremony altered that understanding. The message was clear: 'the people' cannot be properly represented in this way, because 'the people' included women. The king's power to change this state of affairs, to redefine the Moroccan public sphere, resides in the fact that he can do so both theoretically (by announcement or constitutional or legal change) and practically, through his own participation in a social enact-ment, in which he appears as both king and 'man of the people'. The king's authority works in this way because, as Combs-Schilling suggests, it is embedded 'within the intimate lives of everyday people so that exterior power and interior passion in some arenas converge'.[7] This kind of symbolic legitimacy does not necessarily work on the basis of widespread belief in or assent to myth – such as that the king is somehow sacred. Henry Mufson offers a sharp critique of the kind of analysis offered by Combs-Schilling on the grounds that lack of attention to purely political factors (such as coercive force) and a preference exhibited by anthropologists in general for interpretations that involve culture and religion, tends to overvalue the symbolic at the expense of the real. 'For politically conscious, educated Moroccans, the idea that the king is sacred is a relic of the precolonial past. ... Even the many Moroccans who support the king and the monarchy for fear of the alternatives no longer take these beliefs seriously.'[8]

That the king can deploy symbolic power based in religious practice and belief is not the same as saying that he possesses sacred qualities in the eyes of those who recognize his legitimacy. The efficacy of symbolic power does not rest upon the category of the sacred, as such, but rather upon the way in which religious affiliation and its embodied practice in both ritual and everyday life interacts with the hard realities of political power to generate a social consensus in which the degree of support for the status quo exceeds what would be achieved by the exercise of force alone. Or, to put it another way, symbolic effects are real too.

Political legitimacy

This deeply embedded legitimacy – where symbolic value is not merely superficial, like the as-if adoration with which the public spectacles of the Asad cult are filled – creates what it has earlier been suggested is the room for manoeuvre enjoyed by such monarchs. Clearly, such symbolic resources will always be used for broadly conservative purposes: they are unlikely to be mobilized on behalf of radical political change. However, not all political change is necessarily radical. Indeed, the fact that this symbolic legitimacy enjoyed by Arab kings can be closely associated with Arab traditions of social and political consensus building means that a monarchy can, if it so chooses, act as the agent of a process of political change in which the conservation, restoration and enhancement of traditional political relationships are the principal objectives. Put simply, a king with traditional sources of political legitimacy can lead a process of political change if that change is seen in terms of traditional political and social values. If political change can be presented and enacted in line with widely held beliefs about social and political tradition – and not, for example, as the imposition of systems and structures that appear to contradict such beliefs – then the king can be an agent for the development of democracy itself. Of course this is only possible if democracy – in all its manifestations – can credibly be linked to already existing and indigenous political practices and institutions. As we have already seen, both King Abdullah of Jordan and King Mohammed of Morocco came to the throne amid high expectations that they would lead processes of reform. The idea that a new king might be able to renovate tradition in the interests of reform is widespread – even in Saudi Arabia where the prospects for reform are considered among the most remote in the region, the final accession to the throne of King Abdullah, after many years of *de facto* rule as crown prince, has been seen as opening up possibilities for change that were not available before. One of the difficulties facing all three kings, as well as the rulers of the smaller Gulf monarchies, is how to balance an organic and indigenously driven process of political change with the pressures for democratic reform that they experience from outside.

Put in the crudest possible terms, an Arab monarch trying to sell democracy to a conservative population that has become deeply and passionately suspicious of Western motives as far democracy is concerned, needs to sell it under another brand name. Or, at the very least, he must convince his people that it is a local product, not an American export. This is not easy. For the irony of the situation is this: the political change sought by reforming monarchs in the Arab world is, in effect, a form of democracy. It is an indigenous product (based on Arab and Islamic traditions), but it is also, as democracy, remarkably similar to what is apparently on offer from Western salesmen such as the American administration. The task of the monarch then is to retain sufficient symbolic resources based in traditional legitimacy so as to be believed by his people when saying: 'I'm doing this because I want to, not because I am being told to.' He has to make sure that he transmits enough of his own symbolic legitimacy to the process of change, and that the institutions created by the process retain sufficient symbolic resonance with indigenous political culture.

In the current political climate the symbolic legitimacy Arab citizens attach to democracy as such is questionable. While there may be strong aspirations to democratic practice – as evidenced by opposition movements in Egypt and even Syria, as well as among reformers of various persuasions (including many usually described as Islamists) in the monarchies – democracy as a slogan has been somewhat tarnished by its overuse as a rationale for the invasion of Iraq. In some of the countries of the region it seems possible to mobilize popular support around the principle of democracy. In Egypt, for example, there is clearly significant and principled support among the middle classes for political movements such as Kifaya, for which democracy is a founding principle. In the monarchies the case seems somewhat different. Mass mobilization in support of democratic change from the bottom up seems unlikely. In the Gulf, populations are small and social conventions are not conducive to explicit forms of public political association. In Jordan, political parties lack grass-roots credibility. Morocco's demographics and economic predicament (as well as a history of effective party political mobilization) suggest that it could be the exception in this regard. Even in this case, though, democratic change from the top down actually seems more likely, especially when it seems possible that the symbolic resources of monarchy can be leveraged to support such a process.

The idea that the legitimacy of the king is rooted in his membership of the people rather than in his position above them helps us understand important differences between European and Arab conceptions of monarchy, and to avoid confusions that can arise around the idea that monarchical rule is necessarily absolutist. Although the State Department persists in referring to several of the Arab monarchies as 'absolute monarchies', this designation is historically and culturally inaccurate. The conception of the absolute monarch is a European idea, in which the king is endowed with absolute power by virtue of his God-given legitimacy. Absolutism emerged in Europe in the sixteenth century and became decisively established through the seventeenth and eighteenth centuries with the centralization of state power in France, England and Spain. Absolutism replaced a medieval structure in which power was more widely distributed among an aristocratic class and in which the king tended to rule in close association with an informally constituted council of advisers and representatives, among whom bishops and other religious leaders would play a prominent although by no means decisive role. In Renaissance and early modern Europe, however, religion – in this case Christianity – is mobilized as ideological support for absolute rule through the doctrine of the divine right of kings (according to which the king's rule is ordained and consecrated by God).

The contemporary Arab monarchy (with its emphasis on consultation – *shura*) actually resembles the medieval model far more than it does the later European absolutist state, not because it is less modern but because it is more consultative. One powerful obstacle to the establishment of an absolutist monarchy in the Arab world is Islam's prescription that sovereignty always remains with Allah. The ruler therefore only maintains legitimacy so long as he rules in accordance with the principles of Islam. He has no divine right to rule, let alone to rule absolutely. This means that his actions are always subject to the judgement of his fellow Muslims, and that he retains their support only by means of religiously and ethically correct behaviour. In this respect competence and ethics are intertwined. A bad or illegitimate ruler is one who, through a failure correctly to observe the ethical demands of Islam, rules badly and leads his people into danger, poverty and weakness. Such a ruler may be legitimately overthrown.

In practice, the classical formation of the modern state, in which the government retains a monopoly over the means of coercion (military force), means that the contemporary Arab king is far less vulnerable than this theoretical account might suggest. Even so, there have been recent overthrows. One of these, in particular, deserves some attention, for it suggests that the persistence of monarchy has unexpected outcomes. In 1995 the Emir of Qatar, Khalifa al-Thani, was ousted by his son, Sheikh Hamad, while out of the country, reportedly seeking medical attention in Geneva. This event, routinely described as either a 'bloodless' or a 'peaceful' coup attracted some attention at the time, both within and beyond the region. In the West, where the idea of dynastic plotting in

Arabian palaces most certainly appealed to precisely the kind of audience that enjoys fantasies of Oriental despotism, it was initially reported as an entertaining anachronism. The subsequent attempt at a counter-coup by the ousted emir, perhaps with support from within Saudi Arabia, gained attention in as much as it played on similar themes. Reports that faithful 'bedouin' had rallied to the cause of the old emir resonated with dim folk memories of Lawrence of Arabia.

In the years following the 'coup', rather more enduring interest was provoked and sustained by Qatar's development initiatives. These included the success of the country's liquefied natural gas export project, the global fame of the Doha-based (and al-Thani financed) satellite TV station Al-Jazeera, and the attempt to build a major sporting infrastructure by, among other things, hosting the 2006 Asian Games and awarding Qatari citizenship to prominent African athletes. Less remarked upon, but perhaps of more enduring importance, have been the abolition of the ministry of information, the holding of elections to municipal councils in 1999, and the promulgation, in 2003, of a new constitution. Sheikh Hamad's 'coup' was therefore understood retrospectively as a modernizer's move to take the country decisively in a new direction. While this is an entirely legitimate interpretation of the events in question, in retaining the notion that what happened was a 'coup', it fails adequately to understand what these events might reveal about the nature of kingship in the Gulf. Alternative accounts of these events would present Sheikh Hamad's replacement of his father as part of an orderly, if rather unusual, way of managing the succession and as evidence of some degree of political flexibility within a monarchical system.

In thinking differently about the 1995 'coup' one might start by observing that Sheikh Hamad had been gradually consolidating his role as the leading figure in the government for some time, and that meaningful political power was flowing steadily in his direction and away from his father. This was not a process that was conducted in secret. There was no conspiracy behind closed doors. Emir Khalifa will have been fully aware of what was going on.

Because succession in the Arab Gulf is by no means a cut and dried process – there is no tradition of primogeniture and in Qatar at that time the only constitutional stipulation about the succession was that it should take place within the al-Thani family – the question of whether the proposed new ruler is the most capable option is a real one. Once capacity to rule is acknowledged as a factor in the legitimacy of the ruler it is easy to see how a gradual ebbing of the incumbent's powers meeting the rising tide of the successor's might lead to a transfer of power. In the absence of a tradition of voluntary abdication, the 'coup' becomes the accepted way in which a new ruler, assured in advance of receiving *'baya'* (the formal acclaim that confirms his authority) moves to take full control. The 'coup' is a kind of formality, in which the deposed ruler accepts the fact that his successor has the power to replace him. The ruler 'consents' to the 'coup' because he is satisfied that the successor is now, legitimately, the one who commands the consent of those who matter (usually the key members of the ruling family). The coup in Qatar exhibits aspects of this kind of transfer of power, even though Emir Khalifa appears to have sought to reverse it. The counter-coup attempt may well have been more concerned with securing for the former emir a satisfactory financial settlement than with a serious attempt to take back power. A coup in Qatar, then, is a matter of give and take, not just take. It looks like a half-conscious, half-accidental mechanism for managing the transfer of political power in a system where there is a high degree of legitimacy but where only a modest amount of that legitimacy is vested in formal institutions that stand above the ruler. The ruler thus has to participate in the operation of mechanisms that secure his own demise in order for political legitimacy to be preserved.

A second starting point for thinking about the events in Qatar of 1995 is to consider the political situation facing Sheikh Hamad once he had replaced his father. As we have seen, his accession to the throne led fairly quickly to a rapid acceleration of a process of economic and political reform with a lot of highly visible effects. As Andrew Rathmell and Kirsten Schulze observe,[9] there was no significant social or economic pressure forcing these developments. Instead, they argue, Hamad embarked on this process because of the need to consolidate his political position and to enhance his legitimacy in the eyes of his political constituency, characterized by Rathmell and Schulze as 'the often Western educated and more cosmopolitan younger generation of Qataris who populate the bureaucracy, armed forces and private sector'.[10] For this group, political reform was welcomed, not because it extended political participation but because of the way it enhanced Qatar's regional and international profile. Hamad's reforms rebranded the country in colours with which a significant and influential social and economic constituency felt comfortable. What this suggests is that even within the apparently clumsy and distinctly undemocratic event of a palace coup there exists potential for political respon- siveness, for an implicit dialogue between rulers and (some) ruled, and that the monarch's own need for political legitimacy can become a factor that encourages a kind of negotiated political change. This is not democracy, but it is evidence, in a most unlikely quarter, of a dynamic political process.

The energy behind reform in Qatar clearly came directly from Emir Hamad's accession to power, although, as has been suggested, it also responded to desires either latent or present within a politically significant sector of the elite group and beyond it. The phenomenon of reformist energy emerging in conjunction with the passage of power from one monarch to the next has been widely noted in the region in recent years. It has already been noted how both King Abdullah of Jordan and King Mohammed of Morocco generated considerable enthusiasm based on expectations that they would push forward programmes of reform and modernization in ways that their fathers – men of another generation – might not have wished or been able to do, and how, even in the very limited political space of Saudi Arabia, the fact that Abdullah is now king rather than crown prince acting as king, appears to have made some difference.

No one has yet come to power, however, promising their own abolition or even a significant revision of their own constitutional powers. The powers of other political actors have been enhanced in most, if not all, of the region's monarchies in recent years and, in Morocco at least, there is some reason to believe that the king's current position as the arbiter who stands above party political competition has the potential to be transformed into some form of constitutional monarchy. Until and unless such a transition does take place – either in Morocco or elsewhere – it will remain the case that, their legitimacy notwithstanding, the region's monarchs stand in the way of political developments that would really place the choice of government in the hands of the people. In the final section of this chapter we look at how the monarch as arbiter can still be a progressive force, and also at how, at the very same time, this process enhances the political power of institutions that continue to block reform. There is a constant tension between the potential of the arbiter – who intervenes only to conclude a debate in which others set the terms – and the power of the authority that sets the terms of debate. On the one hand, King Mohammed of Morocco can use royal institutions to intervene decisively in favour of progressive measures, against conservative popular opposition (as in the case of the *moudawwana* reform, to be discussed presently). However, the same institutions accrue further power by means of such interventions, which promotes the continued development of parallel structures in which the royal court competes with the government over the pace and direction of change, and usually wins. The power of the court, rather than the king himself, may ultimately be what prevents the king from becoming either a democrat or a constitutional monarch. Reducing or even eliminating the royal court as a political force may turn out to be much more important to the prospects of democracy in these monarchies than the continued development of their present representative institutions.

Kings and parties: negotiating change

The story of King Mohammed's role in the reform of the *moudawwana* is a story of the king as arbiter. The reality of the permanent power structure – the *makhzan* – that underpins monarchical rule in Morocco demonstrates the continued existence of authority as a determining factor in the political process. The issue of the relationship between the king, the court and the democratic process, in both Jordan and Morocco, exhibits how arbitration and authority have a tendency to merge into one another.

Morocco's *moudawwana* is the 1957 codification of its traditional personal status law, adopted following a royal commission decision not to pursue proposals for a more modern legal framework that the leader of the nationalist political party, the *Istiqlal*, Allal al-Fasi, had developed. Its origins therefore lie in the intervention of the institutions of monarchy to prevent developments arising out of the 'popular' political sphere, in this case the main nationalist political party. Although the *moudawwana* allows a woman to own and manage her property, it requires her to obtain the consent of a patron to marry, and of her father or husband to transact business, get a job or a passport. Polygamy is permitted for men and men retain the right to divorce their wives by declaration (*talaq*). The *moudawwana* became the target of organized political activity by left-wing groups and women in the early 1990s, which resulted in a petition of over one million signatures demanding its reform being presented. The key demands of the petition were for equality in the family; full legal competency for women; a woman's right to marry without a patron; the increase in the legal age of marriage from 15 to 18; the equalization of divorce and end of *talaq*; the abolition of polygamy; the legislation of equal rights of guardianship over children; and, the establishment of a woman's right to education and to work. King Hassan turned, typically, to the institutions of the monarchy, and again, a royal commission was appointed, which eventually proposed some very minor changes to the *moudawwana*, which fell far short of what the petition had demanded. Here the authority of the monarchy has been deployed to arrest movement for change. By the time the issue of the *moudawwanna* regained centre stage in Moroccan politics the political landscape had been significantly altered, partly by the death of King Hassan in 1999 but also by what may now be regarded as his final bequest to the nation, the experiment with political *alternance* after the elections of 1997.

The elections of November 1997 followed the adoption of a new electoral code, which provided for the public funding of political parties, syndicates and the press, as well as an explicit prohibition of the use of government resources for electoral campaign purposes, and specific arrangements for media access for political groups. This new code was accompanied by a formal declaration signed by the government and the leaders of political parties affirming their commitment to a democratic regime based on constitutional monarchy. Together with a measure of social and economic harmony these political agreements created the conditions that King Hassan required for his first experience of permitting a change in government following the result of an election – the move that has generally been known as *l'alternance*. Local elections in June gave the combined forces of the Koutla (the grouping of parties of the left) a slender advantage over the Wifaq coalition of the right. In November's parliamentary elections neither the Koutla nor the Wifaq obtained enough seats to form a majority, but the largest party within the Koutla, the Union Socialiste des Forces Populaires (USFP) obtained the largest number of seats of any single party (57). Elections to the upper house in December resulted in small gains for the Wifaq and its allies on the right.[11] These elections did not constitute a significant change in parliamentary representation, merely displaying a greater tendency to fragmentation than seen in the previous parliament. However, with the political forces fairly evenly matched, the experiment with *alternance* could go ahead without handing too much power at once to the opposition. In February 1998 the king accordingly invited the USFP secretary-general Abderrahman Youssoufi to form the new government.

The opposition had become the government as a result of an election. The role of the king in securing what had been widely known to be his own objective – *alternance* – is more than merely that of a constitutional monarch like Elizabeth II who is more or less obliged to invite the leader of the largest party to form the government. King Hassan's pre-planned intervention effectively turbocharged the rather weak mandate that the democratic process had handed the opposition. *Alternance* was not achieved by the success of the opposition in a democratic election so much as with the assistance of the monarch, who thereby reasserted his power over the process, and the continued dependency on the monarch of the political parties within it. The king was conducting an experiment, and everyone was well aware that it could only be declared a success as long as certain limits were still observed. No one had a free hand. What the king giveth with one hand he taketh away with the other.

The *moudawwana* returned as a major political issue with the left in office. The Youssoufi government developed a plan to enhance the social and economic status of women and their role in the development process, and identified the existing *moudawwana* as 'a serious obstacle to participation in all forms of public life for half of Morocco's population'.[12] This plan effectively returned all the demands of the earlier petition to the table. On this occasion the campaign to reform the *moudawwana* not only mobilized the supporters of reform, but also its increasingly vociferous opponents, led by the Islamist movement, in large public demonstrations in 2000. The leader of the Islamist Justice and Development Party, Abd al-Karim Khatib, described the campaign as 'a war between the believers and the apostates'.[13] Once again, the response of the king – now King Hassan's son, Mohammed – was to create a committee that would report to him. This was initially appointed under the leadership of the president of the Supreme Court, Driss Dahak, and few advocates of reform expected that it would recommend significant change. However, in 2003, King Mohammed replaced Dahak with the *Istiqlal* secretary-general Mohammed Boucetta, who delivered a report, believed to contain two sets of recommendations, one very modest, one much more far-reaching. The king revealed his plan to accept the more far-reaching recommendations in a speech to parliament on 23 October 2003. In this instance the king's action seems to have been that of arbiter rather than authority, and this gave him the opportunity to make a progressive move. The plan proposed by the king accepts most of the demands of the initial position, but all the same the king sought to present his decision as non-partisan: the plan, he said, 'should not be perceived as an indication of one side's victory over the other, but rather as gains for all Moroccans'.[14]

One conclusion that might be drawn from the way in which this issue was handled over more than a decade is that it may be difficult to use the explicit authority of the monarchy on behalf of modernization and change, but that this same authority, presented in the form of arbitration, can be used in this way. Authority cannot line up behind a demand articulated from the 'popular' sphere unless there is a clear dispute within the 'popular sphere' that can be arbitrated. Where a plurality of voices does not arise, the authority of the monarchy favours the silence of the status quo, but where there is a hotly contested issue the monarchy can arbitrate in favour of one or other voice – in this case the voice that called for change. Its arbitration will be presented not as a decision that supports the claim it actually supports, but as a decision that seeks to preserve national unity by bringing a dispute to an end. Thus, modernization can be pursued under the guise of preserving the peace. It is hard to imagine how this kind of manoeuvre might be possible without a person or institution standing somewhere above the political process, yet simultaneously being a part of it. The role adopted by King Mohammed over the *moudawwana*, not unlike his father's management of *alternance*, combines elements of two different modes of monarchy: it is partly monarchical government, in which the king is the authority and speaks first and last, and partly a constitutional monarchy, in which the king speaks only, as it were, when spoken to. In one model the king decrees as a matter of course; in the other the king intervenes only when necessary, or when it looks like it might be.

Another significant factor to limit both the capacity of the king to become a decisive force for reform and the ability of democratic political movements to secure power in Morocco is the continued influence of the *makhzan*. The *makhzan* (literally storehouse) was for centuries the traditional resource of court and administration the ruler possessed that gave him sufficient powers of coercive violence to enforce his rule in the face of a range of local and regional sites of resistance. It enabled, crucially, the collection of taxes that sustained the ruler's economic power. In its modern formation, as John Waterbury has pointed out, it remains a powerful conservative force: 'The heritage of the *makhzan* which has been handed down to the new kingdom of Morocco is a defensive preoccupation with survival.'[15] Today the *makhzan* constitutes a significant political power around the king, accountable only to the king, and is a source of policy advice and even decision-making that remains more influential than the government itself in key areas (particularly defence, internal security, foreign relations and constitutional issues). Similar institutions are readily observable in other monarchies, where many formal institutions of power – typically government ministries – find themselves in an often uneven struggle with rivals within the court. Because the court is preoccupied with survival – both of the system it serves and its own – its interests almost always tend to lie with the preservation of the status quo.

In Jordan, for example, it can readily be seen that the group of advisers in King Abdullah's court constitute a significant source of resistance to the king's preference for political reform. In Jordan, the interplay between the court, government and political parties is richly illustrative of a problem that faces other 'modernizing monarchs' in the region too. The problem lies in the fact that the court, government and democratic political process are not properly linked to one another. Each functions as a separate, free-standing wheel rather than as part of a machine that is 'geared' together. Political parties compete in a democratic process for seats in parliament. However, electoral success is not a direct route to political power. First, the king chooses a prime minister and the prime minister a cabinet that does not have to reflect the results of the election. Of course it is important to create a government that can command a parliamentary majority, but there is no obligation on the king to choose as prime minister the leader of a party that wins an election. This is how the democratic process stands apart from the process of government. At the same time, the government faces the reality that it is far from the only power in the land and that there are senior officials in the court who have much more regular and extensive access to the king, so therefore much greater potential influence. Government is thus at one remove from power. One of the consequences of this state of affairs is to discourage the development of effective party politics, which happens to be something that King Abdullah is widely believed to favour.

The weakness of Jordanian political parties, with the exception of the Islamic Action Front (the political party of the Muslim Brotherhood), is thus deeply bound up with the nature of monarchical power and the institutions that exist to sustain it. In the first place, that many political parties had a clandestine past in which, as leftist revolutionaries, they sought to end the monarchy, is a major handicap. In the eyes of those committed to the status quo, political parties carry too heavy a legacy of an unacceptable past. Even ordinary Jordanians far too readily still see a political party as a secret organization devoted to the overthrow of the monarchy. While a political party might see itself as competing for a stake in government or voice in parliament, many citizens are likely to see it as seeking to replace the existing government system altogether. It is difficult for a political party to make itself understood as part of the existing system rather than as a threat to it, especially when elements deep within the existing system tend to characterize parties in this way. So many parties have made exclusive claims on power and have sought ruthlessly to eliminate all other challengers that the idea of political parties competing within an agreed framework does not enjoy widespread currency in the region. The key idea that would flow from such recognition – the idea of a 'loyal opposition' – is even less prevalent and is particularly difficult in a monarchy where, in the eyes of some, 'opposition' is automatically considered an act of disloyalty to the king. Morocco is something of an exception in this regard because political parties have long operated legally and therefore are free from the shadow of a clandestine existence, making a politics based on the principle of 'loyal opposition' possible.

In addition to the stigma of disloyalty, political parties suffer from low social status, especially when measured against the court. Political activism is not regarded as a socially elevated practice, and few party members are drawn from elite sectors of the population. As elsewhere in the Arab world (in Syria, for example), politics is the preserve of the lower-middle-class people who, though often educated and cosmopolitan, lack the instant social credibility of traditional leading families, which, in turn, tend to favour business over politics. In the case of Jordan, the situation is exacerbated by the presence and political activism of a substantial Palestinian population. This effectively combines the problem of class prejudice with the loyalty issue: the history of Palestinians in the Jordanian state has not been an entirely happy one, and some Jordanians remain very suspicious of the ultimate loyalty of their Palestinian fellow citizens. In this context the continuity provided by the Hashemite court represents a line of defence against the perceived threat of the politicization or 'Palestinianization' of Jordanian politics. Political parties can be castigated for being political by a court that retains for itself an aura of legitimacy that masks, to some extent, its own highly political character.

Although parties are not where the real social elites are to be found, they are also not grass-roots phenomena in Jordan. There is almost no mass membership. Instead, parties are often little more than groupings of people around founding individuals, liable to fracture and collapse according to the rise and fall of the personal fortunes of their leaders. Without firm programmes such parties are more or less doomed to be short lived: there is nothing concrete around which they can gather support and sustain political momentum. The central role of individuals in party formation makes political parties very susceptible to being co-opted to the agendas of others: it is easy for a dominant group to acquire the political support of a range of smaller, individual-centred parties when seeking, for example, to form a government or put together a parliamentary coalition. At the same time, since individuals can move into government without having to build enduring political coalitions of their own, there is little incentive, especially given the political weakness of the government when faced with the power of the court, for the formation of political parties that move beyond this stage towards a politics of participation.

A change in the electoral system through the introduction of proportional representation would probably encourage political parties to seek more enduring alliances and thus, over time, might promote the formation of political parties with fairly broad coalitions. This would take Jordan much closer to the situation apparently favoured by the king, in which three or four stable political parties compete, rather than the numerous small parties that exist today. But such a move is currently being resisted, apparently on advice from within the court where it is feared that it would enhance the electoral power of the Islamic Action Front. In fact, since the Islamic Action Front generally benefits from its capacity to maximize its representation in areas where it enjoys substantial support, a system of proportional representation is likely to have the reverse effect. But, in the eyes of the traditional elites represented within the court, the preservation of the status quo is so closely associated with the need to contain or neutralize the challenge of the Islamists that any change is suspect, as is any opening likely to create space that only the Islamists will fill. The fact that an opening of this kind would almost certainly strengthen the hand of political forces opposed to the Islamists is apparently insufficiently appealing to be worth the risk. For fear of the devil a wall is built that keeps the angels out.

This is a clear example of a parallel structure, linked to the monarchy, impeding political developments that the monarch supports. Such contradictions at the heart of monarchical rule will need to be dealt with if the process of political reform to which several, at least, of the region's monarchs appear to be committed is to move ahead. Until there are sufficient incentives (in the form of real power) that would encourage political leaders to build viable coalitions into lasting parties, the monarchs will have to continue relying on their own powers of patronage to promote – often within the court structure, ironically – the modernizing figures whom they would hope to see promote their agenda. What no monarch in the region has yet done is cut the ties of political dependency that might allow a genuine but loyal opposition obtain real power and take up the challenge of continuing the process of reform. Once a king has done this, though, the days of donning disguises to keep an eye on things will probably have to come to an end.

Chapter 6
Oman: Tradition and Change

The Sultanate of Oman is another of the region's monarchies. It is normally discussed within frameworks designed to apply to all six Gulf Cooperation Council (GCC) member states, of which Saudi Arabia, Kuwait, Bahrain, Qatar and the UAE are the other five. This means that its political development tends to be understood in terms that apply across all six – ruling families, the rentier state, the clash of traditional desert culture with oil-fuelled modernity, economic and security cooperation with the West. These inclusive discussions of the GCC tend to lose out on particularity, and our understanding of each of the six countries in question is impaired by this homogenizing. But there is a good case for suggesting that of the six, it is our understanding of Oman that suffers the most because, in several very important ways, Oman possesses a highly distinctive culture.

Perhaps the most important way in which Oman is different is its historical continuity as both nation and state. This creates the context for an intense contemporary concern with questions of cultural heritage and social tradition. This is instantly visible in the startling absence of modern and postmodern steel and glass from the country. It is visible, too, in the country's tourism proposition, in which the restoration of historic forts and the conservation of endangered wildlife play a prominent role. Considerable importance is still placed on the use of national dress in public. This gives Omani public life a distinctively pre-modern appearance: most people in typical modern Western clothes turn out not to be Omanis and Omanis are in the majority more or less throughout the country. It also creates a distictively

Omani impression, since Omani men wear dishdashas with coloured turbans, unlike the white or checkered *ghutra* and black *iggal* familiar through the rest of the peninsula. Less visible, but of considerable importance, is the way in which social and political development is understood as intrinsically linked to long-established conceptions of national identity, and the social practices in which that identity expresses itself. Oman's negotiations with political change are necessarily bound up with its character as a society that places a very high priority on the preservation of tradition as part of (rather than as opposed to) the process of change.

Oman, as a nation, has a history unlike that of its neighbours. The present ruling family, the al-Said, dates back to the 1740s. Under al-Said rule Oman in the eighteenth and nineteenth century derived its comparative wealth (and interesting cultural diversity) from a significant regional empire that included Zanzibar and large stretches of the East African coast. Although late-twentieth-century economic and social change has been rapid (and late by Gulf standards), Oman is the least wealthy of the six GCC states and owes far less of its contemporary identity to the twentieth-century oil boom. It also has a distinctive cultural and religious identity. Its own citizen population is far larger than the expatriate community (the reverse of the situation in Qatar and the UAE for instance), and it is less homogeneously 'Arab' in composition. Trade and empire have created communities in which Persians, Indians, Baluchis and Africans have long become intermingled with one another and with indigenous Arabs. This social composition is also shaped by a unique religious identity in which the country's most significant (and probably largest) group are neither Sunni (like most Qataris, Emiratis, Saudis and Kuwaitis) nor Shia (like the majority in Bahrain, a significant minority in Saudi Arabia and other communities in the region), but Ibadi. Ibadism is a minority sect within Islam and its adherents are found in significant numbers only in Oman and Morocco. They owe their identity – like the Shia – to a decision not to consent to an automatic dynastic succession in the leadership of the Muslim world. Ibadism continues to place a strong emphasis on the practice of *shura* (consultation) because *shura* was viewed as central to the process of determining leadership in the community. Ibadis (like Shias but unlike Sunnis) also accept the continued practice of *ijtihad*, in which the sacred text is open to interpretation in the light of historical contingency. Ibadis also claim tolerance of other religions and cultures as a strong element in their spiritual and cultural orientation. These are traditions, therefore, that contain considerable potential for political change, for they contain within themselves an orientation towards flexibility and an embrace of the new and the other. At the same time, however, they are traditions and have the potential, for good or ill, to stand in the way of change. A routine and uncritical deference towards 'tradition' in general, for example, without discriminating between specific traditions, risks retarding the very processes of change that the traditions proclaim to support.

Much analysis of Oman tends to see the sultanate as slow and staid by comparison with the supposedly more dynamic states of Kuwait, Bahrain, Qatar and the UAE. Part of this may be attributable to superficial features (the steel and glass phenomenon) but it also reflects the fact that in Kuwait, Bahrain and Qatar, at least, more has been made of political modernization and change. Qatar has made publicity around modernization a central plank of public policy. Kuwait's struggles over women's political rights have been widely publicized. Agitation for political representation in Bahrain has a distinctly modern, public character. Oman, by contrast, sometimes looks as though it does not have any politics at all. In fact, the political process in Oman is considerably more dynamic than this superficial impression would suggest, but it is a process in which considerations of conservation are strongly favoured. These considerations – the relationship between change and tradition – are continually negotiated in a culture where *shura* (which is both dynamic in practice and traditional in nature) predominates. *Shura* culture, then, is where Oman works out its political development. It is a tradition designed to permit change.

Shura culture

As this initial sketch of Oman's negotiations with change suggests, Oman's modern political development should be considered in relation to long-established Omani cultural and social traditions. This means paying attention to aspects of Omani social life that are not frequently discussed in the context of political development. While this analysis of the relationships between social life, cultural tradition and political development is specifically about Oman, a similar analysis, taking into consideration comparable features, will be possible for other countries and cultures.

Of particular importance to the present discussion is the traditional practice of *shura*, in which both consultation and participation are highly valued not so much as a matter of principle – though principles of wide involvement in decision making are clearly articulated within the framework of *shura* – but for reasons of efficacy. Decisions agreed upon by all on the basis of a consensus reached through participatory consultation are likely both to be better decisions, because more thought by more people has gone into them than decisions taken by one person alone, and to stand more chance of being effectively implemented. The conclusion of a process of consultation aims to reach a consensus in which those who may have, at one point during the consultation, advocated a different course of action now come to an agreement that the course of action to be taken is indeed the best one. It can readily be seen that this approach to decision making, which prevails in the home and the village as well as in the formal political institutions of the *wilayat* (governorate) and the nation, is different from the more antagonistic approach managed within Western democracies, where it is possible, within the rules of the social and political game, to leave a consultative process agreeing to accept the view of the majority but reserving one's right to disagree with the decision reached. In the Omani framework of *shura* the idea that a course of action might be followed if only a majority agree to it remains problematic: it will only be the right course of action if it commands a full consensus.

Another and related feature of Omani public life is what Fredrik

Barth characterizes as Omani male society's powerfully internalized 'ideology of politeness'.[1] This turns out to be more than just a matter of superficial grace and elegance, but a mode of being integral to a sense of social identity and to the manner in which *shura* is practised. In a traditional Western conception of identity it is possible to conceive of social being as a performance that hides an authentic self. In Oman, Barth suggests, authenticity resides in the social expression of self. A similar argument is made about eighteenth-century European public identities by the American sociologist Richard Sennett, who argues that the subsequent trend towards a clear distinction between public behaviour and intimate selfhood has devalued the public sphere with gravely negative consequences for the quality of public life in the twentieth-century West.[2] Barth's account of the Omani public self will strike a chord with anyone who has spent time in Oman. He suggests that it is customary to order one's behaviour in accordance with

> a code of honor that inhibits the articulation of public opinion about a person's worth, expressed in judgments of criticism and praise, ridicule and scorn or deference. It likewise dampens the assertion of one's own honor, the demonstration of individual excellence, the expression of claims of pride and even denies a person's right to some form of pride in himself.[3]

While this prevailing sense of social self encourages forms of political and social pluralism that offer considerable potential for the development of a distinctively Omani democracy, it also acts to constrain the development of certain supposedly democratic practices and behaviours, such as public disagreement and open policy debate. Understanding the interplay of these factors with the pressures of modernization and the everyday management of policy in a challenging regional environment will be important to a proper appreciation of Oman's political development process.

An important aspect of the Omani social and political micro climate is the pervasiveness of tolerance as a social, moral and religious value: 'A cultural pluralism based on tolerance – such as has eventuated in Sohar – does not insist on the perpetuation of differences; and a praxis of tact accommodates such differences as exist by underplaying them and ignoring them in interaction, not by enshrining them in interpersonal ritual.'[4] This means that those seeking the familiar indicators of a vibrant democracy – familiar that is from the Western perspective – may not readily find what they seek. This should not lead them to assume, in the absence of familiar signs (political parties, public argument), that there is nothing democratic about Oman's politics.

Elections

The conduct of elections for Oman's *majlis ash-shura*[5] is clearly marked by strongly internalized conventions of social grace, which reinforce aspects of the practice of *shura* and give a distinctive character to the election and the elected institutions. Because these conventions operate very strongly and implicitly it is easy to assume that both the elections and the *majlis* are somehow less than fully real. But that would be wrong, an instance of judging the social practices of a particular political ecology and cultural system by the values of another. In the West we expect elections to be noisy and vividly competitive; we probably even enjoy the mud-slinging and attack ads, despite of our oft-polled protestations to the contrary; we expect our parliaments to be organized along adversarial lines, whether that be expressed spatially in the blocs that form up in amphitheatre chambers like Congress or in the face-to-face confrontation organized by the House of Commons. We forget, perhaps, that these arrangements reflect our own cultural traditions, so implicit in our own lives as to be more or less invisible to us, and also the specific histories of the chambers and political structures they were designed to facilitate.

The gradual development of *majlis ash-shura* is one of the most important institutional processes in Oman's evolving political ecology, and there is a dynamic interaction between traditions of *shura* and the requirements of modern government. The elections of 2003 were the first since the establishment of *majlis ash-shura* in

1991 to be held under universal adult suffrage. This fact is recognized, obliquely, in the US State Department's 2005 Country Report on Oman, despite the fact that in the section on Oman's 'Government and Political Conditions' the only electoral mechanism described is that which obtained for the 1991 elections.[6] Since the Omani government, for reasons that are almost certainly to do with cultural conventions regarding the tactlessness of self-promotion, has done little to correct such misperceptions in the public domain or to develop its own authoritative account of its own political development process, these seemingly authoritative statements of the political status quo acquire unwarranted currency.

There is also clearly confusion about the role of *majlis ash-shura* and the powers it enjoys and should enjoy. Michael Herb, in a recent survey of political developments in the GCC states, is right when he observes that it 'has no powers whatsoever specified in the Basic Law.'[7] It neither initiates legislation nor has the defined and specific right to reject legislation proposed by the government. On the other hand, it is quite clear that in practice it has been extending its powers and that, again in practice, it does exercise powers although none are constitutionally prescribed. Measuring the conduct and role of *majlis ash-shura* against the conduct and role of parliaments in Europe, as Herb does, assumes that the Omani process of political development intends an outcome similar to that achieved in Europe. It is far from clear, as suggested above, that this is the case, and this particular rhetoric of comparison is therefore problematic. So when Herb states that 'the Parliament must be given substantial constitutional powers'[8] his imperative is culturally determined not by Omani standards but by Western norms and values. It presupposes a teleology in which a Western constitutional monarchy with a legislating parliament is the aim of Omani development. The actual evidence of Omani political development fails to support the idea that any such teleology exists. On the contrary, the evidence, such as it is, suggests the very opposite – that there is no specific, predetermined end in view, that the sultan's commitment is to the process as such rather than to a particular formal outcome. Critics would observe that an open-ended process could just be another name for a process that is going nowhere. Without an explicit end point the process is heavily dependent on the personal will and capacity of the sultan.

It is perhaps no accident, then, that many Omanis refer to the process of political development as an 'experiment'. Truly experimental method does not seek a specific result, but is open to what will come. The apparent lacunae in Oman's Basic Statue of the State, including the lack of any prescribed constitutional powers for *majlis ash-shura* (and, as we shall see below, for *majlis a-dawla*) could be interpreted as evidence of a commitment to experimental process rather than fixed outcome. One important reason for such openness is a broadly pragmatic approach to the process. While some advocates of democracy – including members of the current US administration – base their advocacy on the basis of principles, such as the premise that democracy is the best, the most ethical and the most just form of political organization currently available – this is not the only reason for experimenting with democracy. An experiment with democracy may instead be guided by considerations of efficacy: democratic experiments will be evaluated on the extent to which they produce good government.

The establishment of *majlis ash-shura* in 1991 was itself an evolutionary move, in that the new *majlis*, with its indirect elections in which the sultan had the power of appointment over the two candidates elected for his consideration in each constituency, replaced the State Consultative Council, a wholly appointed body first set up in 1981. Experienced local observers[9] of the process of political development are unanimous in their conviction that this has been a process of step-by-step development planned out in advance by the sultan, and, indeed, that even earlier consultative arrangements such as the Agriculture, Fisheries and Industries Council, established right back in 1975[10] – were forerunners of *majlis ash-shura* in that they represented early experiments in formal consultation and citizen participation in government decisions. If their analysis is to be accepted this suggests that although there may be no attachment to democracy *per se* expressed through this process of evolution, there is, at the very least, an ethical and social commitment to the value of participation.

It is interesting to see how considerations of governmental efficacy and the ethics of political participation play out in practice. To take just one example from the 2003 elections in the Batinah village of Nakhl, which elects one member to sit in *majlis ash-shura*, the incumbent member Salem al-Ghattami initially found that he was standing unopposed.[11] He was widely held to have been a hard-working and effective representative and there seemed therefore no good reason to stand and compete against him. If administrative efficiency were the only consideration it would not matter if Salem al-Ghattami were elected unopposed. However, from a perspective that includes the importance of the electoral principle, a contested election would be preferable: the exercise of holding a vote was deemed important for its own sake. As we have seen, this was the first time that elections were to be held by universal suffrage and so the process would have an important function in terms of local political education. Salem al-Ghattami therefore cooperated in efforts to persuade other candidates to stand, and eventually a genuine contest took place. Salem al-Ghattami won a clear victory over his rivals, but, ironically, from the point of view of efficacy, it turned out to be important that a contest had in fact taken place, as he was soon appointed to the position of president of the Oman Chamber of Commerce, a position that required he relinquish his seat in *majlis ash-shura*, to be replaced, according to the regulations, by the second-placed candidate (who, had there been no contested election, would not have been waiting in the wings).

The 2003 elections were also the first in which the government allowed overt campaigning, although on a very modest scale. Candidates were encouraged to circulate biographies to indicate their qualifications for election. They did not, however, issue manifestoes or make campaign promises. Such activity seems to be considered entirely inappropriate. Not only does it go against the grain of the culture of politeness, in which overt self-aggrandisement would be vulgar and undignified, it also appears to be regarded as presumptuous and prejudicial to the process of *shura*. The logic of Omani attitudes on this issue seems to suggest that it might be inappropriate for candidates to make specific policy pledges or promises to their electorate because they are seeking election into an institution that is itself consultative rather than executive in nature. This is not simply a reflection of the perceived weakness of *majlis ash-shura* (from a Western perspective) as a body that does not make legislation. It reflects the fact that anyone elected to *majlis ash-shura* is obliged, according to the principles of *shura*, to participate fully in genuine consultation, with a view to reaching a consensus. Under such circumstances it would make no sense to commit oneself in advance of such a process of discussion to a fixed outcome. *Shura* can therefore be seen as a factor that contributes to the fluidity and open-endedness of Oman's evolving political institutions. Again, that fluidity and open-endedness may also be interpreted as a resistance to definitive change.

The absence of political parties in Oman is often cited as a significant obstacle to democratic development. It is even possible to find supposedly factual statements to the effect that political parties are not allowed in Oman.[12] While no parties exist there is no legislation that prohibits their formation, and furthermore, the Basic Statute contains a provision that could easily be used to legitimate their formation.

Article 33 of the Basic Statute grants to all citizens 'freedom to form associations on a national basis for legitimate objectives and in a proper manner, in a way that does not conflict with the stipulations and aims of this Basic Law, is guaranteed under the conditions and in the circumstances defined by the Law.'[13] This means that political parties, if they were to be formed, would be constrained to observe the constitutional status of the al-Said family, to respect the rights and freedoms established in the Basic Statute – including, importantly, freedom of religion – and to support the continued development of the Omani economy along free market lines (guaranteed under Article 11). This means that in the event of political parties being formed in Oman, they would be constitutionally prohibited from full nationalization (although that is not a very likely course of action). It also limits considerably the capacity of any political party organized on a religious basis to operate. Not only could its formation be questioned on the grounds that it was not established 'on a national basis' but along sectarian lines, but it would be prevented from discriminating between Muslims and non-Muslims, and would have to continue to permit the practice of religions other than Islam. Although, in keeping with the open-endedness of the evolving experiment, there is nothing that suggests a specific intention to promote the formation of political parties, it is also clear enough that the space created for their possible formation is a real space, even, perhaps, an intentional space.

The associations that form in this space might not turn out to be political parties in the sense that they are largely understood in Western democracies. Indeed, a certain resistance to at least the nomenclature of political parties can be detected among Omanis who, in common with thinking we have already encountered, view with some concern the historical legacy of 'the Party' in the Arab world. For many Omanis, the idea of 'the Party' suggests either threatening or oppressive structures (like the Yemeni Socialist Party, which supported secessionists in Dhofar in the 1970s, or the Ba'ath Party, the totalitarian tendencies of which are only too well appreciated in the Gulf).

At present, associations with the character of non-governmental organizations either already exist or are being formed – including, for example, women's associations and professional associations for lawyers. When asked whether Article 33 of the Basic Statute might be the basis for the formation of associations that could become political parties, Omani respondents readily acknowledge that this might indeed be possible, although this usually involves a moment's reflection because the possibility had not previously occurred. The extent to which the sultan may be ahead of even the most well-informed citizens may be measured by the time it took a senior member of the Supreme Court to understand the potential contained within Article 33.[14]

There is at least one instance that suggests there are low-key experiments within *majlis ash-shura* that could lead to party formation. This arises because the chairs and indeed the members of *majlis* committees are elected by their peers, and so there is scope and purpose for collaboration and organization (lobbying and bloc formation) within the *majlis*. On at least one occasion, members have taken the opportunity to secure their election to a key committee as part of a slate or team rather than simply as individuals. When questioned about whether this practice could be extended into the domain of elections to *majlis ash-shura*, informed Omanis took the view that this could very well happen, although the tone of the responses suggested that they saw no particular merit in it.[15]

Indeed, as this discussion of the social dynamics of the election process suggests, such organization might not necessarily favour candidates experimenting with a joint 'platform' of this kind. It would not be the 'joint' nature of the platform that would arouse concern, but rather its separation from everybody else. A party in Arabic (*hizb*) carries much stronger implications of division than it seems to in English. A *hizb*, as we have seen, is a group that stands apart from or against all the others, the very antithesis of the coalition, for example, and liable to be seen by others as unnecessarily divisive and contrary to principles of consensus (*ijma*) and national unity. Many political commentators, observing the supposedly degenerate state of party politics in the West, have at one time or another mused on how much better it might be if there were more independent representatives and fewer party apparatchiks, a concern they share with some contemporary Arab observers (like the Syrian, Ammar Abdulhamid). One may also readily see how these arguments against partisan behaviour may be used in a merely instrumental way in order to discourage debate and dissent by characterizing it as socially or culturally deviant.

Representation or consultation?

Are Oman's political institutions representative? By Western standards, the answer would almost certainly be no, and this would constitute a negative judgement about their democratic legitimacy. But by Omani standards the situation is far less clear, for the democratic legitimacy sought by these institutions derives not only from the principle of representation but also from consultation, which, in Oman, also functions as a principle, or as an end in itself. Members of *majlis ash-shura* are elected by constituencies and are almost invariably drawn from the communities that elect them. In this sense they may be said to be representative, although that term does not seem to be used. It is also clear that members of *majlis ash-shura* are encouraged to think of themselves as participating in a national process and that *majlis ash-shura* is not intended to be another mechanism through which local interests can represent themselves at and make claims upon the centre. After all, there are a range of other mechanisms, both formal and informal, in which such representations may be made, either traditional, such as the practice of the local *majlis*, in which local shaykhs respond to community needs and resolve disputes, or more recent formations such as the businessmen's council. It is also important to bear in mind that other organizations, such as the Oman Chamber of Commerce, perform socio-political functions of a representative character, such as facilitating formal meetings between representatives of the business community and government agencies such as, for example, the Royal Oman Police.

This is why it is important to see that the principles according to which such institutions and mechanisms operate are conceived in terms of consultation and participation, rather than representation alone. In some respects it might be said that representation is regarded as a necessary process for the maintenance of social equilibrium, whether it is achieved by means of elections, as in the case of *majlis ash-shura*, or by carefully balanced appointments reflecting tribal and other specific interest groups and social sectors, as was clearly the case with the State Consultative Council. Here the requirement that such institutions be representative of the social whole is regarded by some supporters of political modernization as a difficulty, in that it tends to privilege traditional social status over professionalism in the choice of members. The nature of Oman's rapid social development meant, for example, that there were a number of highly respected members of the State Consultative Council who had been unable to read their oath of office when called upon to do so when taking up their membership because they had not received any formal education.

Further insight into the relationship between consultation, participation and representation in Oman's developing democracy may be derived from consideration of *majlis a-dawla*. *Majlis a-dawla* (the state council) came into existence in 1996 when the sultan promulgated Oman's first written constitution. Conceived and written by the sultan in consultation with Ibadi legal and religious scholars during one of his many retreats into the desert, the Basic Statute of the State is a remarkable document. It establishes a full range of human rights – freedom of speech, freedom of assembly, freedom of religion – and outlaws discrimination on the basis of race and gender. It also, rather unusually, provides constitutional guarantees for the free market.[16]

When it was first issued it was announced that legislation to implement its provisions would be brought in over a period of two years. Although some very significant legislation has followed – perhaps most notably the laws governing the restructuring of Oman's independent judiciary – there has not been a whole sequence of laws defining these core political rights. This has given rise to some confusion among observers, with one typical assumption being that the absence of specific laws regarding these rights means that the provisions of the Basic Statute are not yet in force. This turns out to be a misunderstanding – the Basic Statute is the constitution and, by definition, its provisions are in force. It is clear that, in practice, anyone seeking to base a case in court on the provisions of the Basic Statute would be able to do so and that in the absence of any specific legal prohibitions (a law explicitly forbidding religious freedom, for example), the provisions of the Basic Statute have full force of law. Furthermore, it is clear that if contrary legislation, such as forbidding religious freedom in some way, were enacted, it would be unconstitutional and the courts would be entitled to throw it out.

Majlis a-dawla was implemented immediately, however, even though its precise function and relationship with *majlis ash-shura* was perhaps not entirely clear. Initially, it was imagined by some observers as a second chamber, not unlike the Senate in the United States or the House of Lords in the United Kingdom.[17] Dr Fawzia al-Farsi, a current member of *majlis a-dawla*, suggests that this is not in fact the case and that its emerging role will be specific to the Omani social and institutional situation. Dr Fawzia – formerly undersecretary at the ministry of education – is very clear that *majlis a-dawla* is not simply a place where respected senior officials nearing the end of their careers are given honorary positions.[18] She says that it is only beginning to define its own role, which, she suggests, may be to work as a kind of 'think tank'. She recalls that its founding documents call for it 'to assist the government'.[19] The people appointed to *majlis a-dawla* have been selected, she suggests, because they have a specific contribution to make. Perhaps it will become an accepted way of discharging civic and social responsibilities for leading citizens, scholars and business-people to devote some years to service in *majlis a-dawla*. This way the government will gain the expertise of its citizens without requiring them to pursue the specifically political track of a cabinet appointment. As the Basic Statute requires that senior ministers abstain from business responsibilities, *majlis a-dawla* may become a means whereby those committed to long-term business leadership may still make a high-level contribution to the formulation and implementation of policy. The gradual extension of decision-making of a political nature to include those who have the greatest stake in the success of the country's social and economic development is a tendency that will also be observed in Dubai.

Insofar as the *majlis a-dawla* has an oversight function that might resemble the role of a second chamber, this function seems to be exercised in relation to government policy rather than the activities of *majlis ash-shura*. Dr Fawzia chairs a committee of the *majlis* dedicated to reviewing the implementation of government development plans, for example. In considering the distribution of responsibilities and political functions between *majlis a-dawla* and *majlis ash-shura* it might make sense to think of *majlis ash-shura* carrying more of the burden of representation (with its constituency based electoral system) while *majlis a-dawla* offers a means of expanding participation in particular areas where the government of the country would be improved by consultation with expert citizens.

Women and social tradition

Dr Fawzia also reminds us that there are now nine women among its 58 members. She thinks this is not only because the sultan, who appointed them, wants to ensure that their skills and experience are put to good use, but also because he sees *majlis a-dawla* as a public space into which he can promote women who will serve as role models for the coming generation, and as proof to those who may be worried about the social consequences of the entry of women into public life that they are here to stay and have a significant contribution to make. While we might think that the democratic cachet that comes from being elected would give a public figure greater legitimacy that one who is appointed, it is clearly the case that among many tradition-minded Omanis, the fact that these women have been put in place by their sultan is a significant factor weighing heavily in the balance against their own previous conceptions of what women should or should not be doing. This means that *majlis a-dawla* has an important additional representative value: it presents a picture of the nation to the nation, helping to shape aspirations and to validate aspects of Oman's modern social and political development. *Majlis a-dawla* and its members are representative by means of example.

During 2004 the sultan appointed three women to the cabinet, as ministers for tourism, social development and higher education. These appointments send out clear signals on a number of counts. First, they seem to form part of a strategy of leadership by example, as observed above in the case of *majlis a-dawla*. Second, they offer a clear indication that the promotion and participation of women in national life is a major priority. Third, they indicate a determination to ensure that government positions are filled by the most capable people available. This latest phase in the 'experiment' is certain to have some very interesting consequences, and will, as with so many other recent developments, involve a characteristically delicate Omani modification of social practice and tradition.

To begin with, whatever their elevated position and despite the explicit backing of the sultan, senior women in Oman still have to deal with the realities of a social order that remains strongly patriarchal and conservative in its understanding of gender equality. What may be crucial here is to understand that in Oman a personal commitment to the fact and value of gender equality is not in practice incompatible (for either men or women) with the continuation of social practices that, to Western eyes, certainly seem to reinforce sharp gender inequality. The social segregation of Omani public society along gender lines may not reflect a pervasive belief that women are inferior or make only a limited contribution to the development of the nation, but its practical effects disadvantage women to such an extent that it is very difficult for even the most successful fully to live up to their constitution's statements of equality.

Malak al-Shaibani is one example of Oman's rising generation of successful women, currently employed by Sohar Aluminium Company, but at the time of our interview director-general of the Oman Centre for Investment Promotion and Export Development (OCIPED). She agrees that social custom and patterns of social interaction pose the biggest set of practical challenges to the full participation of Omani women in public life. The law, she points out, provides for equal rights for men and women, bans discrimination and provides for equal pay. In practice, however, attitudes and long-established ways of doing things impede the full implementation of the government's drive for sexual equality in the workplace. The main social gatherings loosely associated with the culture of work and where the real networking takes place, are indeed often all male. When they are not, as in receptions that are officially part of work, they are still predominantly male. The men involved do not, with some exceptions, bring their wives to such functions (although in theory they could do so). Malak mentions that her former boss actively tried to encourage events to which staff brought their spouses, but on such occasions his own wife did not attend. By the same token, her own husband, whom she characterizes as liberal on such questions by Omani male standards, prefers not to attend such events with her and this means that on some occasions she chooses not to attend rather than do so as an unaccompanied woman at a gathering that is otherwise pre-dominantly male. The fact that she does not appear at such events, and much less at the other kinds of non work related gatherings and general socializing that takes place among men, means that she feels she does not spring to mind (appear in the mind's eye) of people launching new projects or seeking to fill senior positions. This low level of visibility is an obstacle to career advancement for women.

This is a feature of everyday life that appears to run contrary to the direction of government policy. Sultan Qaboos has been unusually progressive in his approach to the role of women in Omani society. He has clearly stated that to exclude women from public life, either in business or politics, or in any other sphere, would be foolish and self-defeating. Women make up (almost) half the population and the country will only realize half its potential if women do not play a full part. From the earliest days of his rule the sultan has placed a strong emphasis on making sure girls got an education. More recently he has been quietly and steadily trying to help women carve out a space in the political arena. While Kuwait was still agonizing over the idea of women voting and standing for election to the National Assembly, since the elections of 1994 Sultan Qaboos has ensured that women have been entitled both to vote and to stand for seats in *majlis ash-shura*. Two women were elected in 1994, for Seeb and Bausher (both constituencies in the supposedly progressive capital area). Since then women have continued to participate as voters on increasingly equal terms with men and, in the latest round of *majlis* elections in 2003, the first to be held under universal suffrage, women stood, campaigned, voted and were elected as a matter of course. It is estimated that a third of all registered electors were women. This proportion is almost certain to increase with each round of elections.

It is clear that the sultan's promotion of women in public life is an act of leadership and that his focus on this issue puts him out ahead of many of his citizens in a country that remains deeply wedded to tradition and conservative social values. Since the first election of women to *majlis ash-shura* in 1994, the number of women elected has not increased (in three successive elections in which the franchise has been extended on each occasion). This might suggest that there is some resistance among the electorate – even as it expands and includes more and more women – to the idea of women taking a leading role in such institutions. Clearly, this is part of a more general view of the role of women in Omani society. Many parents are reluctant to see their daughters pursue career choices that would put them in the public eye. A woman appearing at a public social event unaccompanied by her spouse is still considered unusual. Young Omani women are therefore encouraged to take decisions about their education and long-term career ambitions that will keep them out of the public gaze. This means that hundreds of young Omani women leaving school choose to study education and seek careers as teachers rather than, say, journalists or lawyers. While this is good news for the Omani education system, which urgently needs the skills of a new generation of Omani teachers, it is inhibiting the ambitions of the rising generation that still has too few female role models to fire their aspirations. In the particular case of elections to *majlis ash-shura*, it is also clear that some women have faced obstacles in seeking to serve their communities in this way.

In one case at the 2003 elections a woman who decided to stand for election in Al Hamra (in Oman's interior) found that her father was opposed to her standing. Rather than forbid her from doing so – which might have been seen as high-handed, authoritarian and contrary to the spirit of political openness the sultan was trying to encourage – he decided to frustrate her political ambitions rather more cunningly. He persuaded her brother to stand too, in direct competition with his sister. Her brother won. Even without this kind of interference from their families, women have found the task of political campaigning very difficult. Another example from the 2003 elections bears this out. Salem al-Ghattami, now chairman of the Chamber of Commerce but also, as we have seen, a twice-elected member of *majlis ash-shura* for the village of Nakhl, offers a vivid insight into how this process works, even now that formal campaigning has started to occur. At the last elections in Nakhl one of the candidates competing with Salem was a woman. The local women's association organized a series of public events for its members to which the candidates were invited in succession. The woman candidate, finding herself in one of the only social situations in which she felt she had at least some advantage, urged the women of Nakhl to vote for her because, as a woman, she would best be able to represent their interests and concerns. According to Salem, his own tactic of inviting the women to vote for whomever they thought would be the best representative succeeded and several women told him afterwards that they would be voting for him rather than for the woman, who they thought had expected their votes. Gleefully recalling the skill with which he had campaigned he confessed, 'She campaigned very well, much harder than I did, she even went all the way up the mountain to talk to people,' and then, tapping his cell phone, added, 'I called up and spoke to everyone in my address book.' Salem had a great advantage over his female rival because he was so well plugged into social networks that he did not even need to campaign in an overt way. He could afford to appear indifferent to the voters' preferences in a way that his rival could not. To be known to potential electors, a woman seeking election has to put herself forward and, in a culture that retains traditional reservations about women in public life and sets a high value on modesty, discretion and never seeming too pushy, this places her at a double disadvantage.

On the one hand, women with prominent roles in public life know that they cannot, at least now, be part of the all-male networks of social intercourse through which their male colleagues in government frequently conduct informal business and, despite the responsibility and authority vested in them by their appointment, this places them at a disadvantage. On the other hand, as a conversation with the minister for social development Dr Sharifa bint Khalfan al-Yahyai reveals, they will have access to conversations with women of all social groups to which their male counterparts will not be party.[20] The concerns and creativity of Omani women are thus brought more fully into the realm of policy making.

Two other questions open up in the context of these appointments, both of which are about the political ecology of Oman and the interplay between social practice and political expediency. One concerns the nature of existing all-male social networks. There is limited but potentially significant evidence to suggest that social occasions previously segregated according to gender, either formally or by custom or habit, are beginning to be held with both men and women attending. At present this appears to be confined to social groups dominated by a generation that has been educated in the West and for which mixed social gatherings have become familiar or even normal. It is reasonable to suppose that such practices will now spread within Oman, not merely as a result of a continuing relationship with Western higher education, but also as a result of social emulation on the part of modern-minded Omanis without the specific experience of education in the West. The second question, which is intimately related to the first, concerns social codes of honor and politeness. Although Omani women exhibit in equal measure the grace and politeness that characterize their male compatriots, conversations with leading Omani women suggest that there is a greater willingness among women to speak directly. Perhaps this is merely a coincidence, but if so it is a coincidence supported by some additional social evidence, such as that provided by Unni Wikan, that the 'ideology of politeness' is lived out in different ways by men and women. Perhaps women in Oman have found ways of speaking both politely and directly, while men tend to prefer to veil their meaning more fully when speaking publicly or to non-intimate interlocutors. Whether this nuanced distinction is real, and if real significant, remains to be seen. If it has an impact on the conduct of Oman's experiment in democratic politics its impact will certainly be subtle. Once again, the destination of the experiment remains a mystery, even if the direction in which it is heading seems reasonably clear.

It is also, as the experience of Omani women must remind us, an experiment in which we in the West are also still engaged. We can hardly claim, nor would we wish to, that the participation of women in our social, business and political life has now reached its own finishing line. Dr Rawya bint Saud Albusaidi, the new minister for higher education, is swift to point out that even though women have been able to vote in most Western democracies for the last 70 odd years, there are still very few senior women to be found, either in the cabinets of Western governments or the boardrooms of major Western companies.[21] Indeed, many of the problems Omani women face are very similar to the problems with which feminists in the West (where we like to take it for granted that sexual equality rules) are still grappling. The expectations placed on working women, particularly those with children, are very high. They are still expected, in an informal, customary way, to carry out a wide range of key domestic functions, including seeing to their children's education, attending PTAs, visiting relatives, and ensuring the smooth running of the home. Even where husbands are very supportive, the onus is on the woman to do all this, rather than upon her husband to share the responsibilities more evenly.

There is little or no childcare provision in the public or private sector, and women who take maternity leave routinely sense they are disadvantaged in terms of career advancement. The gradual renegotiation of these roles in every family and for generation after generation will be the only way in which change will take hold. It may also, paradoxically, be the way in which certain aspects of traditional life, centred on the family as an extended social unit, will be conserved. The role of the extended family is a vital support for the working woman. In this case social tradition may be harnessed to progressive development. Malak al-Shaibani is certain that a shift towards the nuclear family would be counter-productive. Her own parents and grandmother live in the same compound in which she has her apartment and their practical support is clearly vital to the professional lives she and her husband enjoy. As the population gradually starts to bulge a little at the top end due to improving longevity, the existing family structures may well allow for some inventive merging of tradition and progress in this area.

Like the other monarchies discussed in Chapter 5, Oman's political system contains dynamic elements that function within a traditional social setting. The imperatives of tradition can retard a certain kind of political change – as, for instance, in the social pressures that circumscribe female participation in public life – but they also constitute a force that can lead to change: traditions of tolerance, politeness and consultation make the political arena susceptible to developments that can be demonstrated to build upon those very traditions. It is likely to be through the conservation and extension into new institutions and among wider social groups that Oman's political development will continue, rather than by the introduction of anything radically new to the situation. Change will be negotiated, but with a very careful eye on its compatibility with evolving social tradition. The success of the process may eventually depend on the extent to which this kind of change can meet the needs of those who have not, until quite recently, been active in shaping the evolution of social traditions. Omani women are as much the custodians of social traditions as are Omani men, and as they take a more prominent role in public life, their influence on how those traditions evolve is likely to become more substantial.

Chapter 7
Dubai: The Airport State

When you take a taxi from an international airport to your hotel, especially when you are arriving in a city, or, indeed, a country you have never visited before, this first journey in this as yet unknown part of the world has a special function, evokes a special feeling. It is a kind of air-lock – a protected space of transition, from the familiar 'non-places'[1] of international air travel, the lounges and cabins that are now almost identical the world over, to the unfamiliar new place into which you are about to plunge. Before taking this plunge, however, you glide (or depending on the quality of the transport and infrastructure, rattle) through a sort of preview of coming attractions. You catch glimpses that suggest what this new place might be like. Perhaps, if the weather is warm and the windows open, you start to pick up something of the sounds and smells of the place. But you remain cocooned against it, delivered to the hotel lobby without yet having actually come into real contact with the place itself. Our entries into foreign cities are very often just more mundane versions of this performance. Only once we have unpacked, showered and rested are we ready to venture out into the new location for real, unprotected, and ready to make contact. The moment of first contact with a place is the moment you step out for the first time from the last remnants of international 'non-place'.

Arriving in Dubai is different. Dubai boasts one of the world's most impressive airports. Indeed, the development of this airport, of the airline (Emirates) it serves, and of the vast leisure and commercial traffic that passes through it has been one of the most vivid indicators of the city's late-twentieth-century rise to prominence. Although Dubai is yet to confirm its place among the global cities urbanists and geographers place in first rank, it has the airport to go with its aspirations to global elite status. The traveller arriving in Dubai moves easily through an almost frictionless arrivals system, on the familiar moving walkways, past the familiar walls of glass that allow the gaze to roam at will across the extensive displays of luxury goods and international snack foods, into a carpeted immigration hall where visas are stamped directly into passports with unhurried calm, and out to waiting taxis and limousines – so far, so familiar. The familiar airlock transition is under way, the traveller remains cocooned in the comfort of 'non-place', except, this time, inexplicably, the transition turns out not to be a transition at all. The city of Dubai turns out to be a continuation, by other means, of its own international airport. Dubai, one might say, is the airport state, and its peculiar appeal owes much to the sense of the uncanny to which this gives rise.

The idea of the airport state – a non-place that is perhaps a new kind of place – helps us understand what is taking shape in Dubai and, crucially, gives us a way of understanding its apparently non-existent politics. In the airport state, as in the airport itself, everything is provided. There is a vast and complex infrastructure, expertly managed and staffed by large numbers of workers, many of whom have come from far away. The airport must, of course, maintain a high level of (largely discreet) security, and those who pass through it willingly agree to regulate their actions, limit their freedoms even, in order that the security of the airport and everyone in it can be maintained. Finally, although the airport expends enormous energy and resources on the maintenance and enhancement of the facilities it offers those who visit it, its real mission in the world is to encourage and facilitate international travel: it derives its existence and its livelihood from establishing itself as a hub through which millions of people and many millions of dollars and many millions of dollars worth of goods from all around the world must pass, year after year.

Not only is Dubai international airport and, along with it, the airline Emirates, central to Dubai's project as a cosmopolitan city at the heart of globalization, it is also the model through which we can understand how it functions politically. Just as the self-evident function of an airport ensures that its users (citizens) willingly agree to participate in its security procedures and make no effort to intervene in the management of the operation, so the citizens (and other visitors, both short- and long-term) of Dubai, recognize that they are implicitly bound in a social contract with their rulers, in which economic well-being and comprehensive infrastructural provision provide a way of life that substantially satisfies their basic needs and, in most cases, much more. Within such a political system, civil liberties of all kinds do, can and will develop, based, largely around the freedom to enjoy, without disruption, the prosperity that globalization has brought, but there will be little pressure for greater citizen participation in the actual job of political management. For, as Marc Augé notes in his theorization of the 'non-place', such spaces are engineered for use by individuals; they do not foster a sense of the social, the solidarity between people that is the basis for citizenship.

In *Arabia*,[2] his vivid account of travels on the peninsula in the late 1970s, the British writer Jonathan Raban compares Dubai with an Italian renaissance city-state. His chapter on Dubai is titled 'Quattrocento' (meaning fifteenth century, the highpoint of the Italian renaissance) and the allusion to Italian city-states is persistent – merchant houses are compared with '*palazzi*',[3] and the new building for the Dubai Petroleum Company apparently generates in its staff a feeling Raban suspects is the same as that felt by 'civil servants in Florence when Lorenzo the Magnificent moved them all into Vasari's Uffizi'.[4]

What is at stake in these comparisons between Dubai and the European city-states? From a political point of view the analogy could point in two completely divergent directions. On the one hand, one might use the analogy with Athens to suggest it is within the city-state that a sense of political solidarity most readily takes shape, and where conditions are conducive to the growth of democratic forms of government. Alternatively, one might imagine that it is the autocratic rule of great Italian families such as the Medici – assuredly no democrats – that will most likely thrive in such a place.

Since it was in the city-state that the concept of the *polis* first emerged in Western thought and with it the idea that man is, at root, a political animal, we may be entitled to ask what has happened to politics, to the idea of the *polis*, in this twenty-first century city-state. So we return to the question: what is the analogy between the twenty-first century city-state and their precursors in European history and culture intended to show? Is the analogy of any value? In the account of Dubai that follows it will be suggested that the city-state analogy is only partially sustainable. To begin with, despite its obvious descriptive appeal, as seen in its use by Jonathan Raban, it lacks cultural specificity. The term 'city-state' covers a range of different formations: beyond Athens and the Italian city-states there are other European examples, usually arising from comparisons with Italian antecedents, not to mention other more recent Asian examples such as Hong Kong and, most particularly, Singapore. In its application to Dubai in particular, it tends to preclude any engagement with what might be specific to an Arab city, for example, or a Gulf city. The term is too general in that it already brings with it too wide a range of analogies and it does not attend to the specifics of Dubai and its historical moment. To attempt to account for Dubai solely within the framework offered by the city-state idea would be both too vague and too confining. It would be rather like trying to import 'one size fits all' democratic solutions into every Arab Middle Eastern state, which is precisely what this book is seeking to avoid. In the case of Dubai it is also probably worth trying to avoid the opposite tendency: that of trying to think of Dubai within a strictly Arab Muslim conception of the city. Despite the presence of typical elements of the Arab city – the souq, the mosque, the sequestered private space of the domestic courtyard – Dubai is a hybrid, perhaps a unique hybrid, which needs to be analysed on its own terms.

That is why, rather than adhering to the conventional

description of Dubai as a 'city-state', the new concept of 'airport state' works better. The idea of the city-state seems to carry with it no decisive political implications (as suggested above, it could come in either democratic or autocratic forms). The idea of the 'airport state', arising out of an experience of globalization but also respectful of the specifics of Dubai's local history, offers, as we shall see, some specific pointers about the nature of the politics that are coming into being in Dubai.

Pearls and Persians

Some 100 years ago Dubai was just one of a number of similar small coastal towns in which the inhabitants made their living from pearls and date palm cultivation. Like other such towns, Dubai had a creek that snaked inland through the sand flats of the Gulf littoral. During the nineteenth century Dubai's pearling and a certain amount of internal trade had drawn an immigrant population from other locations along the coast and, indeed, from similar settlements along the Persian shore. This population growth meant that by the first decade of the twentieth century Dubai already had a population that was considerably more diverse than those of either Sharjah or Abu Dhabi. While families of the dominant local tribe, the Bani Yas, occupied over 400 houses, an almost comparable number were occupied by Arabs from further afield – from Bahrain, Kuwait and the Persian coast. Other significant groups included Baluchis, Persians and Indians (both Muslim and Hindu). Already the 'local' Arab population con-stituted a minority within the total population of the town. The souq in Deira (one of the main neighbourhoods of the growing town) was reported to have had over 350 shops, making it the largest souq on the Trucial Coast.[5]

In her account of the development of Dubai as a trading centre, Frauke Heard-Bey, trawling the rich details provided in *Lorimer's Gazetteer*, finds early evidence of the liberal economic practices that were to characterize Dubai at the key moments in its twentieth-century history. While the size of Dubai's pearling fleet was comparable with those of other such towns, with just under

7000 people working on 335 boats, it turns out that 210 of these boats were, for one reason or another, exempt from taxation.[6]

This meant that Dubai was exceptionally well placed to take advantage of high new customs duties imposed on all imports and exports passing through the ports on the Persian shore of the Gulf. This had the predictable effect of driving traders away from the Persian ports, like Lingeh, which had profited from a substantial entrepôt trade. Goods from India, which had previously arrived on the Trucial Coast via Lingeh or other Persian ports, now came directly to Dubai, which became the centre for their distribution into the interior of the Arabian Peninsula. From 1904, with the establishment of a weekly steamer service from India, Dubai became a centre for re-export trade.[7] This accelerated the expansion of Dubai's population, with further influxes of merchants, craftsmen and traders to the city. The official response to this potentially only transient shift in population was perhaps important: Shaikh Said, ruler of Dubai, offered many of the new arrivals an area of town in which to settle permanently. Not only does this opening of the right to permanent residence beyond the local tribal groups constitute an important move in its own right – a long-term investment in an outward-looking attitude rather than a short-term exploitation of foreign enterprise – it also contributed directly to further growth.

However, as with the rest of the region, Dubai was to suffer an acute economic crisis, provoked first of all by the development of cultured pearls in Japan. This radically transformed the global pearl market and made Gulf exports disastrously uncompetitive. Fewer and fewer boats were able to earn enough income even to set to sea in the 1920s and 1930s and, with the onset of the Second World War at the end of the 1930s, the re-export trade dried up too, for merchant shipping could no longer safely ply the seas between India and the Gulf, or between the Gulf and Europe. The strategic location between India and Europe that had promised to bring reliable economic development to the lower Gulf turned out to be a poisoned chalice. It was at this moment in Dubai's history that a political crisis developed that holds some further keys to the nature of Dubai's contemporary identity and, possibly, even to its future political development. This was the short-lived Dubai Reform Movement of 1938–39.

Reform

Clearly, the economic crisis constituted a significant root cause for growing dissatisfaction with the state of affairs in Dubai. Historians have suggested that a range of factors other than this basic malaise may have contributed to the emergence of a political opposition to the rule of Shaikh Said. Rosemarie Said Zahlan suggests that incipient (and tribal) hostility between communities facing each other across the creek allowed factional divisions within the ruling family to acquire weight (and political support) beyond the family. Most importantly, she argues that the Reform Movement came to represent the interests of the merchant class, which had been permitted to establish itself as a significant political constituency and was now starting to chafe against the remaining restrictions and limitations placed upon the conduct of its business by the rule of Shaikh Said: Dubai's growth was driven by a combination of agitation for greater commercial freedom and a cosmopolitan political identity that took shape out of interactions with foreign merchants.

This is important, not just for understanding the Reform Movement but also for the wider theme that this history of Dubai is designed to illustrate. Democracy in Europe and, indeed, in the United States is widely regarded as a political development that arose out of the growing political, economic and social power of the capitalist middle classes. Middle-class economic activity starts to become the dominant mode in which wealth is created, and those who are creating the wealth start to identify, within the structures of their society, impediments to the extension of their wealth-creating capacities. To pursue their own economic interests, they increasingly need to find a way of articulating their demands publicly. Middle-class political groupings take shape, demanding a place at the decision-making table, whatever shape that table might take in their society. This basic requirement soon grows as it becomes apparent that the table has been designed to ensure the continued monopoly on political power by those who own land (at least in Europe).

The extension of the franchise to include the economically empowered middle classes takes place on the basis of property. In Britain, for example, representation in parliament used to be on the basis of the ownership of land, a situation that by the nineteenth century had clearly become both anomalous and corrupt. The famous 'rotten boroughs' and 'pocket boroughs' of pre-Reform British parliaments were geographical entities that had either lost any place in the economic order (some had even fallen into the sea) or had as their member of parliament a man put there 'from the pocket' of the local landowner. The major extension of the franchise that took place in 1832 involved not only the abolition of these anomalies but also the creation of a new criterion for the right to political participation. Instead of just land, the ownership of other forms of property and sources of income became the basis for the right to vote. Middle-class enfranchisement in Europe – the process of democratization – came about not just because of a political principle but also because of an economic logic. It made sense to the reformers of nineteenth-century Britain that a man should take part in and contribute to the political life of his country if he had a substantial stake in its economy. The idea that a man should take part and contribute if he had no such stake – a peasant or labourer without property – did not make sense. Democracy emerged as a way of representing new economic interests.

This is what Zahlan means when she refers to 'the political and social consciousness' that the Dubai merchants acquired. It is the consciousness of economic interests to be protected and advanced by social and political action. It is not simply that the merchants were coming into contact with foreigners who had interestingly different ways of doing business and politics back home, although the cosmopolitanism of the Dubai merchants was obviously a factor in this new 'political and social consciousness'. They were not simply seeking to import foreign ideas to which they had been exposed on their travels or in their dealings with foreign travellers, they were developing a 'political and social consciousness' particular to their own situation.

Two crucial points emerge from this. First, it reminds us of the importance – to the emergence of new and democratic politics – of an organized and organizing middle class with distinct common business interests at stake. Second, it emphasizes the important of local and indigenous factors in the emergence of democratic politics. Dubai's Reform Movement of 1938 was not simply a local attempt to copy or transplant what was being done elsewhere: it arose out of its own political ecology as a native growth. That part of its native environment was cosmopolitan in nature was perhaps significant, but not, perhaps essential. If the movement was, as Heard-Bey suggests, 'an attempt to bring into harmony the paternalistic authority structure of the City-state with the require-ments of a multinational merchant society',[8] this should not be understood as the imposition of foreign ideas or requirements on Dubai. The 'multinational merchant society' describes Dubai and Dubai's interaction with the wider world: it is an internal environ-ment, rather than an external climate. Or, to put it another way, the outside had come inside: Dubai's openness to the world at large had been folded into the internal dynamics of its social and political life.

This is perhaps a third and potentially decisive point to emerge from this initial movement towards economic, social and political reform: in the case of Dubai, the multinational or cosmopolitan are features of the internal landscape, not part of the external context in which Dubai operates. In contemporary terms this is self-evident: Dubai does not simply swim successfully in the currents of globalization, globalization swims through every corner of Dubai. There is a good deal of boosterist rhetoric associated with Dubai's current expansion projects, but it is a rhetoric that has a basis in fact. The idea that the world may be found in Dubai is expressed with grandiosity in the construction of 'The World', the new collection of sand-bar islands fashioned in the shapes of our planet's land masses, available for purchase and presumably leisure and domestic development by the world's super rich. The precise quality of Dubai's participation in the processes of globalization will have to wait until later: what is important to recognize in its earlier history is the way in which, in certain key ways, Dubai's social, political and economic structures turn out to have pre-programmed Dubai for receptivity to the new global economic order, and that this has made it very easy for the world to come to Dubai.

While part of this pre-programming of Dubai arose from the international dimensions of its mercantile activity and the merchants' increasingly cosmopolitan cast of mind – a mentality shared with other merchants around the region, on the Trucial Coast and in seafaring Oman – a more tangible and obvious element of the way in which Dubai seems, uncannily, to have prepared for its destiny as a global city, has been the emphasis placed by successive waves of reformers and developers upon the provision of infrastructure. Elsewhere in the region, the development of the kind of infrastructure capable of supporting the development of a modern industrial society had to await the arrival of oil. In many cases, the oil companies took substantial responsibility for providing and maintaining infrastructure (the role of Saudi Aramco is perhaps exemplary in this respect)[9] and oil revenues, naturally, financed its construction (most notably in Kuwait and Abu Dhabi). In Dubai, and this may be another reason for Dubai's exceptional degree of compatibility with current globalizing trends, the development of infrastructure of all kinds both preceded and remained largely independent of oil revenues. It appears that it was infrastructural reform rather than (or at least as part and parcel of) political reform that most strongly motivated the Reform Movement of 1938.

As Zahlan points out, the movement's leaders used the language of an emergent nationalist bourgeoisie, normally associated with a narrowly political agenda. Mani bin Rashid, the chief spokesman for the *majlis* and Dubai's director of education during the brief reform period used the term *wajibat wataniyah* (national duty) in correspondence with Shaikh Said and *majlis* members spoke routinely of their duty to *biladina* (country).[10] However, the main activities of the 15-member *majlis* established in the 1938 agreement between the Reform Movement and Shaikh Said involved the improvement of both the administrative and built environment in which Dubai's business was conducted. They established a new financial regime, which allocated a specific sum of city-state revenues to the ruler, and required that decisions taken about revenues more widely should be taken by majority vote of the *majlis*.[11] Reforms of commercial practices appeared to have been the first priorities, with particular emphasis on reform of customs services. These reforms should be understood as a sustained attempt to create a level playing field for businesses by establishing regulatory frameworks and a culture of accountability. Responsibility for running customs services was placed in the hands of 'elected' officials. Comprehensive lists of employees and their salaries were drawn up and maintained; import taxes were specified and a council of merchants was established to preside over their implementation and to disburse tax revenues for educational projects and municipal improvements. A municipal council was established to oversee such expenditure. Port enlargement and road widening were among the other projects proposed by the *majlis*, but they failed to secure Shaikh Said's support for these initiatives.

It is important to note here that there is little evidence to suggest that a 'democratic' impulse, based on political principle, was at work here. The use of 'election' in the case of senior customs officials needs to be seen in the context of local traditions of 'election' to office as well as a pressing need to eliminate corruption arising from nepotistic and monopolistic practices with-in the customs service. The *majlis* was selected, according to Zahlan, by the 'principal people'[12] of Dubai – an arrangement that seems to resemble the processes of *majlis* selection widely used by Arabia's tribal societies for centuries. The emphasis would have been on ensuring competent administration and a degree of consensus and accountability, thereby enabling the trouble free operation of business, rather than on the extension or establishment of political liberties for their own sake. It is important to recognize the degree to which such arrangements continue to command broad social consent today. Reform of a democratic character will be subject to intense and sometimes sceptical scrutiny in smoothly functioning societies such as Dubai's, and will only gain momentum and broad support among the citizenship to the extent that it can be shown to promise more effective and better managed social and economic sectors. Until and unless things start going badly wrong for the business community there is unlikely to be much weight behind calls for an extension of political decision-making powers to people who are not considered *ahl al-hal wal-aqd* (the group of influential citizens, not formally constituted, who exercise *de facto* decision-making powers within many traditional Arab political cultures). It may well turn out to be the case that political reform elsewhere in the GCC will be similarly constrained.

The Reform Movement was short lived, foundering apparently on competition for advantage among its various components. Shaikh Said successfully rallied bedouin supporters from the interior to his side and ousted the *majlis*, sending Mani bin Rashid into exile, first in Sharjah and then in Ras al-Khaimah. In establishing his authority over Dubai again, Shaikh Said gradually handed over more of the day-to-day running of the city to his son Rashid bin Said, who was to succeed him on his death in 1958. Frauke Heard-Bey argues that when he took power in 1958, Shaikh Rashid bin Said was, in effect, implementing Reform Movement policy 20 years on: 'Shaikh Rashid bin Said became Ruler in 1958, and when funds became available to improve conditions in the shaikhdom he initiated changes which had much in common with those proposed in 1938.'[13]

Boom town

Thus the idea, very popular in discussions of Dubai's more recent development, that Dubai is Rashid and Rashid Dubai, turns out only to be partially true. While there is no question that Rashid's energy and vision were essential to the steps Dubai took and to the particular and idiosyncratic approach to economic and social development that has made it what it is today, it is equally clear that such an approach drew on a logic that was both internal and intrinsic to Dubai as Rashid inherited it. By the same token, the recognition that Dubai is exemplary of now familiar patterns of economic (and cultural) globalization overemphasizes the novelty of its position. As we have already seen, Dubai entered the era of globalization pre-globalized. In understanding what has happened since Rashid assumed control of the government in Dubai, it is important to recognize not only that Dubai was pre-programmed in this way, but also that Rashid's development strategy was constructive rather than responsive. That is to say that the planning of Dubai's economy and, above all, the crucial decisions over investment priorities, seem to have been guided by a vision of what might become possible. While other, later regional engagements with the facts of globalization appear to be in responsive mode, involving modifications to existing plans to account for new realities, Rashid appears to have been in a position to anticipate these new realities. One very plausible explanation for this otherwise uncanny capacity to predict the future may have been that key elements of the future were already in place in Dubai. Just as *déjà vu* turns out to be the effect of a perceptual mis-sequencing, in which we see someone coming round a corner, fail to register it fully in the brain and then, when we finally do register it fully, experience a fleeting recollection of what we had in fact already seen, so Dubai's engagement with globalization only looks like the consequence of supernatural powers of anticipation if one forgets or fails to realize that it was always already under way when one first noticed it.

Also very popular in everyday conversation about the Dubai boom is the idea that there is something disreputable about it. You hear this everywhere else in the Gulf. Dubai is where you go when you want to get away from your own country's more conservative restrictions on everyday social life. Since the Iranian Revolution of 1979 there has been a nervous imposition of supposedly 'traditional' social and religious rules throughout the Gulf. The situation in Saudi Arabia is the most acute. Here the government, frightened by the revolution in Iran and then almost immediately thereafter traumatized by the Grand Mosque siege, has maintained a deeply uncomfortable alliance on social policy with religious extremists of a highly puritanical disposition, resulting in a viciously obsessive public culture of conformity. But, even outside Saudi Arabia, cities where once, in the 1970s, women went unveiled and enjoyed nightclubs, where alcohol was readily available to those non-Muslims who wished to consume it, even during Ramadan, have become deferential towards conservative social attitudes. In this context, Dubai has become to the Gulf states what 'speakeasies' were to Prohibition America, or, in a widely used analogy that also draws on Dubai's spectacular postmodern architecture for its appeal, an Arabian Las Vegas. Both metaphors reveal attraction and repulsion. The speakeasy, Las Vegas and Dubai are all appealing because they seem to offer a space of liberation from unnecessarily restrictive social norms. They are also repulsive because this space of liberation also allows the development of social practices that offend the moral sensibilities of the people who enjoy the freedoms on offer. Thus, alongside the freedom to drink alcohol (the speakeasy), to gamble (Las Vegas), or to go to nightclubs (Dubai) come other more unpleasant freedoms: prostitution, drugs and organized crime. Not only is there a sense, in each of these cases, that such unacceptable liberties flourish alongside more licit pleasures, there is also a suspicion – by no means unfounded – that sometimes the space for licit pleasures has actually been created by the criminal elements. Thus harmless social pleasures turn out, worryingly, to be partly dependent on international organized crime. The most austere anti-capitalist and anti-Western critics of globalization would no doubt observe that this is in fact the case the world over, and that we simply choose not to see it that way.

As Michael Field notes in *The Merchants*, his absorbing study of Arab family businesses, 'the trade that blossomed under Sheikh Rashid's enterprising rule was gold smuggling. When business reached its peak in 1970, the flow of gold totalled 259 tones. This accounted for slightly more than 20 per cent of the non-communist world's new gold supply that year.'[14] This trade was based on the longstanding commercial and family ties between Dubai merchants and communities in India, where large quantities of gold were the essential element in putting together an appropriate dowry for daughters about to be married. This was a social custom by no means exclusive to the wealthy and a practice widely condemned by Indian modernizers and feminists even today. Despite federal legislation in India designed to prohibit excessive dowries, passed in 1961, it has continued, sometimes in a clandestine manner, throughout the era of modern India.[15]

Quite apart from the money this lucrative trade brought into the Dubai economy, it was of considerable significance for the way in which it tied Dubai into the heart of commercial networks that embraced Bombay businessmen, London gold markets, Swiss financial institutions and international airlines. It also helped develop and create networks that sustained the existence of other trading activity, most particularly a massive re-export trade, initially in goods like cloth and cigarettes, sold in Iran and Pakistan, but more recently (and still today) capital goods such as cars and, perhaps most prominent of all, consumer durables. Anyone who has spent any time in Gulf airports will have seen evidence of this trade. It is both massive and small-scale and is intimately associated with the Dubai–South Asia connection in all its manifestations, including the most recent phenomenon of expatriate labour. When you see expatriate workers checking in to fly home with huge boxes containing televisions, CD players, washing machines and dishwashers, you are not looking at someone who has spent all his wages on his own domestic improvement project in Kerala; you are watching the re-export trade at work. The consumer goods are the means by which the expatriate worker finances his trips back home. He (in most cases it is men who do this) is buying these goods in Dubai, over the counter, for resale at a profit in the Indian consumer marketplace.

Field, writing in the mid-1980s, reckons that 'this trade accounts for three-quarters of all the consumer durable goods brought into Dubai.'[16] Expatriate labour thus supports Dubai's economy in a double way: not only does it build all the spectacular new buildings and maintain the modern infrastructure upon which the economy is based, it also provides an army of hundreds of thousands of electrical goods salesmen, fanning out across the consumer markets of the subcontinent, each one of them feeding income straight into Dubai. Not only is Dubai one of the shopping capitals of the world, this network allows it to service main street in every small Indian town too, selling to customers who could never imagine actually visiting Dubai. It is not just expatriates who do this: ordinary middle-class, modest-income Dubaians do it too. The place of such trade in the texture of everyday life in Dubai is evident in Muhammad al-Murr's short stories: writing from Bombay to his brother back in Dubai, Muhammad complains: 'The things I brought with me – the recorder, the radio and the two watches – I have sold at cost price, so I have not made a single rupee. I think the dealer must have cheated me: better luck next time.'[17] Later his Uncle Salim, the invalid he has accompanied to Bombay to get medical treatment, laments: 'All my friends became merchants. They sold sugar, smuggled in gold, bought wine and contraband hashish and made thousands and thousands. I had no such luck and remained an obscure grocer.'[18] The idea that the ordinary man might make it in business, by hook or by crook, is clearly one of the driving forces behind Dubai's success, as well as a perennial source of disappointment for those who recognize they have missed out. Although Dubai today may look like the top–down creation of vast multinational corporations, down at street level, outside the new high rises, there is plentiful evidence of this bottom–up entrepreneurialism, a culture that contributes massively to Dubai's continued economic vitality and is likely to secure its future.

Rashid at work

There has been plenty of top–down development too. In building on the legacy of the Reform Movement and Dubai's incipient state of globalization, Sheikh Rashid was swift to initiate major infrastructure development projects. In 1958–59 the Dubai Creek was systematically dredged so that if could offer sheltered anchorage for local and coastal shipping of up to about 500 tons. These ships were able to bring cargo off much larger vessels that had to stay about two miles out to sea (the waters of the Gulf are very shallow), whatever the state of the tide. This opened up Dubai port to a much more continuous traffic of merchandise, which included the developing re-export trade and gave the city a new advantage over Sharjah. The development of Dubai Creek was followed by the construction of a Creek bridge and the start of work on the international airport. As Frauke Heard-Bey notes, these projects are powerful evidence that Dubai under Rashid was engaged in a proactive development project that seemingly anticipated economic developments that analysts less familiar with the peculiarities of Dubai's existing economic structure might not have anticipated:

> Both these communications projects, the airport and the bridge, showed clearly that in Dubai infrastructure planning was hardly ever just a response to the immediate needs of the community: it was clearly linked to ambitious ideas about the future development of Dubai. Much of this development seemed to foreign experts to be over-optimistic at the time of conception but in the event the economic situation changed very rapidly during the time it took to implement the projects; the influx of foreign companies, the growth of imports and of turnover realized by businessmen more than justified this daring optimism.[19]

The programme of port development, both at Dubai Creek and later at Jebel Ali, meant that the Dubai Port Committee was gradually established as one of the primary locations for the determination of development policy. That economic policy in Dubai should have been driven by a body whose clear economic and professional interests lay with the expansion of the city's maritime trade capacity is obviously a significant distinguishing feature. The energy and commitment demonstrated to the extension of this conception of Dubai is also exemplified in the successive phases of the development of Dubai's international airport:

> This has been achieved by means of continuous expansion, development, and modernization of Dubai International Airport. In 1997, the total number of passengers arriving, departing and in transit at the Dubai airport exceeded 9 million, an increase of 13.7 per cent over 1996 (Government of Dubai 2000). With the completion of the second terminal in April 2000, the airport's capacity was enhanced to 22 million passengers a year. A third terminal is planned that would increase capacity to between 40 million and 45 million by 2018.[20]

This particular focus and commitment is related to another striking aspect of Dubai's development under Sheikh Rashid. Compared with most of the region's ruling families, the Maktoum are only modestly wealthy, yet, as David Hirst commented in 2001 in an article on Dubai's ambitions for 'internet era' economic development, 'they commit a much higher proportion of it to constructive purposes'.[21] Despite some rather spectacular evidence that might suggest otherwise – such as the externally beautiful and internally grotesque hotel folly that is the Burj al-Arab – expenditure on glamorous fripperies has not been a characteristic of Dubai, either under Rashid or his successors. Instead, relatively modest purses have encouraged a rational rather than an ostentatious use of resources, an ethos more in keeping with a profit-driven public company than an oil-rich private fiefdom. Michael Field, one of a number of admiring commentators who praises Dubai for having 'pulled itself up by its own bootstraps',[22] strikes another familiar note[23] when he describes the city as a corporation:

> Until very recently Dubai was not so much a state as a diversified industrial, banking and trading enterprise, headed by Rashid as chairman of the holding company. In this corporation, as in any other, there was a sensible emphasis

on keeping down costs and making departments pay their
own way. This meant doing without a government in a conventional sense and relying on a few long-serving and trusted
lieutenants to oversee particular bits of the affairs of state.[24]

It is not entirely clear what might have happened 'very recently'
to Dubai, to bring this state of affairs to an end. If there is any
significant shift in this configuration of interested parties it is most
probably the increasing involvement of international capital in the
decision-making process. For one immediate effect of the mode of
'corporate' governance adopted by Dubai has been the involvement
of the private sector in decision making and in public provision
normally the responsibility of the state. Even though Dubai's
neighbours, from Oman to Kuwait, operated market economies on
a capitalist basis, the role of the state was not only highly *dirigiste*
in the economic sphere (until the liberalizations that began in the
1990s), but the responsibility for providing public services has
until very recently indeed been the undisputed preserve of the
state. But in Dubai, as Frauke Heard-Bey notes, 'many of the services which had become desirable or necessary for the City State
were not provided or organized by government or municipality but
by private companies.'[25] Once again, a predisposition to adapt to or
engage positively with the processes of globalization seems to have
arisen in Dubai, not as a result of crystal-ball gazing, but as a
logical product of the given social and economic circumstances of
the city.

While this absence of 'a government' is now a familiar idea in the
context of twenty-first-century neo-liberalism and globalization, it
does not necessarily imply an absence of politics. It simply points
towards a new or perhaps just a different kind of politics. The aim
of the concluding section of this chapter is to suggest what this
new or different kind of politics might be and who precisely might
be taking part in it. That there is such a scarcity of literature about
Dubai's politics as such should not be taken to mean that there are
no politics there, merely, perhaps, that the models of political
activity routinely available to the political scientist do not offer

anything that promises to explain what is going on in Dubai, or how it might develop.

Dubai: global city

The *Arab Human Development Report*, first published by the United Nations Development Programme, identified the inadequate development and distribution of knowledge and information as one of the most significant obstacles to the full human (social, economic and political) development of Arab countries.[26] Restricted media, limited and restricted use of the internet and other tools of global communication, poor standards of higher education and low levels of English language skills were all cited as impediments to the kind of development needed in the era of globalization.

Dubai, as ever a few steps ahead of the game, had already launched its bid to base the next phase of its economic development on the establishment of a knowledge economy. Three new industrial parks are under development, twenty-first-century equivalents of the free trade zones of the recent past.

The first of these to commence construction was Dubai Internet City, which aims to make Dubai the information technology hub of the Arab world (a virtual sister to the other two hubs, Jebel Ali Port and Dubai International Airport). Among tenants who have already committed to take leases on regional HQ buildings in Dubai Internet City are Microsoft, Oracle, Dell, Hewlett-Packard and IBM. According to the chief executive officer of Dubai Internet City, Omar bin Sulaiman, interviewed for *Wired Magazine* by Lee Smith, 'the goal is to have five million knowledge workers by 2010.'[27] The second is the Dubai International Financial Centre, due for completion in 2010. The aim here is to create a regional stock exchange, operating according to international norms, rather than within a framework created by local regulatory regimes, which many potential foreign investors have suspected lack transparency and effective regulation. The third is Dubai Media City, which is using its free zone status to permit uncensored programming by international broadcasters. CNN and Reuters have both established operations there, and MBC, formerly based in London, has now set up its headquarters in Dubai. Media City has also facilitated the establishment of Dubai's own rival to Al-Jazeera. Al Arabiya, as the new station is called, is funded by MBC (Saudi-backed) and by the Lebanese Hariri Group. Like Al-Jazeera, it is modelling its news coverage on Western operations like CNN and BBC World.

The historical account of Dubai's development has identified minimal government regulation across a broad range of activities, a commitment to meaningful infrastructure planning and develop-ment and a private sector rationale for economic development, both bottom–up and top–down as the key features of Dubai's prior globalization. These factors turn out to be essential for the develop-ment of a knowledge economy. It is conventionally supposed that a knowledge economy, based on computing and communications technology can, in some miraculous sense, exist in virtual space. The internet finally abolishes space and instant electronic markets obliterate temporal distinctions. You can be anywhere at anytime and still take part.

Of course this is fantasy. As Saskia Sassen rightly insists: 'There is no fully virtualized enterprise nor fully digitalized industry. Leading economic sectors that are highly digitalized require strategic sites with vast concentrations of infrastructure, the requisite labour resources, talent and buildings. This holds for finance but also for the multimedia industries, which use digital production processes and produce digitalized products.'[28] What this means is that the processes of globalization produce not just dispersal and virtuality, but a new form of hyperconcentration to support it, in which global cities performing strategic functions in relation to economic space become 'command points in the organ-ization of the world economy, key locations and marketplaces for the leading industries of this period (finance and specialized services for firms), sites for the production of innovation in these businesses.'[29] What has to be reckoned with in terms of imagining and, indeed, planning Dubai's knowledge economy is the asso-ciated growth of specialist production and services to support core new economy businesses.

These might involve anything from copy shops, interior

designers, janitorial services, water cooler suppliers, photocopy maintenance and repair services, scooter sales outlets, CD burning, flower shops, restaurants and sandwich bars, to international accountancy, advertising, digital film production, actors, night-clubs, sports facilities and cinemas. Knowledge workers the world over are notoriously exacting and specialized in their leisure time demands. All the apparently virtual businesses not only need their own infrastructure – even a dot.com needs a sewage system to plug its flush toilets into – but the ancillary and incidental businesses that emerge to service them are also businesses with people in, that need places to put these people and things for these people to be serviced with and to buy. Just like any international air traveller arriving at Dubai International Airport.

In thinking about the politics that might stem from such a situation one of the things one might want to do is think about who these people are, how they identify with Dubai, what they want from Dubai and, finally, what they might want to do for, as well as in, the city. David Hirst suggests, usefully, that Dubai, as a global city, is 'definitely not a melting pot, more a new polyglot polity in the making'.[30] A melting pot is perhaps the predominant metaphor by which the mixing of cultural and national identities is described in the United States, and seems to rest on the assumption that all the different 'ingredients', once thrown together in the pot, fuse and blend to produce a substance that may be addressed as a politically homogeneous mass. Although retaining a sense of different 'flavours' this metaphor of multiculturalism aims to insist upon the viability of a democratic politics, Western-style. Everyone is free to proclaim and enact their own specific cultural identity on condition that, as citizens, they place their loyalty to the United States of America and its constitution above such allegiances to culture. The resistance to dual nationality in America's citizenship laws is further evidence of the way in which American representative democracy demands that the 'melting pot' produce a society of formal equals, a society in which a Chinese-American can both be and feel legitimately represented in the processes of government by an African-American and vice versa and so forth.

Furthermore, the fantasy, if not the reality, of this melting-pot and this version of citizenship is that wherever they come from, Americans all at least try to speak some English. If Dubai is not a 'melting pot' of this kind, but rather some kind of 'new polyglot polity in the making', what are the identities by which its citizens, and indeed its other residents, visitors and stakeholders more generally, define their relation to its political organization?

Jonathan Raban found his own sense of identity dissolving in Dubai. Not, it seems, an uncomfortable or unwelcome sensation, but one against which he seemed to need to protect himself just occasionally by dipping his mind back into that most English of cultural products, the Victorian mystery novel:

> The crowd absorbed strangers easily: Indians, Iranians, Pakistanis, Arabs congealed into the careless cosmopolitanism of an old port which has always been used to beaching the tidewrack of the Gulf and Indian Ocean. European faces do not stick out with any special prominence from that duncoloured mass of different skins and styles of dress. The noise of the crowd, too, was a muted Babel, an indecipherable mutter of Hindustani, Urdu, Persian and Arabic. My own language seemed to melt in freely enough; I had precious little occasion to use it, and after a day or two I began to feel that its loss was no particular burden. It was the language of the book I was carrying, and every so often I would read a paragraph or two of Wilkie Collins, just to remind myself who I was.[31]

Saskia Sassen suggests that the processes of hyperconcentration in the new command centres of the global economy are bringing into being a new kind of place, one in which Raban's self-forgetting becomes the norm for most people, rather than a kind of exotic exception. One of the striking things about spending time in public spaces in Dubai, as Raban hints without actually specifying, is that there is no single lingua franca. Arabic, Hindi, Urdu, English, Russian, Farsi flow equally readily through the polyglot space. Even in cities famous for their multiple languages and language communities – one thinks of both London and New York – there is still a strong sense that the community as a whole is English speaking. But in Dubai, there is little or no sense that a community is moored to the land through the pervasive use of a single language (in the way that Arabic still functions as such a tie in the rest of the Arab Gulf). Sassen suggests that this uncoupling of a person's sense of identity from a particular territorial location or origin is one of the characteristic experiences of the new places being created by globalization: 'I would argue that another radical form assumed today by the linkage of people to territory is the unmooring of identities from what have been traditional sources of identity such as the nation or the village. This unmooring in the process of identity formation engenders new notions of community, of membership, and of entitlement.'[32]

This seems of enormous importance in the case of Dubai, the airport state, where identity formation may not generate communities, memberships and senses of entitlement that lead to the formation of anything we might recognize as conventional democratic institutions, but that still exist and exert their power, possibly towards the formation of new kinds of systems for political self-management. These systems will develop as the political institutions of supermodernity. It may be that Dubai, as well as prefiguring in mid century some of the key elements of late twentieth-century globalization, will, in establishing its super modernity, be one of the places where these new political arrangements are first attempted.

It is almost impossible to imagine the passengers at an airport – each of them engaged in his or her own individual set of contractual relations with an ever-expanding array of international airlines, as well as temporary contractual relations with the suppliers of other goods and services on site (Starbucks, for example, or Giorgio Armani) – banding together to form a democratically representative organization designed to improve services at the airport, or to demand that the airport be turned over to some alternative function. Likewise, the airport state. This is not to suggest there are, or can be, no politics in Dubai, for although no representative politics based on the kind of communities and collectives that have constituted democratic organization in the West may arise from such a social and economic scenario, there are, nonetheless, meaningful political claims that users of such a city, whether permanent or transient, corporate or individual, might start to make more explicitly. As Sassen notes, such claims are already being made in global cities:

> Yet another way of thinking about the political implications of this strategic transnational space anchored in cities is the formation of new claims on that space. As was discussed earlier, there are indeed new major actors making claims on these cities over the last decade, notably foreign firms that have been increasingly entitled through the deregulation of national economies, and the increasing number of international businesspeople. These are among the new 'city users'. They have profoundly marked the urban landscape. Their claim to the city is not contested, even though the costs and benefits to cities have barely been examined.[33]

If we were to think about this in relation to a possible democracy in Dubai, we would have to ask first on what basis there might be entitlement to a vote or votes. If stakeholders in the success of the city, those who have 'invested' in its development, might also be said to owe some responsibility to each other for how things are organized, some agreement, perhaps even a mechanism of some kind, may be necessary to mediate the various claims that might be made upon the city by the city. What might be the qualifying criteria for participation in such an arrangement or mechanism? Citizenship, limited as it is, hardly looks like the sole candidate, for citizens are only one group among cosmopolitan Dubai's potential stakeholders. Residency might be an alternative or additional basis. Such criteria might qualify the participant for different levels of rights and responsibilities. This differentiation, in which everyone remains equal before the law but exercises unequal political responsibility proportionate to the extent of their social and economic role in the airport state, opens the door then to corporate participation. What major transnational actor would wish to see himself or herself excluded from the rights that might start to accrue to the managements or owners of Dubai-only enterprises, when the issues at stake might be of billion-dollar significance?

Is it possible, then, to imagine a scenario in which stakeholders 'opt in' to the politics of Dubai, a macrocosmic version of a residents' association or property-management company? One might also imagine a separation of the social from the political in Dubai. Generally speaking politics in the states of the Arab Gulf continue to be strongly marked by traditional forms of social cohesion, often tribal. It is important not to forget that tribal politics remain very important throughout the UAE, and Dubai, despite its modern corporate identity, is no exception to this. But, given the very small number of people who are members of tribes as a proportion of the total population of Dubai,[34] the social alliances and affiliations created by tribal structures may continue to be important among the citizens, but if political participation is not dependent on citizenship, and some kind of non-territorial democratic or managerial politics starts to take shape, this split starts to look possible. One could hardly imagine such a split becoming total: after all, tribes and economic elites are often to be found in one and the same physical body. But, with an increasingly highly educated, media-savvy, polyglot workforce, more or less permanently engaged in the business of the airport state, one can most certainly envisage increasing demands for more active involvement in the running of the corporation from its stakeholders.

Chapter 8
Turkey: Islamists in Power

The victory of Hamas in Palestine and the strong showing of the Muslim Brotherhood in Egypt have placed the question of political Islamism very firmly back on the table, despite sustained and credible intellectual attempts to pronounce its failure and imminent death, perhaps most famously by Olivier Roy.[1] These election successes have no doubt renewed anxieties in many of the countries already discussed here – Morocco and Jordan come most readily to mind – about what might happen if election systems were opened up in such a way as to allow the Islamists to gain further ground. It is a different story in each country. In Jordan, it looks as though a further opening of the political system might disadvantage the Islamic Action Front, although it is easy to see why the guardians of Hashemite continuity are reluctant to find out. In Morocco, it seems almost certain that further liberalization of the political system can only benefit the fairly recently legalized Justice and Development Party. The consequences of Islamist advances in these countries, and the prospect of Islamist parties taking power or at least forming part of government, are also uncertain and will vary again from one country to another.

There is no doubt that, with few exceptions, Islamist parties and movements represent the best organized, most popular and therefore most credible political organizations in the region. They get things done: they run clinics, schools and other social services. They get the vote out. In many situations they are the only people offering the prospect of political change. Only where there is very modest pressure from below for political change can one confidently claim that there is only a negligible Islamist opposition movement. Most of those cases are to be found in the Arab Gulf, where political Islamism is limited on the one hand by the social and religious conservatism of the existing governments and societies, and on the other by the limited nature of political pluralism. This means that political Islam is either relatively quiescent (sitting peacefully within the establishment) or clandestine. Elsewhere, though, it is organizing, building mosques, recruiting supporters, mobilizing around social issues, publishing newspapers and running successful election campaigns.

The responses from governments in Libya, Algeria, Tunisia and Syria have involved various levels of suppression. In Morocco, Jordan and Egypt there have been various combinations of suppression and concession. Among opposition movements the question of whether and how to deal with the Islamists has been a difficult one (for Iraqis, and now for Syrians). None of these engagements has been entirely satisfactory and many of them might be described as disastrous for everyone involved – governments and Islamists alike. It remains to be seen quite how these questions will play out among the Syrian opposition and the new rulers of Iraq.

In Palestine special circumstances applied. First, national resistance compelled Fatah to allow Hamas to operate, despite repeated demands from the United States and Israel that it should act to shut down the militants. Second, in the democratic scenario, the government (Fatah) had no response available, since, in losing the election, it ceased to be the government. This is the only situation in which the relationship between government and opposition Islamists has not (at least yet) resulted in some form of disaster or impasse. It suggests that there might be some virtue in a response to the Islamists that involves letting them in, rather than going through contortions to keep them out, which has largely been the way it has been done so far.

It is clear that politics in the region has been distorted by the desire to exclude or constrain the 'Islamists'. Even where they are permitted to exist, they must not be permitted to take power. The situation is not unlike that of Italy between 1945 and 1989, where the golden rule of politics was the exclusion from government of the Italian Communist Party on the grounds that western Europe could not run the risk of another country falling out of the capitalist democratic camp and into the clutches of the communists. Both the deep corruption and the endless recycling of coalition governments in Italy during this period can be directly attributed to the application of the 'no communists in government' rule in a country where up to a third of the electorate regularly voted for the Communist Party, and any manoeuvre or shady deal was justified because it kept the communists out.

With this kind of logic in operation the 'Islamists' are a problem for regional democracy on two counts. On the one hand, you have the problem that the 'Islamists' cannot be trusted to be proper democrats. It will be 'one vote, one time' and after they are safely in power they will throw off their democratic sheep's clothing to reveal themselves as the sharia-hungry wolves they really are. On the other hand, the 'Islamists' are so clearly sharia-hungry wolves that they must be kept out of government at all costs, even if that means abandoning all pretence to democracy (as in the case of Algeria). But what if things were different? It is surely possible that pluralist politics would positively benefit, as it has already been suggested may be the case in Palestine, by the full and unconstrained participation of the Islamists. In fact, whisper it only, this might turn out to be the most effective means for proving Olivier Roy to be right after all, and to hasten the failure of political Islam. A pure and ideological position is easy enough to sustain when you are in the business of manufacturing slogans for opposition. 'Islam is the Solution' is unlikely to be a credible policy response to each and every challenge facing a politician who holds real power. The failures of the Islamic government in Iran demonstrate some of the limitations of an approach to politics that believes that religion holds a monopoly on correct answers. It is too early to see what an Iraqi government in which SCIRI and the Dawa play a significant role will turn out to be like. It will surely find that it faces enormous problems, whatever role religion is going to play.

Yet another way to explore this possibility is to look at Turkey, where the 'Islamists' are firmly established in government, and appear to have been reasonably successful. Since 2002 the Turkish government has been led by the 'Islamist' Justice and Development Party (henceforth referred to by its Turkish acronym, AKP), first under Abdullah Gul as prime minister, and then by the party's real leader and current prime minister, Recep Teyyip Erdogan.[2] Given that Turkey has historically been the regional country most steadfastly committed to a purely secular politics, and that has worked as hard to keep religion out of politics as the Italians worked to keep the communists out of government, this development is perhaps surprising, and certainly alarming to many. The AKP is the successor to a series of 'Islamist' parties that have participated actively in Turkish politics since the inauguration of multi-partyism in 1946. Indeed, this is by no means the first time that the party has participated in government.

Under its previous leader Necmettin Erbakan, it formed part of a coalition government from 1995, in which Erbakan was prime minister. Like many Turkish governments, the one led by Erbakan was brought to an end by means of the intervention of the military establishment (which views itself as the faithful custodian of Atta-türk's secular republican legacy), although the intervention this time did not take the form of a straightforward coup (as it had in 1960, 1971 and 1980). Erbakan had previously served as deputy prime minister in governments during the 1970s, initially in coalition with the leftist Social Democratic Party, despite the fact that his own party, which was initially established as the National Salvation Party, has been repeatedly banned by the Turkish state. In response to a series of bans the party has been re-established successively as the Virtue Party, the Welfare Party (the name under which it shared power from 1995) and now as the AKP. Like many 'Islamist' parties in the region, it draws its political strength from grass-roots activism and the successful provision of local welfare services, to the extent that it may be seen as constituting a kind of counter elite. Erdogan had served as a very successful mayor of Istanbul from 1994.

Lakhdar Brahimi thinks that the Turkish situation is a singular one. Brahimi is an Algerian diplomat (and former foreign minister) who has played a key role in some of the region's most difficult political crises – including serving as the UN's chief representative in Iraq in the months immediately after the overthrow of Saddam Hussein. In October 2004 he was emphatic in his defence of a strongly secularist vision of the region's politics. Of the Algerian election in which the FIS was poised to take power before its cancellation, Brahimi insisted that 'that was an election that should not have taken place': FIS leader Abbas Madani 'and his crowd' had not demonstrated they were willing or able to 'work within the system'. He had told the Algerian president (Chadli Benjedid), 'either you have an election where you may have to give power, or you don't have to have an election.' He resists any suggestion that there might have been a deal to be done between the government and the FIS: 'There was no leadership in Algeria and the president was very very weak.' On this issue Brahimi, as a committed secularist, is out of step with many analysts, both in the region and outside it who claim that some kind of deal that would have allowed the FIS a share of power would have been a reasonable solution, and who now warn of the dangers of repeating the Algerian experience. It has become almost an orthodoxy of regional political analysis to say that it would have been better to have let the Algerian Islamists win. For Brahimi, though, the risk was too great, and rather than the botched solution in which the cat was let halfway out of the bag, only to be stuffed, snarling and biting, back into it, he would have preferred to have kept the bag firmly tied with the Islamist cats inside it. In Turkey, though, the cats are right out of the bag and well and truly among the pigeons. How come this does not fill Lakhdar Brahimi with foreboding? Does he not fear Erdogan? 'He came as the mayor of Istanbul who had already established himself as part of the system. He was a very successful, the most successful, mayor of Istanbul. He had established his credentials as someone who could live within the system.'[3] This was quite an achievement given that the system is based on a secular constitution and one of the region's most powerful armies has regularly intervened to restore proper 'republican' order whenever mere elected politicians have looked like they might be losing control.

The fact that the Islamists have come to power in Turkey first, rather than in the Arab world, needs to be addressed, particularly if any lessons are to be drawn from the Turkish experience. On the one hand, it might be considered odd, given Turkey's secular traditions. On the other hand, given that Turkey's democratic system (the occasional military coup and serious civil liberties deficits notwithstanding) is rather more robust than, say, Egypt's, it is not so surprising. Where there is a tradition of governments accepting election defeats (or even allowing them to happen) it is harder to rip up the rule book when the result turns out to be one you really did not want. That the Turkish Islamists won an election in which a large percentage of the population (79 per cent) cast votes considerably undermines the claims made on behalf of the Egyptian government that the percentage of the vote won by the Muslim Brotherhood in 2005 would not be repeated if the turnout were more than 25 per cent.

That the Islamists have come to power in Turkey also has very significant implications, in particular for the relationship between Islam and the West, or rather, Islam in the West. With Turkey on a course designed to end with accession to the European Union (a policy actively pursued by the Islamist government), the rise of Turkish Islamism has helped focus political attention not simply on the Turkish Muslims who will one day be part of 'Europe', but also on the many millions of Muslims who already are, and who in many cases struggle to have their views and aspirations represented there. Istanbul, where Europe and Asia so famously meet, will be one of the key locations for the development of European Islam in the twenty-first century. This question will be addressed briefly here in the hope that some idea of the potential of this development might be given, while recognizing that democratic politics of European Islam is a whole new topic that cannot be done justice here.

Turkey, October 2005

It is Ramadan in Turkey and the chancellor of Germany is in town. In fact he is not in town yet, he is delayed at the airport and he is not going to be chancellor for very much longer. Gerhard Schroeder, Social Democrat chancellor of Germany since 1998 has been narrowly defeated in an early general election, but the inconclusive election result means that political wrangling over the formation of a new government is taking longer than ever. Schroeder has just conceded for the first time in public that he will not lead the new government. As he flies into Istanbul for what is certain to be his last visit to Turkey as the head of the German government, it is far from clear who will succeed him, though it still seems likely that the job will eventually go to the leader of the Christian Democrats, Angela Merkel. Merkel is the first woman to lead a major German political party. At the start of the election campaign she and her party held such a commanding lead over Schroeder's exhausted and discredited Social Democrats that a convincing victory seemed assured. The final result was nail-bitingly close, and Merkel's rivals within her own party have already started to blame the indecisive outcome on her failure of leadership. These recriminations clearly have a strong sexist component. In German democracy, at least, some candidates are still more equal than others. Indeed, like all democracies, in Europe and beyond, Germany's system is not without its imperfections. In spite of these, Merkel is finally confirmed as chancellor in a vote in the Bundestag on 22 November.

As Chancellor Schroeder makes his way from the airport to the *iftar* reception the Turkish government has laid on for him, prayers are delayed and the breaking of the fast is put on hold. Is this simply the accommodating nature of Turkish hospitality or is there special regard in Turkey for this nearly-departed but not yet arrived chancellor? There is perhaps something unusual at work here. After all, one of the most egregious imperfections in Germany's postwar democracy had been the position of Turkish Gastarbeiter (guest-workers) in first West Germany and then in the post-1989 reunified republic. German laws on citizenship, dating from before the First World War, stipulated that citizenship was a question of both blood and soil. The millions of Turkish workers who migrated to Germany to fill low-paid jobs that helped underpin the 'miracle' of postwar development would never, by definition, become citizens of the country to which they had permanently committed themselves; nor, astonishingly, would their children. Early in his first administration, Schroeder put forward new legislation that would entitle the children of Turkish residents born in Germany to German citizenship. Since most of the Turkish community entitled to vote in Germany already strongly favoured Schroeder's centre-left SDP over the Christian Democrats of the right, there was a clear pragmatic gain for Schroeder in such a move. It also reflected, however, a genuine commitment to an inclusive politics that rejected restrictions based on categories such as race.

This was a political vision that subsequently informed Schroeder's approach to Turkey's application for membership of the European Union. Under Schroeder's leadership Germany had gradually became a supporter of Turkish accession, arguing successfully against the far more reluctant French. France has traditionally operated its own idiosyncratic and potentially disastrous version of an inclusive politics in this regard, effectively refusing to acknowledge at the political level any difference of race, ethnicity or religion. All citizens of France are simply French. They are expected to assimilate fully into mainstream French society and to refrain from any behaviour – like, for example, wearing head-scarves – that might indicate affiliation with any particular religious or ethnic identity. Ironically, this hardline secular republicanism finds its strongest echo in Turkey, where it is also illegal to wear headscarves in state educational establishments and where nationality is held to subsume all differences of religion or ethnicity. France clearly harboured deep reservations about Turkey's accession to the EU, apparently concerned that the entry of 70 million more Muslims into this supposedly secular European polity would make the task of republican assimilation ever more difficult, and that the supposedly secular nature of European modernity would be undermined. Germany, on the other hand, committed under Schroeder to a politics of inclusion that recognized and respected difference (of race and religion) rather than seeking to ignore or efface it, could readily accept Turkish aspirations to European membership.

So the welcome extended to the German chancellor here in Istanbul, in Ramadan 2005, is a welcome based on a shared understanding of what an inclusive democratic European politics might mean. The depth of this understanding depends not just on Schroeder's politics, but also on the very important political reality embodied in the person of his host for the evening, Turkish Prime Minister Recep Teyyip Erdogan. For, although Turkey has for so long mirrored France in its fiercely enforced state secularism, Prime Minister Erdogan came to power in 2002 as the leader of the supposedly Islamist AKP – a development that many feared would bring a raft of unwelcome religious considerations into the politics of the Turkish Republic. In particular, the business and political elite, which was wholeheartedly committed to a European policy, feared that Erdogan and his colleagues would either reverse the policy, or, by their actions, persuade Europe that Turkey must be kept out. Such fears seem, so far, to have been largely unfounded, and, in fact, Erdogan's government had already done more to remove obstacles to Turkish membership of the EU, in its first year in office, than the avowedly pro-Western administrations of the preceding five years.

Both Schroeder and Erdogan represent an open and democratic approach to the politics of a multicultural, religiously diverse Europe that stands in stark contrast to the closed and decidedly authoritarian approach offered by the traditional secular republicanisms of both France and Turkey. One of the main purposes of this chapter is to show that when we are thinking about the benefits that will come as a result of Turkish membership of the European Union, we should be thinking not only of those things that will benefit Turkey, which is the usual approach, but also, vitally, of the benefits that Europe will win from Turkey joining. In a year when French cities burned for more than two weeks, and the French interior minister and likely future president of the republic called for the North African and mainly Muslim 'scum' responsible for the unrest to be 'sandblasted', it seems painfully obvious that Europe's future must lie with the politics of inclusion and difference, rather than with the desperate rearguard action of compulsory assimilation (conducted, strangely, hand in hand with urban ghettoization) and homogeneity. Seventy million new Muslim citizens are actually just what Europe needs right now. Ask not what we can do for Turkey, but what Turkey can do for us.

Schroeder finally arrives for the *iftar*. As he steps up to the podium to address the assembled accompany, the music played is Mozart's *Rondo alla Turca*. He is followed to the podium by Erdogan – Beethoven's *Ode to Joy*. On the surface, at least, the idea of Turkey as part of Europe seems an entirely natural historical development. One might imagine that even Mustafa Kemal Attatürk, architect of the modern Turkish Republic and diehard secularist, would have smiled with satisfaction at this ostentatious display of Turkey's European modernity, orchestrated as it was by his 'Islamist' inheritor.

History and mythology

In the longer perspective of the whole twentieth century, it is tempting to think that Turkey's eventual accession to the European Union will stand as the fitting conclusion to 100 years of 'Westernization', beginning with the establishment of the Turkish Republic following the collapse and dismemberment of the Ottoman Empire. Crucial to this 'Westernization' is the subjugation of religious culture and practice to the demands of a new secular politics. To become 'Western' is to abandon Islam. To hold fast to Islam is to remain incurably 'Eastern'. The East, furthermore, is the land of the past, while the West is the future. No doubt much of the elite anxiety over the rise of 'Islamist' parties can be attributed to the casual association of modernity and democracy with the West, and pre-modern, pre-democratic politics with the East. As we have already seen, this simple set of equations does not reflect reality elsewhere in the region, and it does not stack up, despite a powerfully mythologized history, in the case of Turkey.

Turkish historical mythology is powerful, and it is transmitted with great vigour in the teaching of history to Turkish school-children. Turkish school history textbooks tell an uncomplicated version of Turkey's history, a version that is widely accepted not only by those who share its authors' ideological stance (Kemalist republican secularists), but also by critics of this ideology. In this simple version of Turkish history a group of Western-influenced modernizers, led by Mustafa Kemal Attatürk, gains control of Turkey in the 1920s and sets about a programme of radical secularization in which every trace of religious tradition is system-atically expunged from public life. Western dress is imposed; Arabic script is replaced with the Latin alphabet; the lodges of Turkey's once powerful religious orders are closed and a legal system based on Swiss and Roman codes replaces a system based on sharia. According to this version of Turkish history, then, the rise of Islamism in electoral politics is a recent and alarming development. From somewhere in the middle of a modernizing nation, perhaps fomented by external agitation as well as fuelled by poverty and the familiar pattern of mass migration from the countryside to the cities, a powerful new religio-political force has taken shape. Fiercely ideological, committed to the decisive overthrow of Turkey's secular advances of the twentieth century, this Islamist force is determined to turn Turkey away from its path towards the European Union, to enforce sharia law, to ally Turkey with Middle Eastern states like Iran, and to bring about the creation of an Islamic Republic. This new Islamist politics threatens a well-established democratic politics. Back to the past; the forward march of heroic Turkish modernization reversed.

Two main points need emphasizing to counter this prevailing mythology. First, the modernization undertaken under Attatürk was entirely consistent with longstanding patterns of thought in Ottoman Turkey in the mid-nineteenth century. The modernizers were themselves the result of a process of prior modernization. Second, the exclusion of religious elements from the political process was in fact part of the non-democratic trend in Turkish secular politics. It was the opening up to competitive pluralism that allowed their return to the scene. For as long as Turkey has practised democratic politics the people and organizations now called the 'Islamists' have been part of the process. There is underlying continuity here: the process of modernization has been a trend in Turkish politics for twice as long as is often imagined, and the religious character of some of the participants in the political process has been a constant element, and is part of the development of democracy rather than a factor that opposes or challenges that process.

Who is Erdogan?

How is the new prime minister regarded by his compatriots, especially by people who might be thought of as his political opponents? The view of the military establishment is surely significant. After all, this could really matter, given the military's track record of political intervention. If the military establishment thought that Erdogan was really a threat to the Turkish national interest, it would surely be prepared to take steps to ease him from office or at the very least make him mend his ways. Who better, then, to test the temperature of this powerful behind-the-scenes constituency than Admiral Isik Biren? Last time the military stepped in to save the nation from itself, back in 1980, Admiral Biren had been secretary-general of the National Security Council. In a rather strange remark, the admiral says he had not known of the impending coup until hours before it took place. All the same, he was chosen to serve as secretary to the junta once the coup had been accomplished. This was a coup that is generally thought of as having taken a year to plan and that Nicole and Hugh Pope describe as executed with 'practised ease'.[4] Biren is clear about his priorities though and, in a typical turn of phrase that carries with it the weight of its own self-evidence, he matter-of-factly observes that 'the rule of law comes before democracy'.[5]

This is clearly a man who would have no political scruples about countermanding the democratic rights of an elected government if the government in question were perceived as a threat to the law. In this respect, Biren is confirming that members of the military establishment view Erdogan's election and continued premiership with considerable suspicion. They do not like him. Some of this may be a matter of class and background. Erdogan and his close circle of political and social intimates are poles apart from the urbane sophisticates who still dominate the upper reaches of Turkey's civilian and military elites. Elite mistrust of Erdogan and his people may involve a degree of snobbery. There is almost no real communication between Erdogan's inner circle and the military leadership. If this is an uneasy cohabitation, which it clearly is, the partners seem to be living on separate floors, and without even an internal telephone system. They are getting on with their separate lives, each hoping that the other does not sell the house out from under them or call in the demolition crew. But, if it is uneasy there is no sign of out and out conflict. The establishment attitude is clearly not outright hostility. Admiral Biren captures rather beautifully the ambivalence with which he and his colleagues seem to view Erdogan as prime minister. 'He is the wrong guy doing the right thing,' he says. As the political scientist Ilter Turan has commented in an assessment of the first year of the new government, Erdogan has displayed energy and commitment in pursuit of what is surely now the Turkish elite's top priority – EU accession:

> From the very beginning, the AKP government has shown a keen interest in enacting legislation needed to bring the laws of Turkey into conformity with those of the EU. Arguing that much work needed to be done in this area, the prime minister kept the parliament working throughout most of the summer in order to get through many bills that had been waiting to get enacted. The dedication with which he has acted has won him recognition in EU circles, including comments that these policies have moved Turkey closer to the EU negotiations than ever before.[6]

So the traditional military establishment may find living in close proximity to Erdogan a little distasteful, as though the wrong class of people had started changing the character of a previously elegant neighbourhood. They actually seem rather pleased, though, with what the new arrivals are doing to the place. It seems that the new neighbours have somehow managed to improve street lighting and refuse collection after years in which the old residents had simply written long-winded letters of complaint that nobody ever read. Perhaps these pushy newcomers are not so bad after all, and we can just sit back and let them get on with doing those things we wished we had been able to do ourselves.

But what about the left? Surely the left would find Erdogan's politics equally distasteful. After all, he is not only the leader of a supposedly religious party, but a politician who mobilizes electoral support on the basis of a standard issue right-wing populism, mixing an appeal to business with the promotion of traditional conservative (and distinctly macho) social values. Cengis Cedar is a self-confessed sixty-eighter, a radical of the modern European new left. He was wholly opposed to the military interventions in Turkish politics and fled the country in 1971, spending most of the 1970s in Beirut and in Syria, the classic destinations for Middle Eastern Marxists. He first encountered Erdogan back in 1993, when Erdogan was chair of the then Welfare Party's Bosnia solidarity group. Cedar is something of an Iraq specialist. He is fluent in Arabic and was Turgut Özal's envoy to the Iraqi Kurds. Erdogan called him in when he was dealing with the critical decision of whether Turkey should offer military assistance to the American invasion of Iraq in 2003.

Iraqis are always asking him about Erdogan. One can see why an Iraqi might find Erdogan intriguing: faced with US occupation on the one hand and an unconvincing array of local politicians unable to command anything like a popular consensus on the other, the idea of an elected leader who might straddle the secular–religious divide looks very appealing. So what does Cedar tell them? 'He is close to people, to the people. People identify with him. They think of him as incorruptible.'[7] Cedar also talks about the importance of

Erdogan's grass-roots support, the AKP's social activism and the character of its supporters. There are a lot of people of Arab origins in the party, and like so-called 'Islamist' parties and movements in the Arab world, the party is active on the ground, providing services, helping people with day-to-day problems. In this respect it is 'like Hamas', he says. The leadership is rather 'closely knit', a bit of a cabal, perhaps (again, not unlike Hamas, which can at least cite operational reasons for such a structure) but Cedar sees this starting to change already, as the realities of office kick in. This is a familiar descriptions of the AKP and its predecessors, of a party dominated by a rather secretive inner circle (of men) but with a family network in which wives and their social circles also form a kind of closed community that outsiders find hard to penetrate or understand. Erdogan is not a man of any great education, but he has 'strong instincts', Cedar says, and he gets things done. Cedar is not the first person to say that Erdogan is like Turgut Özal.

Turgut Özal was perhaps the last big man of Turkish politics and is often regarded, especially by his supporters, as the most important Turkish political leader since Attatürk. He led the Motherland Party to electoral success in the 1980s and, as prime minister, played a major role in transforming Turkey from an inward-looking country with a state-dominated economy into a dynamic mixed economy fully engaged in global trade and competition, and enjoying rapid economic growth. He also massively enhanced Turkey's international profile, winning the admiration of the first President Bush for his stance, as president, at the time of the first war with Iraq, and promoting Turkey's accession to the EU with great energy and chutzpah. His career in politics actually began in the late 1970s, after a substantial career in economic planning (under the powerful Prime Minister Suleiman Demirel), when he campaigned in Izmir as a candidate for the Necmettin Erbakan's National Salvation Party (of which his brother, Korkut, was a leading member). After the coup of 1980 he became deputy prime minister, with special responsibility for the economy, a post from which he resigned when his liberalizing tendencies clashed with the statist proclivities of the military.

However, he soon sought to create a new political party, with a broader appeal than the National Salvation Front, and launched Motherland for the 1983 elections – the first after the 1980 coup. Fighting against two parties more or less created by the military establishment, Özal's Motherland won an overall majority in the new parliament. As Engin Güner, a close friend and key political aide to Özal explained, he was a man whose charisma and vision, combined with his practical experience, could bring together people from the right and the left, both conservatives and liberals (and, although Güner did not add this himself, the religious and the secularists). Güner, like Cedar, thinks that Erdogan is following the same path, and no doubt attracts many of the same people, including, crucially, many in the business sector.

Like Özal, Cedar explains, Erdogan has the capacity to move politics forward. He does the unexpected: he is not bound by political convention and has a strong tendency to take risks, to be daring and radical in his choices. Özal, who started his political life in the National Salvation Party (the historic antecedent of Erdogan's AKP) was also a genuinely pious man and performed the *haj*. It should be said that, despite his personal piety, Özal, with his exuberant personality and taste for a showy lifestyle, was no ascetic. As with many men who enjoy a straightforward relationship with the faith of their own tradition, Özal could effortlessly combine earthly pleasures with genuine piety. Erdogan, Cedar suggests, is the same. Perhaps the most important point of similarity though is that, like Özal, Erdogan is the 'master of big tent politics'. He knows how to pull people together around simple and clear policies and to keep them there, not bothering with details or the factionalism that has bedevilled Turkish politics throughout its democratic period. If his tent can look like a plausible home for someone like Cedar, an old time leftist, and at the same time not entirely beyond the pale to an old coup hand like Admiral Biren, then it is a capacious tent indeed and not at all like the narrow, doctrinaire space that we might expect to find being built by a so-called 'Islamist'.

It is perhaps a clear sign of Erdogan's interest in playing modern big tent politics that he has appointed Akif Beki as his director of communications. Beki was recruited in June 2005 from a prominent position as a news anchor and journalist on Turkey's Kanal 7. Clearly, Erdogan understands the importance of communicating as widely and effectively as possible. In person, he is relaxed and clearly enjoys being in company. Erdogan talks first about his early political career:

> I was born and raised in Kasimpasa, a metropolitan district of Istanbul, and that's where I started my work for the party [the National Salvation Party] and for another NGO, the national students' organization of Turkey, which I got involved in when I was in the second year of my studies. And of course I was involved in sports a lot at the time too.

Kasimpasa is on the European side, on the Golden Horn, and was once the site of the Ottoman imperial shipyards. In Erdogan's formative years it was a busy inner city neighbourhood with a decidedly macho street culture, in which only the most canny and confident rise to the top. Erdogan is happy to indulge a little misty-eyed nostalgia for his youth. It is widely claimed that he used to be a professional footballer. 'Those were the times', he says, 'I played as a striker first, later on in midfield, and in the last couple of years, as a libero. But it was all amateur, not professional.' Football has long been one of the key ways in which Turkey plays out its relationship with Europe. Turkey's most celebrated contemporary novelist, Orhan Pamuk, reminded British readers of the *Guardian* that 'since childhood, my football team, Fenerbahçe, has played in the European Cup.'[8] Nicole and Hugh Pope explain how when Turkish clubs like Fenerbahçe (or Galatasaray, Besiktas or any of the other leading teams that 'qualify for Europe', as they say) play a European team, it seems as though the whole nation is absorbed in the contest – a contest in which the fact of playing makes Turkey part of Europe but in which victory will always be experienced as a triumph of the marginal, the underdog against the overrated might of the Europeans: 'Typical headlines after a victory against a European team show how blurred is the Turks' sense of being inside or outside Europe. "Galatasaray roared, Europe groaned, the Earth was shocked", or "We have become Europeanized", or "We have entered the European Palace Accompanied by our Lion".[9] Perhaps the Turkish 'lion' from Kasimpasa possesses the right combination of Turkish muscle and cunning to march his fellow citizens proudly into the waiting (and groaning) palace.

Was Erdogan disappointed when his father refused to let him turn professional? 'Yes, but if I had turned professional I wouldn't be here now! Anyway, there were players who were better than me. Turkish football has come on a lot in the last few years [indeed, Turkey reached the semi-final of the World Cup in 2002]. My political career, that began as chairperson of the party in the city [of Istanbul].' That modern, respectful 'chairperson' is probably not a natural turn of phrase for the man, but one he may have got used to choosing, depending on to whom he is talking. Did he ever imagine, back then, that he would end up in power in Ankara?

> To be honest, back in those days I wasn't thinking. You don't set yourself the target of becoming prime minister. That's a target that's set by the people. My most important thing was to be sincere. When you achieve that, the rest comes naturally. When I decided to read the poem [The mosques are our helmets and minarets our rifles] and was sentenced to prison, when I was on my way to prison, there were posters put up, and flyers, tens of thousands of them, with this one sentence, 'The song is not over', and I am still singing that song with my people.

This is a man who is proud of his popular origins and of the fact that he has retained a popular touch:

> Of course being mayor of Istanbul is not a small achievement, and taking Istanbul was very important, Istanbul is a summary of Turkey. A positive deed done in Istanbul can immediately mean a great deal, not just to the people living in Istanbul. When I took over in Istanbul the rubbish was piling

up, the water was not running properly, and these problems were solved.

This focus on the nuts and bolts of local politics is hardly unexpected. It is in local politics that the 'Islamist' parties have always built their political foundations. In fact, it could be said that it is this rather than their supposedly 'religious' character that really distinguishes them from other political parties in the region, which, as we have seen, are often little more than elite formations organized around a single individual or group of like-minded colleagues. Parties like Erdogan's AKP (as well as the Muslim Brotherhood, Hizballah and Hamas) are political parties of a different kind, grounded in grass-roots activism, participation and popular appeal. This is a startling phenomenon at a time when the apathy of the electorate in the West is a source of perpetual hand-wringing from the political classes, and where party membership has been declining sharply for decades, leaving the business of politics in the hands of a class of managers and administrators. While the mass party politics upon which so much European and American twentieth-century politics was based might be coming to an end there, it seems to be enjoing a renaisssance in Turkey. While European politicians grow increasingly anxious about the 'democratic deficit' that has led electorates in a series of European countries to reject outright proposals for a new European constitution, some attention might perhaps be directed towards a political situation in which the people still seem to engage in the business of politics, and where, accordingly, democracy might be imagined to be flourishing as a result of mass interest rather than withering from lack of care. As Erdogan talks about the transition from local to national politics, it seems reasonable to wonder whether it might be the prospect of democracy rather than the appeal of Islam and Islamic political solutions that has mobilized the AKP grass-roots.

In the Council of Europe the AKP is part of an umbrella grouping of centre-right parties, along with Germany's Christian Democrats (Angela Merkel's party). No one thinks of the Christian Democrats as a religious party. Perhaps in Italy the Christian Democrats (now defunct) could have been (and often were) accused of being too cosy with the Vatican (but such accusations were usually of financial rather than religious impropriety). European Christian Democrats are an entirely secular formation, even if some of their members would readily identify themselves as Christians. Party leaders certainly do not make any use of religion in their appeals for support. So it seems reasonable to suggest that Erdogan might see the AKP in a similar light. Might the AKP be an example of what we might call 'Muslim Democrats', I wonder?

> First of all we have to define something. First there is the person. You and I are real persons but parties are organizational. A political party cannot be a person, cannot have a religion. But if we as a person are trying to be religious but taking our personal beliefs and putting them in front of this organization we ought not to. There were people who asked us, why are you not calling yourselves Muslim Democrats and there have been questions like this from our European friends as well and we told them this would be taking advantage of religion.

This distinction between the religious beliefs of the person and their role as a member of a political organization is orthodox secularism. Secularism is not the imposition of non-belief or atheism, but rather, the separation of religion, as a matter of personal conscience, from the collective institutions of political life. The separation of religion and state inaugurated by Attatürk certainly does not look under threat here.

> As Turkey we are a democratic secular state. We are never going to use religion. We are a Conservative Democrat party, not Muslim Democrats. If we called ourselves Muslim Democrats we would be taking advantage of religion. We are never going to make any party politics because of religion. But we will be respectful of religious values. And we will be at the same distance from people of all beliefs, and people

who do not believe at all. In order for them to practice their beliefs freely, and we will show how sensitive we are to this issue. We do not accept regional nationalism; we do not accept religious nationalism; we do not accept ethnic nationalism. We have Christians; we have Jewish members as well – all ethnic backgrounds. We are not allowing any kind of discrimination. And from the ethnic background we have Turks, Kurds, Armenians. We are the number one party in the southeast part of Turkey.

His comments on ethnicity constitute an important claim. Without going into any detail here about the genocide of the Armenians and the political suppression of the Kurds (and other non-ethnic Turks) suffice it to say that the Turkish Republic has historically framed nationality as though it were identical with Turkishness – hence the strong tendency to efface and deny evidence of distinctive non-Turkish culture. Kurds, whose language was banned from public discourse, were routinely referred to in official language as 'mountain Turks'. The AKP has proved to be far more open to the recognition of diversity in unity, reframing the conception of the nation in a way that is far less homogenizing. The Attatürk legacy contained within it the seeds of a worryingly familiar 'modern' approach to ethnicity: the idea that diverse cultures and attachments to the past within the present can all be subsumed in a progressive, rational orientation towards the future.

Such thinking was a feature of Soviet communism as well as of various strands of European fascism. It is also, it should be said, evident in many traditional modern Arab political contexts, particularly among nationalists who identify the modern future of their republics with a homogeneous Arab identity. Even in relatively benign Arab polities, there is a reluctance to admit to the realities of cultural and ethnic diversity in the interests of developing and sustaining a modern Arab identity, of identifying the Arab with the modern. The idea of the Turk as a new kind of republican citizen seemed to require the effacement of the Kurd, the Armenian, the Greek, the Arab or the Laz (to mention just the most prominent non-Turkish identities of Turkish citizens). Perhaps because this kind of ideological mobilization around the concept of Turkishness as a shared identity is not necessary for a political party for whose members the shared identity is cultural and religious (even if the party is not), the AKP has liberalized Turkey's laws on 'minorities' considerably. Since respect for the rights of the minority constitute an important aspect of what many democrats would demand of a democratic politics, the AKP's claims to inclusiveness, while it may not speak the language of liberalism and think in terms of minorities (people in the Middle East do not tend to calculate identities this way, anyway), might seem to offer a route towards the kind of self-determination that liberal democracy promises. Inclusiveness is a matter of practical social policy and recognition of reality rather than a position dictated by an ideological commitment to 'rights' as such or 'minorities' as such. The results may be the same, though.

The end of 'Islamism'

Erdogan is a practical politician, and a politician above all. Ideology does not come into it. This is crucial to an understanding of the role of religion in Turkish politics. Despite what one might think, given the apparent 'rise of the Islamists', religion is actually not a determining factor. Yes, there is a strong religious element in the language and life of the AKP, but this is because, as a party, it reflects and expresses the experiences of ordinary people, many of whom continue to cherish the values and traditions they have acquired through their identity and religious practice as Muslims. To embody and express a set of values that are religious in origin, and to wish to apply those to the conduct of social and political life, should not be confused with the desire to make religion the dominant priority in political life. Under Erdogan, Turkey's AKP is simply not caught up in the rhetoric of the *umma*, the reactive politics of identity, or reflexive anti-Westernism of the kind that can sometimes characterize the statements of Islamist leaders elsewhere.

The Turkish experience may also be a clue to the meaning of the so-called 'Islamist' phenomenon in the politics of the region more generally. The particularity of the Turkish context needs to be acknowledged, and it would be rash to generalize too freely from this situation. The Turkish experience has been different perhaps most of all because of the long time the 'Islamists' have spent within the system. It has not been, at least at the level of its rhetoric, an especially hospitable system for 'Islamists' to spend time within, and this seems to have acclimatized the movement to the political art of compromise. Time and time again, in order simply to be permitted to remain within the system, the AKP and its predecessors have compromised, accommodated their aspirations to the realities both of the power held by others (such as the military and the secular establishment), and their own power. They are, in effect, purified of the trappings of rhetorical Islamism, or perpetual opposition. They do not have the luxury those who have no responsibilities (or aspirations to govern) might enjoy, the luxury of indulging in self-gratifying ideological purity. To get anywhere near power they have had to demonstrate a commitment to the system; and to govern they need to be flexible enough to maintain the support of the very broad and diverse popular base that elected them in the first place. So the Turkish AKP is different, but in its difference it also points out a possible way forward, both for 'Islamists' elsewhere and for those (governments and liberals) who might be their political opponents. The clear message of the Turkish experience is about the big tent. The more the 'Islamists' are encouraged to work within the system, to contribute to it and to feel its constraints as political realities, the more likely they are to respond responsibly to the system, to invest genuinely in its continuity and to play by the rules of whatever democratic game is in town. It is far better to have them mending the streets, fixing the sewerage and clearing away the refuse, than to have them mouthing off on Al-Jazeera, or worse.

Although an Islamist in Turkey is a different creature from an Islamist in Jordan, Morocco or Kuwait, let alone Palestine or Lebanon, there may still be some value in thinking of connections and continuities. These turn out to have nothing to do with a supranational, religiously motivated mass movement in favour of the Islamization of the region's politics, and nothing whatsoever to do with fantasies such as the export of the Islamic revolution (a short-lived Iranian fantasy that lives on only in the febrile imaginations of frightened Americans). Instead, it is the appearance, in a range of local ties, of a particular form of social and political conservatism. Yamama Shalaldeh in Sair described herself as a devout and conservative Muslim, and showed herself actively committed to a set of values in which public duty and social responsibility feature highly. This conservatism is conservative in the original sense: it is about the preservation and nurturing of traditional values, values inherent in established social relations, in the face of the challenges of change in modernity. It is neither reactionary – it does not consist in an unthinking rejection of change – nor is it associated, as conservatism in the West generally is, with liberal or neo-liberal economics. Indeed, this kind of social and political conservatism often places a great deal of emphasis on the importance of public service, welfare provision, local government spending, the eradication of poverty, and the development of education. The conservative face of this movement is to be identified in its attachment to values and practices modernity threatens to erode and that the movement seeks to restore, reactivate and resuscitate, in order to give new meaning to public life in communities where public life, in all its forms, has been largely degraded, eviscerated. This is therefore a kind of progressive conservatism, paternalistic and a little authoritarian, even, in which religion is of central concern primarily, if not only, because it is a central part of the everyday life of ordinary people. And, as real politicians, its genuine exponents, like Erdogan and Shalaldeh, are interested in the everyday life of ordinary people, and how, above all, they might help make it better. To call it 'Islamism' is in fact deeply reductive and misleading. So let us stop, now.

Coming at this phenomenon from a liberal Western perspective – replete with anti-authoritarian, secularist reflexes – one might be reluctant to agree with the world-view of such politicians. We are used to thinking, for example, that the restoration of religion to political discourse and practice is a move that only the reactionary right can make. It is certainly not something with which any self-respecting leftist in Europe, the United States or even the Middle East would wish to be associated. However, a political movement that seems to express the aspirations of ordinary people and that takes convincing action on their behalf on key bread-and-butter issues such as health, welfare and local services, seems to stand for precisely what traditional leftists have always stood for. If conservatism stands for protecting vulnerable communities, improving the basic standard of living for ordinary people and resisting some of the depredations of neo-liberal globalization, perhaps these are conservatives with whom a genuinely democratic Western left might wish to find common cause.

At the moment the rather disquieting truth is a kind of political culture shock. It is a culture shock because it is these conservatives (conservatives who currently offer some of the best practical solutions and conservatives who offer the best practical alternatives to their own governments) who seem willing – perhaps out of a sense of altruism and public duty that a religious faith sustained in a supportive community can foster – to undertake the difficult task of day-to-day politics. If we can handle that shock then we might begin to realize that even movements like Hamas and Hizballah, best known to us for their role in armed struggles, are part of this wider political constituency. That Hizballah and Hamas have engaged in armed struggles has been entirely due to the specifics of their political situation, and in particular to the basic fact of Israeli occupation. Without Israeli occupation both Hamas and Hizballah would still exist, but they would not be waging armed struggle. In this sense they are genuine and legitimate political agents, completely different in character, logic and rationale from the various groups and clusters of individuals who operate as terrorists within the loose Al-Qaeda network.

The fear of Islam in the region's politics thrives today off the sense that there is a simple continuum, or perhaps a slippery slope, between parties like Erdogan's AKP on the one hand and Al-Qaeda on the other. There is no such continuum and it is hard to imagine organizations further apart in tone, ideology or social values than the AKP and Al-Qaeda. In order to dispose of this continuum altogether, the line needs to be drawn so that Hamas and perhaps Hizballah are on one side of it, along with the AKP and the Muslim Brotherhood in Egypt and the various other legitimate democrats in the region, and Al-Qaeda (inasmuch as it actually exists) on the other. The historical accident of armed struggle in Lebanon and Palestine must not obscure the more fundamental difference between conservative political parties committed to democratic practice on the one hand, and military organizations that have no commitment to democracy and seek only military objectives on the other. The retention of the word 'Islamism' prevents us from seeing that distinction.

Chapter 9

Iraq: Democracy under Occupation, Revisited

T he story of how America went to war in Iraq and tried to introduce democracy has already been told many times, even though it is a story without, yet, the satisfaction of an ending. I do not seek to add to the many versions of this story already in circulation. Many of the versions note that it starts badly, and many tell that it has continued worse. The initial aims of the war do not seem to have included the introduction of democracy at all. The war was to rid Iraq of its weapons of mass destruction (which famously turned out not to be there). Alternatively, the war was to counteract a burgeoning (but non-existent) alliance between the regime of Saddam Hussein and the terrorists of Al-Qaeda. In both these versions the war started to become a matter of getting rid of Saddam Hussein. With the second President Bush in the White House, the rationale for war sometimes looked personal, with the son charged with the mission of completing business left unfinished by the father.

It may be the case – and several writers[1] have argued this per-suasively – that behind the various ostensible reasons for the war (weapons, terrorism, Saddam), and behind even some of the rationales attributed to the project by its political opponents (oil, global hegemony, civilizational antagonism), there lay an ambi-tious and idealistic project of democratic transformation. In many accounts, both sympathetic and hostile, this project, nurtured by a group of like-minded enthusiasts for American democracy, involved the systematic capture of the foreign policy apparatus of the United States, in order that Americans should, for the first time in their history, take up a mission of active democratization on a global scale. Iraq became their first major combat mission.

This consideration of the prospects for Iraqi democracy will largely leave to one side the rights and wrongs of the war itself, concentrating instead on what is being done in the political situation created by the invasion and occupation of Iraq. But, in doing so, it seems essential to recognize from the very beginning that all current political efforts, by Americans and Iraqis, to build democratic political institutions are overshadowed by the continuation of both occupation and war. These are far from normal conditions in which to try to construct democratic politics. If Iraq really is to be regarded as a kind of experimental subject or test-bed for democracy in the Middle East, the conditions of the experiment are anything but representative.

The relationship between occupation and democracy is far from straightforward. It is not a matter of one or the other, but of both at the same time, a combination with unpredictable conse-quences. The occupation will not suddenly be wrapped up once democracy is established. How, in any case, would one determine that it had been? Nor is it a matter of democracy being impossible until the occupation ends, although for many Iraqis the two are entirely incompatible. This means that resistance to the occu-pation will continue alongside democracy, while at the same time the resistance will be both for and against democracy. In fact, just as in Palestine, two systems will coexist – a democratic system sitting within a broader system of occupation and resistance, with each system impacting upon the other. In Palestine, recent developments suggest that democratic success will come to those who can claim to offer the greatest resistance to occupation. The profoundly uncomfortable situation facing the United States in Iraq at the moment is that this pattern looks likely to be repeated. The democratic will of the Iraqi people would end the occupation tomorrow if it were allowed to reveal itself in sovereign action. But without the occupation there would have been no prospect of that democratic will even expressing itself. The Americans in Iraq are the architects of a process that would defeat them if it could. They can only achieve their aims by departing from the scene. In departing from the scene they abandon their aims. The Americans cannot, themselves, break this impasse. The fate of Iraqi democracy does not lie in American hands but in the hands of the Iraqi people. But the fate of the Iraqi people is still in American hands for as long as the occupation continues. In this chapter I seek to establish whether there might be in Iraq's recent history, political culture and present situation sufficient resources of pluralist politics to enable the Iraqi people to find a way out of this impasse. First, however, it is necessary to understand how the impasse was entered, how and why an occupation without a political solution was planned and how post-invasion politics have remained trapped within the terms of the paradox of democracy under occupation.

Plans

There is only one place where plans can really be made for the political and economic arrangements that are to follow a successful invasion, and that place is where the invasion itself is being planned. Plans conceived in Baghdad, or for that matter Amman or Tehran, are all very well, but they are unlikely to command the kind of backing an occupying power provides. It is therefore perhaps inevitable that all the key preparation for post-Saddam Iraqi politics should have taken place in the United States. Plans conceived in Washington and, as we shall see, in other parts of the United States, not only enjoy the prospect of implementation because the American authorities will call the shots when the time comes, but they also enjoy a significant advantage in terms of time. People working in and with the Pentagon and State Department on how Iraq might be governed after the fall of Saddam Hussein will almost certainly have been working within a realistic timetable, shaped by what the Pentagon and State Department knew or believed about the likely timing of the invasion. Circumstances, then, dictated that preparations for the development of an Iraqi democracy would be located in the United States. The route to democracy by means of a purely local, grass-roots, bottom-up and culturally specific itinerary was simply not available.

The post-invasion planners would have to rely on the work and expertise of people who either already lived in the United States or who were able to travel there. Given the nature of the Iraqi regime, there would not be many Iraqis resident in Iraq ready and able to travel to and fro between Iraq and the United States to participate in such planning, with the exception of those, mainly Kurdish, who enjoyed the protection of the no-fly zones over northern Iraq. Richard Perle, questioned on this issue in 2003, dismissed out of hand the argument that Iraqis within Iraq could and should have played a significant role in planning the post-invasion transition.

> Oh, this is complete rubbish. It would be hard to imagine a sillier argument. Iraq was a place where, if you were an opponent, you were dead. Now how are we supposed to find people in Iraq that we can talk to, and whose judgement we can repose any confidence in? People who kept secret and managed to survive their opposition to Saddam all those years? What are we talking about?[2]

So the work would have to be done by those who had already, by accident or design, escaped alive from the regime and were free to travel. Not everything would need to happen in the United States, but close coordination with the planners in Washington will have been vital for everyone involved. As we shall see, other locations outside Iraq would feature in the itinerary of the planning process, including Kurdistan, which had been functioning as an effectively autonomous region beyond Baghdad's control (or at least beyond its military reach). That Iraqi democracy was conceived, planned and prepared in Washington is not to claim a malign conspiracy, but simply to state an inevitable state of affairs. While it is hard to see how such planning could have been done otherwise, it is clear that the leading role played by exiles in the conception and execution of Iraq's post-invasion transition to democracy has been problematic, to say the least.

To begin with, there was the problem of the Iraqi National
Congress (INC). This was initially formed in the wake of the
1991 war by a coming together of diverse Iraqi opposition figures,
including the Kurdish leaders Masoud Barzani and Jalal Talabani,
members of both the main Shia religious groups, the Dawa and
the Supreme Council for Islamic Revolution in Iraq (SCIRI), as
well as leading secular, nationalist and liberal figures (Kanaan
Makiya, Ahmed Chalabi, Laith Kubba). According to Laith
Kubba, by the time the INC had held its first major conference (in
Vienna in 1992) it was already starting to fall apart. There were
those, such as Kubba, who had envisaged that the INC would be
an open and inclusive forum, in which diverse views would be
heard and debated. They found, to their dismay, that others,
particularly Chalabi, saw it as a vehicle for engaging the US
administration in search of financial backing. By 1996, Dawa,
SCIRI and the Kurds had all withdrawn from the process, and the
INC had become, in effect, Chalabi's political party.

Chalabi, widely described as able and persuasive by Washington
insiders, despite persistent allegations of financial misconduct in
the past, successfully won the support of key players in Washington, but not quite enough to win State Department backing for his
proposal for a coup attempt in 1996. Whatever Chalabi's
ambitions, it is not hard to appreciate the dilemma facing those in
the US administration interested in supporting opposition to the
regime in Baghdad. On the one hand, they had a loose grouping,
several players among whom were in receipt of direct support from
neighbouring Iran, who were unlikely to agree a coherent political
programme and plan of action. On the other hand, they could deal
with a much more narrowly defined group, of a secular pro-
Western complexion, apparently focused on a specific course of
action. It is perhaps inevitable that anyone in Washington seriously
interested in pursuing regime change in Iraq in the late 1990s
should have opted for Chalabi and the INC. Whether they were
wise to do so, and whether, in any case, the contemplation of Iraqi
regime change was a sensible way to spend your time is in the late
1990s is another matter. Laith Kubba sees this choice as a wilful

and ignorant refusal to engage with the realities of Iraq and the existence of the Iraqi people:

> I have heard it actually in meetings, where the whole of Iraq has been reduced to only the Iraqis who are in exile, because the 22 million Iraqis who are inside have all been destroyed by Saddam Hussein. So the only Iraqis left are the two million abroad, and those two million abroad are in the INC or in the opposition. The opposition is the INC and the INC is a very narrow circle of people, and we are going to design for Iraq and Iraqis what they need. We know best.[3]

It was against this background – in which one narrowly-defined group had apparently seized the agenda and monopolized political and financial support in Washington circles by the end of the 1990s – that planning for a post-Saddam Iraq began in earnest. One of the most substantial efforts was launched by the State Department in 2002, in collaboration, initially, with the Middle East Institute. The Future of Iraq Project brought together a wide range of Iraqis and Iraqi-Americans, with a view to devising strategies for implementing a new government structure in Iraq. It created a sequence of working groups with remits ranging from working out the logistics of postwar environmental protection to devising constitutional arrangements and the basis for a new legal system. Once again, and perhaps again out of necessity, much of the available expertise came from the exile community (with, as in the case of the original INC, significant contributions from the Kurdish autonomous regions).

The achievements or otherwise of this project have been hotly debated by a range of participants, particularly once it was effectively sidelined by the Pentagon in early 2003. In its place Assistant Secretary of Defence Paul Wolfowitz assembled a new organization called the Iraq Reconstruction and Development Committee (IRDC); and many of its members were drawn from among the large Iraqi expatriate community in and around Detroit. Despite the bitterness surrounding this move – apparently a function of the now well-documented inter-agency struggle between the Pentagon and State Department – the IRDC comprised many of the same key personnel and carried with it similar deficiences as those evident in the Future of Iraq Project. It may be the case that detailed programmes drawn up by the Future of Iraq Project, which Jay Garner had intended to use until Rumsfeld ordered him not to, would have prevented some of the early chaos following the fall of Baghdad on 9 April 2003 (bitter advocates of the project frequently claim that this was the case). Since the complete breakdown in law and order that followed the fall of Baghdad is now reckoned to have been one of the most serious impediments to the subsequent establishment of legitimate and eventually democratic government in Iraq, this may come to be regarded as one of the crucial early missteps of the whole American enterprise in Iraq.

In any case, the problem of the origins and background of the planners remained. As in the case of the Future of Iraq Project, it is probably fair to say that the exile community involved in the IRDC was not entirely representative of the Iraqi diaspora as a whole. It was overwhelmingly staffed by people resident in the United States, and selected to work with civil servants on technical-administrative projects. Its members appear to have been mainly secular in orientation, college educated and middle class. Many of them were American citizens who, in their personal journeys from Iraqi repression to American freedom, would have almost inevitably and quite justly acquired a deep emotional and intellectual attachment to American democratic values. This brings with it problems of perspective. Committed, idealistic and secular, would they really prove the best judges of how to deal, on a day-to-day basis, with, say, village spirituality and social conservatism, the ex-Ba'ath apparatchiks or the mass urban poor who have since rallied to the Sadrist cause? To what extent would the realities of Iraq in the twenty-first century correspond with the Iraq of their memories, imaginations or dreams? And to what extent would the American occupation government under Jay Garner and then Paul Bremer listen to them even when their imaginations and dreams started to encounter realities?

History

It is April 2005 and Iraq's deputy permanent representative to the United Nations is giving a talk at the Kennedy School of Government. It is not, however, his role at the United Nations that brings him here. Feisal Istrabadi, a lawyer based in Chicago, is responsible for leading the drafting of an interim constitution for Iraq, a document that came to be known as the Transitional Administrative Law (TAL). He was a member of the Future of Iraq Project and also of the Iraq Reconstruction and Development Committee. Barbara Bodine, who had worked under Jay Garner in Iraq, is chairing the session and commends Istrabadi to the gathering of students, faculty and visiting fellows as someone from whom the United States would do well to learn about democracy. The idea that the United States might have something to teach Iraqis on this score is derided. Istrabadi makes no such claim, but is determined to dispel what he regards as damaging myths about Iraq.

The first of these is that Iraq does not really exist, and the second that Iraq has no history of democratic political life. The first myth is based on the now familiar story that Iraq was a late colonial formation, forcibly imposed by the British under a mandate of 1920, and bringing together three former provinces of the Ottoman Empire, Mosul, Baghdad and Basra, which as Elie Kedourie bluntly states were 'three quite different provinces, which had previously never been grouped together'.[1] What this story fails to acknowledge is the development of a distinctive Iraqi national identity forged, in part out of opposition to the British presence in the country, but also a product of late nineteenth-century integration into world markets, exposure to European nationalist ideas and the emergence of a distinctively Iraqi national intelligentsia among the professional middle classes. The existence of a political class that agitated over a long period of time in favour of independence points to a conception of Iraq as a nation state, with aspirations to join the League of Nations, govern itself, secure the integrity of its borders and exercise all the prerogatives of national sovereignty. This political class was not agitating for the formation of three distinct states based on the previous Ottoman provinces. The revolution of 1920 was known as the Great Iraqi Revolution and, according to historian Eric Davis, it generated a 'sense of unified national consciousness' and 'united Sunnis and Shi'is in a manner that had not been seen before in Iraqi history'.[5]

The idea that the nation of Iraq is an inauthentic colonial imposition compared with the prior authenticity the administrative structures of the Ottoman Empire had conferred on Basra, Baghdad and Mosul is an illusion. It is an illusion that is only made possible by an a priori privileging of the British over the Ottoman Empire, as though 'history' only begins in a place like Iraq when the British (Western) colonial power arrives. The three provinces of Basra, Baghdad and Mosul were just as much historical products of imperial jurisdiction as was Iraq. They do not acquire greater moral or political legitimacy by virtue either of having preceded British intervention or because the Ottoman Empire somehow does not count when we are talking about colonial or post-colonial history. While the motivations behind the insistence that Iraq was a victim of British imperial maladministration may include a desire to make rhetorical atonement for past Western misdeeds, the effect is oddly 'orientalist': only the oppressions we Westerners imposed on others really count (because these are the only ones we can feel guilty about). This is a complex psycho-political reflex that has been much in evidence during Western political debates over the invasion and occupation of Iraq. For Istrabadi, then, there is a viable and legitimate political entity called Iraq; it has been in existence under various forms of government for about 80 years and that, surely, is enough continuous history for a country to be taken seriously. Things change over time and it would be surprising indeed to find more than a handful of Iraqis who would describe their primary political identity in terms of long disbanded Ottoman provinces. The fact that these three provinces map roughly onto what many Western observers continue to see as a three-way ethnic/sectarian division of the country into Sunnis, Shias and Kurds perhaps contributes to the persistence of the myth that Iraq does not exist. As we shall see later, this image of Iraq as irredeemably sectarian in composition is an 'orientalist' myth. Both myths maintain Iraq in a fictional version of its own past.

The further myth that Iraq has no experience of democratic politics must also be dispelled according to Istrabadi. Many analysts tend to interpret the establishment of Iraq under the British mandate, the installation of the 'foreign' Hashemite King Feisal on the throne and the series of 'monarchist' governments that came and went between 1924 and 1958 as a period in which a narrow elite, initially serving British interests, wielded unaccountable power and eventually created the circumstances that allowed the Ba'ath Party to come to power. Istrabadi suggests otherwise, claiming that it was during this period – the period in which the idea and practice of Iraqi politics in an Iraqi state took hold – that Iraq enjoyed a meaningful experience of democratic, or at the very least constitutional, politics.

Elie Kedourie is typical of the version of Iraqi history Istrabadi wishes to revise. Writing of the defects in the Iraqi polity of this period he claims that

> the largest part of the population, whether Arab or Kurdish, was tribal, whether composed of nomads or semi-nomads, or settled fellahin. It was illiterate, unable to understand unfamiliar concepts such as elections and parliamentary representation, and accustomed to obey their tribal leaders and such government officials as came into contact with them and, in the case of the Shi'a, also revering the religious divines residing in Najaf, Karbala and other shrine cities in Iraq sacred in the Shi'i world.[6]

Few Western commentators would now dare to dismiss an Arab population (past or present) in such terms. It is a characteristic of the debate about the relationship between Arabs, Muslims and democracy more generally that some of the most pessimistic views of the prospects for Arab or Muslim democracy are held by Arab intellectuals.

A more sympathetic observer, such as the historian Matthew Elliott, offers precisely the kind of revisionist account of this period that Istrabadi might be looking for (or may, indeed, already have read). Elliott recounts the process by which a constitution providing for a bicameral parliament was adopted in 1924, and chronicles the ups and downs of the various governments that came and went during the years that followed under this system. 'The royal plebiscite of 1921 and elections first to the Constituent Assembly and then to its successor, the Chamber of Deputies, hardly took place in the spirit intended by the constitution. Nor did the Chamber of Deputies operate as envisaged. Nevertheless, as we shall see, both elections and parliament worked after a fashion.'[7]

While Elliott recognizes that this system fell far short of modern Western democratic norms, he argues that even the limited democratic or constitutional political space, which allowed for the formation of political parties after 1946 and brought with it lively parliamentary debate and electoral defeats for government candidates, was worth having. From Istrabadi's point of view, this modest experience of electoral and parliamentary politics may be considered in similar terms to the formation of an Iraqi national political identity: it made it possible to cultivate democratic practices, even within a relatively narrow elite group. Democracy working 'after a fashion' is better than no democracy at all, and it constitutes a real historical legacy. Elliott's work suggests that we should avoid thinking of the politics of this period wholly in terms of a pretend democracy masking British and Iraqi elite domination, without succumbing to the idea that Iraq enjoyed some golden age of liberal freedom: 'The phrase "free elections", which sometimes appears in embassy records of conversations with Iraqi politicians or their pronouncements, should neither be taken too literally nor dismissed altogether.'[8]

Adeed Dawisha, explicitly describing his approach as 'revisionist' in relation to a dominant narrative in which Iraq has no significant historical experience of democratic practices or institutions, insists that this dominant narrative misrepresents the Iraqi political reality of the monarchical period by measuring it in relation to an 'ideal' of Western democracy. He suggests that during this period the

political system was open enough to allow for 'a multiplicity of
political opinions and orientations', that parliamentarians could
oppose the government 'without fear of retribution' and that
political parties and parliament exerted genuine influence on the
direction of policy.[9]

For Elie Kedourie, the whole process was tainted and, towards
the end of the period, he argues, the gradual fixing of the system
in favour of the court and against the constitutional institutions
led to 'a further concentration and centralization of power,
making constitutional and representative government even more
of a mockery than before'.[10] Whereas Elliott and Dawisha appear
to be arguing that the baby need not be thrown out with the bath-
water, Kedourie, by pointing out the baby's frailties and
inadequacies, seems to wish it had never been born. Istrabadi sees
some life in the old baby yet.

Aside from these narrowly political considerations – from which
it would be reasonable to conclude that only the potential for
democracy rather than its successful implementation can be
attributed to Iraq between the fall of the Ottoman Empire and the
rise of the Ba'ath Party – there is the much wider and perhaps
more significant question of what Eric Davis calls Iraq's 'incipient
civil society'.[11] New political parties enjoyed real social bases,
professional associations and clubs made political debate
'commonplace', trade unions were organized, and a wide range of
newspapers and other periodicals contributed to the kind of
distributed print culture typical of an emergent national identity.
Coffeehouses, too, came to life as sites for political and other
intellectual (cultural, literary, artistic) exchange. Davis also notes
that the urban national press started to pay close attention to
rural society during this period as an indication of a conscious
effort to bring into being the 'imagined community'[12] that
constitutes the affective and experiential basis for national
identity and nationhood. He also, in an observation of particular
resonance given that it was looted in April 2003, identifies the
struggle for Iraqi control over the Iraq Museum in the 1920s as a
powerful sign of an incipient yet purposeful Iraqi nationalism,

determined to control this important and symbolic repository and articulation of a specifically national heritage.[13]

The national museum becomes a prime location for the development of a sense of national identity (think of the relationship between the British Museum and Britain's imperial identity, or the museums that make up the National Mall in Washington DC). It is a key element in the 'invention of tradition'[14] that constitutes the development of national historical narrative and memory. If you have a museum that can actualize historical memory – in the display of artefacts in a chronological sequence, supported by explanatory narrative – you have a highly visible and publicly accessible political and pedagogical tool for the promotion and maintenance of a widely shared sense of national identity. That such institutions – from the party, to the newspaper and the museum – were brutally suppressed and then crudely regenerated and perverted in support of the Ba'athist regime after 1968 should not prevent us from recognizing something genuine and potentially positive in this history of Iraqi nationalism. It is precisely this refusal to acknowledge the existence of a benign Iraqi modern nationalism that leads to dangerous political fantasies – that Iraq never did and never can exist, that sectarian division and civil war is inevitable, that only totalitarianism held an otherwise untenable nation together. All these fantasies deny Iraq its own history, its own indigenous modernity and play into the hands of those who would now deny Iraq its right to democratic government.

The big unanswered question arising from a consideration of this historical legacy is whether or not the Ba'athist regimes from 1968 to 2003 succeeded in eradicating, perverting or discrediting this legacy to such an extent that it has no purchase on contemporary reality at all. At Harvard, Faisal Istrabadi ruefully noted recent electoral evidence suggesting that this may indeed be the case. Istrabadi is close to the former Iraqi foreign minister Adnan Pachachi, who returned to Iraq after the 2003 invasion, was appointed to the Governing Council set up by the Coalition Provisional Authority (see below), and established a liberal democratic political party, the Iraqi Independent Democrats. Not only was Adnan Pachachi foreign minister in the mid-1960s, but his father and uncle had both been prime ministers in the 1940s. His father, Muzahim, was also the founder, in 1913, of one of Iraq's most notable newspapers, *Al-Nahda*, which Adnan Pachachi revived in 2003. At more than 80 years old, Pachachi was regarded by supporters as a living embodiment of the liberal tradition of the pre-Ba'ath era. This meant that to many he looked a complete anachronism. In the elections of January 2005, Pachachi's Iraqi Independent Democrats, for which Istrabadi had also worked, polled a miserable 2 per cent of the vote and secured no seats in the transitional national assembly.

Sitting in the comfort of the Kennedy School reflecting on this history and the process of drafting a modern liberal constitution for Iraq, one was inclined to wonder whether we were slightly divorced from what the pragmatists like to call 'reality on the ground'. What price historical legacies and written constitutions while Baghdad still burns? Perhaps optimism about the prospects of democracy being established in Iraq was simply wilful disregard of the unpleasant fact that decades of dictatorship had destroyed Iraqi political and civil institutions, and that an illegal invasion had then spawned a series of violent insurgencies. Or worse, perhaps such optimism was tacit acquiescence in the propaganda peddled by Cheney and Rumsfeld in which a grateful and inherently democratic Iraqi people would embrace the American troops as liberators. When Cheney floated this bizarre expectation on Meet the Press, citing Kanan Makiya as the man who had convinced him that this would happen, Istrabadi felt his heart sink: 'I knew nobody who spent four decades in exile knew what was going on in Iraq. I didn't and Kanan didn't. The only difference was I was a hell of a lot more cautious.'[15]

Perhaps nobody knew what they were doing. Throughout 2004 and much of 2005 it seemed as though the two constant themes of conversation with people who had recently been in Iraq were their insistence that 'however bad you imagine it is, believe me, it's far worse,' and their absolute conviction that 'nobody knows what's going on, not the Americans and not the Iraqis.' The worst thing to do in such a situation must surely be to pretend: to pretend you know what you are doing and to pretend you know what is going on. To some extent at least, the Coalition Provisional Authority, under Paul Bremer, stands guilty of both pretensions in the way it handled the establishment of Iraq's post-invasion political institutions.

Government

On 13 July 2003 the CPA announced the establishment of a Governing Council, with a membership of 25, from whom were drawn a group of nine leaders who would serve as a rotating presidency, with each member taking a one-month turn as president. Its role was to advise the CPA, appoint interim government ministers and set in motion the process of drafting a new constitution, to replace (but build upon) the TAL. Its leading figures – Iyad Allawi, Ahmad Chalabi, Masoud Barzani, Jalal Talabani, Ibrahim Jaafari and Abdel Aziz al-Hakim – would all go on to play prominent roles in the transition to democracy. They would be the leaders of the main competing political blocs at the elections of 2005, and they would take top government positions. The composition of the Governing Council – supposedly a transitional body with no permament political mandate or democratic legitimacy – would turn out, perhaps inevitably, to be a self-fulfilling prophecy about the nature of the Iraqi democracy that would emerge in its wake.

The formation of the Governing Council – the first post-Saddam national political institution, and the body set up to manage the transition towards an elected government – therefore offers a rich illustration of the problems encountered trying to convert admirable intentions and a carefully constructed constitutional framework into political reality.

It is inevitable that the first step would be difficult. The first step would establish a direction and would therefore shape the democratic future in significant ways. Yet the first step was not democratic in character. To what extent was it appropriate that a political institution appointed by the CPA rather than elected by the

Iraqi people should exercise such potentially long-term influence over the shape of the coming democracy? How could the new appointed body claim political legitimacy and a meaningful say in Iraqi political affairs and yet at the same time remain a temporary institution? It was essential that it should be regarded as temporary, and not pre-empt the democratic choice of the Iraqi people. But it should be able to claim the kind of political authority that usually only permanent bodies command. The task was perhaps impossible. The only way to achieve this kind of separation might have been to appoint a Governing Council composed entirely of people who would promise in advance that they would not seek to be part of any future and permanent government. But none of the major political leaders would be likely to make, let alone keep, such a promise, and nor would any of them pass up the opportunity to be part of the Governing Council. From the perspective of the CPA it was essential that those leaders who had support on the ground should be included in the Governing Council. Since support on the ground, particularly at this early stage, largely meant financial backing from external sources and/or the capacity to mobilize armed militia, the choices were to some extent predetermined. Both Kurdish parties would have to be represented, as would both Dawa and SCIRI, and exile groups that had been working directly with the United States would also require representation. It is easy to see that once the decision had been taken to appoint such a body, the CPA was far from having a free hand in determining its composition.

The logic of the situation also seemed to demand consideration for ethnic and sectarian interests. In the absence of a democratic foundation for the formation of the council, some other political rationale had to be used as a representative principle, for the council, to have any political legitimacy, must in the eyes of the CPA at least appear to represent the Iraqi people. This may turn out to have been an unfortunate miscalculation, for it appears to have given institutional legitimacy to the sectarianization of Iraqi politics, which many Iraqis feel is alien to the texture of Iraqi social reality and risks abandoning the path of genuine democracy in favour of a confessional/ethnic polity. But the combination of the realities of power on the ground (guns, men and money), the legacy of Saddam's exploitation of ethnic and religious divisions and the CPA's entirely understandable desire that the Governing Council should in some way be 'representative' seems to have permitted no alternative. A bad choice may have been the only choice under the circumstances. As so often in complex political situations, the only answer to the obvious question 'What would you do instead?' might have been 'I would not start from here.' A nation under occupation, as we have already seen, is a difficult place in which to start trying to build democratic institutions. There will always be a powerful rejectionist tendency and a strong impulse to wonder 'What's the point?'

The implications of this forced choice were clear. The 25-member Governing Council was selected and appointed on the basis of American calculations about the relative strengths and imagined constituencies of political groups based in ethnicity and sect. The nine-member 'rotating presidency' would replicate this attempt at national representation. There would be no real political space for actors who represented constituencies other than those based on ethnicity and sect. This is one of a number of ways in which the Americans repeated the errors of the British 80 years earlier. As historian Toby Dodge warned, rather accurately, before the Governing Council had been formed, there was a real risk that 'the United States, like the British in the 1920s, will succumb to "primordialization". This would involve them reimagining Iraqi society as dominated by the supposedly premodern structures of tribe and religious authority. However, in doing this, US administrators will not be discovering the "essence" of Iraq.'[16] The British reimagination of the 'essence' of Iraq was of a country divided between city and countryside, with the city dominated by the effete and corrupt remnants of Ottoman-era bureaucracy and the countryside held together in traditional formations by conservative sheikhs who were authentically connected to the aspirations and values of ordinary rural Iraqis. 'British colonial administrators, aware of the short time they would be in Iraq, set about devolving power to indigenous Iraqis they believed had social influence. Resources were channelled through these individuals in the hope that they would guarantee social order at the lowest possible cost. The resulting state was built on extremely shallow social foundations.'[17] The British reimagination of Iraq was clearly nurtured by cultural fantasy. It is not hard to see this strong preference for 'authentic' sheikhs as opposed to 'effete' urbanites as consistent with, if not actively shaped by, the kind of encounters that British explorers, adventurers and colonial administrators had already for some time both preferred and romanticized.

The Americans brought their own cultural fantasy to bear on the Iraqi situation and therefore acted with acute and perhaps debilitating awareness of the ethnic and sectarian divisions they believed to characterize Iraqi society. Having successfully overcome an historical reluctance to engage with the Shia (largely shaped by recent experiences of getting their hands badly burned in Tehran and Beirut) they saw their immediate task as ensuring that the Shia majority – for so long the victim of minority Sunni oppression under Saddam – should be properly represented. This reading of Iraqi society, as comprehensible primarily in terms of this and other sectarian or ethnic divisions, is far from adequate. As Faleh Jabar argues in his study of Iraqi Shia politics, this kind of approach gets Iraq wrong because 'the tribe, the clan, extended families, urban guilds, status groups, city neighbourhoods and city solidarities all split religious spaces and cut across such totalizing categories as Sunnis, Shi'is or even Kurds.'[18]

But this 'totalizing' vision, in which all complexities and alternative affiliations and socialities are ignored in favour of a single grid of social, religious and political identity, has clearly dominated the way in which the American establishment, and the defence establishment in particular, chooses to view polities like Iraq's. 'A simplistic image of Iraqi society has emerged, largely under the influence of Middle Eastern "experts" of the US defence establishment, of "Arab Sunnis" supporting the "Sunni" regime of Saddam Hussein and the allegedly "somewhat less Arab" Shi'is (a sort of Iranian fifth column) bitterly opposed to it.'[19]

This 'simplistic image' was not just accepted by the CPA, but extended. In a sense, American analysts may have seen this extension of a very 'simplistic image' as a way of making the image more complex, by adding other identities to the mere binary of the Sunni–Shia split. But the effects were simply to replicate such thinking, rather than to move genuinely beyond this kind of reductive categorization. Pursuing the false logic of ethnic and sectarian division, of which the 'simplistic' Sunni–Shia division was the easiest and crudest version, the Americans proceeded to attend to and institutionalize in their planning, every available ethnic or sectarian division, with an almost obsessive concern to ensure that every group that could be identified and named on these terms should be properly represented. This involved a strange historical conjuncture between an imaginative 'primordialization' of Iraq, in which only 'ancient' and 'traditional' social divisions were recognized as authentic, and a late twentieth-century American self-consciousness around the politics of identity.

Although the 'politically correct' American practice of ensuring visible representation for minority identities is more readily associated with Democrats than Republicans, the Bush administration had already displayed its considerable political sensitivity to identity politics in some of its most important senior appointments (Colin Powell, Alberto Gonzalez and Condoleezza Rice). An almost reflex concern for making sure that ethnic diversity was properly and visibly accounted for in representative institution building appears to have influenced CPA thinking. Neither the reimagination of Iraqi society as intrinsically sectarian nor the application, conscious or unconscious, of contemporary American notions of identity politics were appropriate to the realities of contemporary Iraq. Therefore, the imposition of a Governing Council that was obviously based on ethnicity and sectarian affiliation failed as an attempt to 'represent' Iraq politically. Many Iraqis, particularly educated, middle-class ones who might in both the short and long term be the most effective and enthusiastic advocates for and participants in democratic politics, simply did not see themselves 'represented' in such a body. Not only did it institutionalize ethnic and sectarian divisions that many Iraqis did not fully recognize, but it also very visibly confirmed the leading role of exiles, many of them dependent on either Iran or the United States for their political strength.

The Governing Council therefore institutionalized a false and sectarian understanding of Iraqi politics, predetermining a largely sectarian formation of political blocs for elections. At the same time it cemented an exile dominance over the visible political sphere, so even the imaginary 'authenticity' of the council's representation of Iraqi identities was fatally compromised by the widespread perception of the council's members as 'puppets'. Of the nine members of the rotating presidency, only one had been resident in south or central Iraq (the area under direct rule by Saddam Hussein) between the end of the first Iraq war in 1991 and the US invasion of 2003. The observations of the Iraqi blogger, riverbend, might be taken as representative of a significant trend in Iraqi political attitudes to the Governing Council.

It is a way of further dividing the Iraqi population. It is adding confusion to chaos and disorder. Just the concept of an ethnically and religiously selected council to run the country is repulsive. Are people supposed to take sides according to their ethnicity or religion? How, nine months down the line, are they going to select one president ... or will we always have 9 presidents to govern the country? Does every faction of the Iraqi population need a separate representative? If they do, then why weren't the Christians represented? Why weren't the Turkomen represented? Would two more members to add to the nine really have made that big a difference? ... The most infuriating thing is hearing Bremer talk about how the members of the rotating presidency represent the Iraqi people. In reality, they represent the CPA and Bremer. They are America's Puppets (some of them are Iran's). They do not govern Iraq or Iraqis in any way – they are merely very highly paid translators: Bremer gives the orders and they translate them to an incredulous public. The majority of them were trained using

American tax dollars, and now they are being 'kept' by the
CPA using Iraqi oil money. It's a bad start to democracy,
being occupied and having your government and potential
leaders selected for you by the occupying powers.[20]

The American democracy specialist, Larry Diamond, who was
drafted in by Condoleezza Rice to assist the CPA in managing the
transition towards democratic politics is less harsh in his
evaluation of the Governing Council.

The GC was not bad as a first step, but it was hobbled by
serious flaws. First was the image problem caused by the
inclusion of too many controversial Iraqi exiles, particularly
Chalabi, in widely visible and powerful roles. Second, the
CPA failed to move rapidly enough toward the creation of a
more representative and legitimate body. And third, it failed
to encourage GC members to reach out and develop constituencies. During its tenure, it was not uncommon for the
majority of the council to be out of the country at any given
time. Most Iraqis never saw any of the council members. As a
group, the GC did not distinguish itself.[21]

But Diamond's critique has further implications, because the
government chosen to replace the Governing Council so clearly
resembled the Governing Council. A leadership already suspect
because of its flawed representation of Iraqi society and the widespread belief that it was largely composed of 'puppets' of either Iran
or the United States, further damaged its credibility by its poor
performance as the Governing Council, failed to broaden its own
political constituency, and yet went on to form the core of the next
government, a development that was not lost on riverbend: 'The new
government isn't very different from the old Governing Council. Some
of the selfsame Puppets, in fact.'

The foundations laid for Iraqi democracy have been deficient in
two principal respects: they were not democratic enough and they
were not Iraqi enough. Perhaps they are, however, as good as they
could have been, under the circumstances. The conditions under

which these foundations have been established could hardly have been less auspicious. Let it not be forgotten, furthermore, that the American government was the sole author of the inauspicious circumstances in which the foundations of Iraqi democracy have been laid. It is not just that Iraq is still at war, which is a state of affairs that offers powerful incentives to undemocratic behaviour of all kinds. The fact that the initiators of the war are the same people now trying to promote democracy is deeply damaging to the integrity and credibility of the democratic project, and places serious limits on the occupation's capacity to encourage participation. Nonetheless, in a period of just over a year, at two elections and one referendum, the Iraqi people have demonstrated a genuine will to take control of their future by means of democratic institutions. The war and the occupation, as well as the particular constraints those circumstances have imposed on the shape of the political institutions that have been established, have limited the extent of the control they have been able to exert. Once these institutions start to develop an enduring life of their own, more Iraqis may come to place faith in them. It is hard to see how this can happen, however, until the occupation comes to an end.

Although a new government is yet to be formed at the time of writing, riverbend's scepticism about the legitimacy of the 'puppets' still holds good. The arrangement of political furniture created by the formation of the Governing Council is being preserved for the time being. One way or another, Iraq's short-term future is going to depend on some combination of 'puppets' and ethnic and sectarian considerations will dictate the terms of political debate. These will be the men (and they are nearly all men) on whom the responsibility for government will fall. They will have to negotiate the perilously narrow path between the resistance and the occupation, and they will have to carve out some kind of autonomous political space between these two powerful forces. The best thing that could happen in that space might be the emergence of previously unrepresented political constituencies and, with them, new leaders who, at some election several years from now, might have secured

enough legitimacy from within Iraqi society to allow them peacefully to replace the 'puppets' and make Iraqi democracy a little
more Iraqi.

The future
From where might an authentically Iraqi democracy come? One
answer to that question, which needs to be taken seriously not just
for its relevance to the Iraqi situation but also for its wider
implications for democracy in the region, is that it is from within
Iraq's Shia clerical leadership, and the culture it represents, that the
best prospects for lasting democratic politics in Iraq are to be
found. The reader will doubtless recall the suggestion offered
earlier that the United States cutting itself off from one of the most
dynamic and fruitful sources of political and religious innovation,
and most interesting prospects for democratic politics in the form
of Iran's traditional Shia clerical culture, has been a tragic irony.
The situation in Iraq, therefore, offers what we might term, in the
strictest sense of the word (that is, involving happy endings rather
than laughter) a comic irony.

Having invaded Iraq, the United States comes face to face with
the tradition embodied, most importantly perhaps, in the figure of
Grand Ayatollah Ali Sistani. Sistani was born in Iran, is a Persian
speaker and, like all major Shia clerics including Ayatollah
Khomeini, studied at both Qom and Najaf. He is undisputedly the
most senior Shia cleric in Iraq and, all other things being equal,
might be considered to outrank any living Iranian ayatollah were it
not for the distortions of political power that give the otherwise
rather minor religious figure of Ali Khamenei that particular
distinction. If there is an Iranian to rival him for influence it would
probably be Ayatollah Montazeri, once Khomeini's designated
successor but currently languishing under effective house arrest in
Iran because of his criticisms of the Iranian theocracy.

The United States entered Iraq recognizing the importance of
engaging with the Shia, whom they realized formed a majority of
the population. We might attribute this to happy accident alone, if
this recognition came only from the understanding that with

Saddam being Sunni, the most enthusiastic supporters of his overthrow might well be Shia. But we might imagine it to have been more a case of design if, guided by the secular Shia Ahmed Chalabi, the administration had pinned its hopes on being able to build support for a new government from within the Shia community. Perhaps it also recognized fairly early in the proceedings that the likes of SCIRI and Dawa simply could not be excluded from the process for fear they would then constitute a powerful new front in the ranks of the resistance. In any case, those who feared that the United States would come unstuck because of an irrational fear of the Shia were to be proved wrong.

Effective Shia domination of political structures was more or less guaranteed, as we have already seen, by the way in which the CPA and its advisers guided the formation of the new Iraqi polity. It is critics of the administration who have developed an advanced and perhaps irrational fear of the Shia, warning that with SCIRI and Dawa calling the shots in Baghdad and the Iranians funding all manner of troublemaking in the south, Iraq risks falling into Iran's lap or becoming a replica of Iran's mullah-driven regime. Such critics can point to the very real fears of ordinary Iraqis that this might be the case. Women, in particular, are gravely concerned about the kind of social restrictions a government dominated by religious Shia leaders will bring, and has done for many already. This is not simply a matter of government and legislation. There are countless examples of religously-motivated attacks on the freedom of women that have no basis in law, but come from newly confident Shia men taking the law into their own hands, in the streets, in education and in the workplace. This does not augur well for the role of religion in the everyday politics and social life of a Shia-led country and, as with all arguments here and elsewhere about the democratic potential of Islamist movements or parties, Sunni or Shia, this doctrinaire strand of reflex social conservatism at a popular level introduces a serious reservation about the desirability of their continued advance. Isobel Coleman has argued, convincingly enough, that there is no reason to believe that the constitution, even if interpreted by religiously-minded Shia, can

provide a legitimate basis for the suppression of women's rights in
Iraq.[22] But others, who note ironically the advanced protection for
gender equality in the Saddam-era constitution, point out that not
only does the present constitution (which the Shia parties had a
significant hand in drafting) represent a step backwards in respect
of the earlier one, but that bullies and bigots on the streets of a
country where personal security is almost nowhere guaranteed pay
little heed to written constitutions when trying to enforce their will
on Iraqi women.

So, despite reservations about Shia religious values gaining
forceful political expression in the new Iraqi democracy, the
Americans also seem to have recognized – at least to some extent
– that Ayatollah Sistani may be a crucial source of moral and
political support for the project of Iraqi democracy, even if they
have found it frustratingly difficult to deal with him directly. Paul
Bremer never met him and regarded him as an obstacle to the
implementation of his own plans, both for creating the appointed
Governing Council and for the complex caucus-based system by
which it was initially proposed the transitional national assembly
would be elected. On 30 June 2003, Ayatollah Sistani issued a
fatwa, calling Bremer's plan for an appointed body (the Governing
Council) 'fundamentally unacceptable' and stating that 'general
elections must be held so that every eligible Iraqi can choose
someone to represent him at the constitutional convention that
will write the constitution.'[23] Bremer ignored this *fatwa* and, as
well as proceeding with an appointed Governing Council, also
overruled Sistani's calls for more democratic participation by
cancelling municipal elections in Najaf (where Sistani lives and
works) and other towns across Iraq, even though preparations
such as voter registration had already taken place. According to
Diamond, one of whose key criticisms of the US government is
that Sistani repeatedly took up positions that were more
democratic than those taken by the CPA, Sistani's position
'stemmed from a philosophical conviction, deeply embedded in
his religious teachings, of the importance of a contract in social
relations. He thus could not endorse as legitimate any form of

rule that was not freely arrived at – that had been arranged by or under a political occupation'.[24]

Diamond also takes the view that Sistani represents an essentially 'quietist' approach to politics, typical of most Shia clerics and quite unlike the activist role promoted by Ayatollah Khomeini. He therefore views Sistani's interventions on such occasions as atypical, and signalling a desire to keep the Iraqi clergy out of the political arena where possible. Nonetheless, he accords great significance to what Sistani will say or do in the future, claiming that, for the time being at least, 'much of the future of Iraqi politics will turn on who Ayatollah Sistani really is.'[25] Diamond retains some scepticism, acknowledging a repeated tendency to seek political compromise, but suggesting that it 'remains to be seen how much of this was tactical and how much an acceptance of basic principles of democracy'.[26]

This ambivalence is a familiar stance and to some extent it reflects a widespread caution that recalls Edward Djerejian's oft-cited warning about relations between 'Islamists' and democracy, namely that religious politicians in the region might turn out to support a 'one man, one vote, one time'[27] democracy. In Diamond's ambivalence about Sistani one hears also a familiar suspicion of the motives of unfamiliar political actors. Whenever 'Islamists' are seen displaying behaviour that suggest they value consensus, com-promise, political deal-making, coalition building and pragmatism – all wholly admirable, it seems, when engaged in by modern secular (Western) political actors – there is always someone suggesting that they are not really to be trusted, that they do not mean what they say. There is something similar at work in claims that Iranian and other Shia political movements are practising *takiye* (dissimulation) whenever they make moderate statements. Such claims are pre-emptively suspicious, and seem, at least to some extent, to betray a cultural preference for viewing non-Western political action as unusually secretive, inscrutable and cunning, when compared with the notorious lack of duplicity for which Western democratic leaders are universally recognized. It also fails to recognize the extent to which words are action, especially in the political domain. If someone repeatedly proclaims themselves to be a democrat and starts engaging in discussion of democratic politics as a result, he or she is actually participating in democratic politics, not just pretending to do so or talking about it. The more democratic you talk, the more democratic you usually have to act. The process of democratic give and take sucks you in. That is the nature of political negotiation. What you say has consequences and creates new realities. You are held to your word in the real world. That is why we still believe in constitutions and treaties, and recognize that they are often worth more than the paper they are printed on.

In the specific case of Sistani issuing a *fatwa* (which is, after all, one of the world's most compelling instances of words that are actions) even if his support for democracy were merely tactical (which seems improbable) and its consequences therefore unintended, there can be little doubt that it will have consequences. What a Grand Ayatollah says today, many Shia faithful will seek to implement tomorrow. Reuel Marc Gerecht, a former CIA analyst, now a scholar at the American Enterprise Institute, is perhaps the most enthusiastic of all contemporary Western analysts in the welcome he accords to democracy Sistani-style. He describes Sistani's June 2003 *fatwa* as 'revolutionary'[28] for its implicit separation of religion from politics: 'Sistani has done what Iran's pro-democracy dissident clerics have dreamed of doing: He has taken the all-critical moral imperative in Islamic history – *al-amr bi'l maruf wa an-nahy an al-munkar* ("commanding right and forbidding wrong") – and detached it from the Holy Law.'[29]

In Gerecht's analysis of Sistani's position, it is now the duty of all Muslims to take free political decisions and to choose the government by which they are to be ruled. One might think of this as a decisive widening, in the political sphere, of the right to practice *ijtihad*. Formerly, only properly qualified scholars would interpret the word of God and reach a consensus (*ijma*) on its meaning and application in any given contemporary situation, but now this responsibility to produce consensus by the exercise of free rational decision falls on all Muslims, and democracy is the contemporary mechanism by which they are enjoined to do so. According to Gerecht, this means that sovereignty is to be shared by God and Man. One suspects that Gerecht's interpretation of Sistani's *fatwa* might go further than Sistani would imagine. But words are actions, and they resonate with consequence in many places. For this reason, Gerecht sees Sistani's position, and the implicit support it lends to the Shia parties of the United Iraqi Alliance, as constituting 'Iran's worst nightmare'.[30] By 'Iran', here, he refers to the conservative establishment, which will see growing next door in Iraq a democratic politics explicitly legitimated by the *fatwa* of a leading (perhaps the most senior) ayatollah, a politics from which Iran's Islamic left will draw a confidence and authority that might restore political innovation to its second rightful home, in Iran itself. The introduction into the region's politics of a democratic tendency underpinned by Shia culture and tradition could have even wider-ranging implications, which will be greeted with both enthusiasm and anxiety beyond Iraq and Iran (hardly negligible powers in the region) in Lebanon, Bahrain and Saudi Arabia, where there are substantial Shia political constituencies. It is also likely to have a significant impact, as yet hard to predict or evaluate, on democratic movements and thought in the many non-Shia communities of the region. The laws of unintended consequences may yet bestow some kind of pardon upon the makers of war.

Conclusion

There was once a time when Cairo was the place to go to if you wanted to be part of the wider public debate, at least in the Arab world. Cairo was where books were published and discussed, where newspapers carried polemics and debates and where coffee-house conversations were thick with the news and views of the day. Versions of this Arab public sphere existed elsewhere – in Beirut, Damascus, Baghdad, to name just three cities where cosmopolitan urban elites and others have engaged passionately in issues that mattered to them. Autocratic leaders like President Asad know full well that such places spell danger for authoritarian projects. In a society that needs conformity, they must be monitored closely or closed down altogether. Even in the more relaxed political environment of Mubarak's Egypt, where the regime is still pretty jumpy about such things, recent years have seen a serious decline in the quality and scope of the public sphere. As part of a strategy of simultaneous accommodation and repression of its Islamist challenge (which resembles Mustapha Barghouti's characterization of Fatah as swinging between madness and capitulation) the Egyptian government has permitted a creeping puritanism and censoriousness to pervade the country. The murder of Farag Foda, the stabbing of Naguib Mahfouz and the persecution for alleged apostasy of Nasr Abu Zeid are just three of the most widely publicized and shocking examples of the way in which public discourse has been narrowed and confined in Egypt. Similar accommodations with conservative efforts to limit freedom of expression can be observed across the region, alongside courageous struggles to resist such encroachment.

From time to time newspapers, blogs and satellite television have provided source material and evidence for this exploration of the new politics of the Middle East. Hossein Derakhshan's observation that the newspapers and blogs cannot compete with the mass audience claimed by satellite television is worth taking up further, because there is a convincing case to be made that, for the Arab speakers of the region at least, the public sphere that once was only accessible to literate city-dwellers, has recently opened up in a new and unprecedented way. The emergence of what the scholar (and blogger) Marc Lynch calls, in a deliberate echo of Habermas, the Arab public sphere could be one of the most important factors shaping the way in which the people of the Arab Middle East negotiate among themselves in search of political change in the years to come.[1]

As Lynch shows in his study of discussions about Iraq and related issues broadcast on Al-Jazeera between 1991 and 2004, the public sphere constituted by Al-Jazeera and other more recent satellite stations is one in which opposing arguments are constantly and vigorously aired, interrogated and tested in debates in which ordinary viewers, members of the Arab public, are encouraged to participate by phoning in. Lynch shows that Al-Jazeera is far from being the stereotyped propaganda station of myth. Indeed, how and why would a conservative, though modernizing, Gulf ruling family like the al-Thani in Qatar support such an operation while at the same time providing extensive military facilities to the American armed forces? Al-Jazeera has not only provoked opposition (and perhaps even military assault) from the United States, but it attracts criticism from within the Arab world too. There are commentators who find the tone of its debates too strident. They step over the boundaries dictated by some ideas of good taste. Much the same might be said of comparable television stations in the West from the BBC to Fox News. That is one of the things that television does: it magnifies and it sometimes simplifies. Hostility to the debates on Al-Jazeera is, at least to some extent, a manifestation of an anti-democratic prejudice, namely that only those who really know what they are talking about have the right to talk about it in public. That is a short step from saying that only the experts should have the vote.

Satellite television is not democracy. But, as Hizballah with its own al-Manar station, and Mehdi Karrubi with his attempts to set up Saba TV have shown, it is the medium through which the twenty-first-century political public is most likely to engage in thinking and talking about politics. One of the principles underpinning the practice of *shura* is that the more widely you consult the better the eventual outcome of the decision-making process. Since the prospects for democracy in the Middle East ultimately lie in the hands of its people – democracy is after all the name for the political system in which the people rule – it is their understanding of the political issues that face them that matters most. The expansion of the public sphere does mean that more citizens in the region are better informed and more engaged in genuine debate than ever before. That is surely likely to lead to better *shura*, to continued negotiation and to politics in which change is always a real possibility.

This expansion of the public sphere represents an opportunity. It is noticeable that the West – and the United States government in particular – has proved so far unwilling to intervene constructively in this sphere and make a contribution to the debates and discussions that are taking place there. Senior American officials do not generally appear on Al-Jazeera, where they might be compelled to enter into debates from which they might gain a fuller understanding of the region's politics. Instead, following the invasion of Iraq in 2003, the United States government sought to establish its own media presence in the region, specifically to promote its own agenda of support for the new Iraqi government and for so-called 'reform' elsewhere in the region. Perhaps, not surprisingly, the satellite television channel Al-Hurra, set up to present news and opinion in the region with a broadly pro-American perspective, has failed to win either audiences or credibility. There are signs in early 2006, however, that at least this aspect of public diplomacy may be changing. It is not necessary for the politics of the region that the US government should be appearing regularly on Al-Jazeera, but it is most certainly a necessary part of the political education that American policy makers need to acquire in the region's politics.

Western public diplomacy in support of democracy in the Middle East needs to change. At the moment it still sees its task in terms of advocacy. Public diplomacy still apparently consists in appearing on television and other media to advertise the merits of a certain kind of politics. Instead, it should take on a new dimension, one that will only become possible by entering into genuine dialogue. Western public diplomacy needs to listen. Policy makers need to hear and start to understand the diversity of voices available to be heard in the regional public sphere. It may seem a strange thing to suggest, but the fact is that American government officials need to get on Arab satellite television, not to be heard, but to hear, and to be seen to be hearing.

From such a change a new politics of the region might become possible. A posture of listening rather than preaching could become the basis for meaningful negotiation. If the West is to play a helpful role in any of the complex negotiations that could lead to political change in the region, this is a prerequisite. The current stance, based on talking rather than listening, is a real obstacle to change, for it constantly reaffirms the unwelcome association of democratic politics with the intransigent assertion of Western power. If only the West is given the right to speak when it comes to the debate on democratic change, then small wonder that those with the greatest stake in such change come to view the whole process with scepticism or hostility. As part of the process of removing this obstacle and gradually uncoupling democracy as an idea from Western power as a reality, it is incumbent upon Western policy makers to accept the limitations of their own power. The West cannot create democracy – in its own image or in any other – in the Middle East. It may be able to help, but only if it genuinely hands leadership of the process over to the people who really can make it happen, the people of the region in question.

This will be uncomfortable but worthwhile. It will mean listening and taking seriously voices and opinions that many Western policy makers will find troubling, or, at best, difficult to understand. It will mean accepting the legitimacy of political actors previously categorized as unacceptable and illegitimate (Hamas, Hizballah and the government of the Islamic Republic of Iran). It will involve recognizing that the region is socially and culturally complex and diverse, that solutions that work in one country may not work in another, and that each and every solution will arise out of the particular historical, social and cultural circumstances of the country in which it takes shape. The countries of the region are not all heading towards a single finishing line. Each will find its own path; some of these will lead to new institutions and practices that the West may readily recognize as democratic, but some may appear unfamiliar or solve issues of legitimacy and representation in ways that have not been explored in the West. This is not just another argument for a complacent moral and political relativism in which no distinction is established between one outcome and another so long as each is consistent with its supposed cultural context. There is no fixed or determining relationship between cultural context and forms of political representation. It is perfectly possible, for instance, to imagine democratic and profoundly anti-democratic forms of government both being entirely compatible with the cultural traditions of, say, Egypt or Saudi Arabia. The important thing is to encourage those developments that appear both democratic and culturally and socially viable. At the moment it looks as if the most likely contenders for democratic and socio-cultural viability are the broad-based social, political and religious coalitions like Hamas, the Muslim Brotherhood and Turkey's Justice and Development Party. It seems unlikely that liberal secular opposition groups will be major agents of change, either in Iran – where reform still looks more likely from within an Iranian Shia political context – or in the region's monarchies, where the monarchies *per se* still look likely to be capable of maintaining a social consensus around gradual change.

If there is to be a new politics in the region it will involve negotiation. If Western governments and their representatives are to play any positive role in such a politics they will have to deal with the consequences of negotiation. In a process of negotiation you are likely to find yourself talking to people with whom you may profoundly disagree. As part of that process of negotiation you may be called on to give up something you hold dear, or agree to something over which you have deep-rooted misgivings. Finally, you will not know the outcome in advance. The new politics of the Middle East, if and when they take substantial shape, will almost certainly look very different from anything imagined in the West.

Notes

Introduction

1. Providence Journal/Brown University/Public Affairs Conference, 3–4 April 2005.
2. Danielle Pletka, American Enterprise Institute, February 2006.
3. Henry A. Kissinger, 'Intervention with a vision', in Gary Rosen (ed.) The Right War? The Conservative Debate on Iraq, Cambridge: Cambridge University Press, 2005.
4. Noah Feldman, After Jihad: America and the Struggle for Islamic Democracy, New York: Farrar Strauss and Giroux, 2003, pp. 32–7, 76–8.

1. Egypt: Mosque and State

1. Kifaya website, http://harakamasria.org/manifesto_english (accessed 1 March 2006).
2. Jonathan Steele, 'Egyptians urged to boycott presidential election', Guardian, 21 July 2005.
3. Amr Hamzawy, Al-Ahram Weekly, 26 May–1 June 2005, accessed online at http://weekly.ahram.org.eg/2005/744/focus.htm, 1 March 2006.
4. Baheyya, 'Pessimism of the intellect, optimism of the will', 10 September 2005, at http://baheyya.blogspot.com
5. Olivier Roy, The Failure of Political Islam, New York and London: I.B.Tauris, 1999.

2. Iran: Innovation Impeded

1. Ayatollah Khomeini, cited in Roy Mottahedeh, The Mantle of the Prophet : Religion and Politics in Iran, Oxford: Oneworld Books, 1985, p. 243.
2. The term given in Shia Islam to the series of leaders of the community of the faithful, the last and twelfth of whom (at least for the majority 'Twelver' branch of Shia thought) has disappeared (gone into occultation) to return eventually as the saviour of the world. President Ahmadinejad, as we shall see, is widely believed to be strongly influenced by Shia clerics who believe that the return of the Twelfth Imam is imminent. This is just one respect in which he seems to resemble rather strikingly his most prominent global adversary, President George W. Bush.
3. Roy Mottahedeh gives a rich portrait of this culture in The Mantle of the Prophet.
4. See Ali M. Ansari, Modern Iran since 1921: The Pahlavis and After, Longman: Harlow, 2003, pp. 221– 2.

5. Ansari, *Modern Iran*, p. 221.
6. See Ansari, *Modern Iran*, p. 226
7. It is Mohsen Kadivar who has perhaps articulated this view most strongly from a religious standpoint. Clearly, all secular opponents of the regime would also reject *velayat-e faqih* out of hand.
8. Mustapha Moin, cited in 'Fraudulent Election Results Claimed', *Iran va Jahanh*, <http://www.iranvajahan.net/cgi-bin/news.pl?l=en&y=2005&m=06&d=19&a=1>
9. Mehrdad Mashayekhi, *A New Era for Iran's Democracy*, opendemocracy.net, 21 April 2005.
10. Jürgen Habermas, *The Structural Transformation of the Bourgeois Public Sphere: An Inquiry into a Category of Bourgeois Society*, translated by Thomas Burger, Cambridge, MA and London: The MIT Press, 1991.
11. Nasrin Alavi, *We Are Iran*, London: Portobello Books, 2005; Azar Nafisi, *Reading Lolita in Tehran: A Memoir in Books*, London and New York: Fourth Estate, 2003.
12. Karl Marx and Friedrich Engels, *The German Ideology*, New York: Prometheus Books, 1998.
13. See Markman Ellis, *The Coffee House: A Cultural History*, London: Weidenfeld & Nicholson, 2004.
14. See Dale F. Eickelman and Jon W. Anderson (eds) *New Media in the Muslim World: The Emerging Public Sphere*, Bloomington: Indiana University Press, 2003.
15. See Hossein Derakhshan's account of this amazing 'revelation', *Editor: Myself*, www.hoder.com, 29 September 2004.
16. Nahid Diamdoust, 'Iranian blogger returns from exile for vote', *Los Angeles Times*, 23 June 2005.
17. Hossein Derakhshan, *Editor: Myself*, www.hoder.com, 25 June 2005.
18. Hossein Derakhshan, *Editor: Myself*, www.hoder.com, 31 October 2004.

3. Palestine: Democracy under Occupation

1. It has been a long 'year of elections' after the death of Yasser Arafat, between January 2005 and January 2006: Iraq twice (January and December 2005), Egypt twice (September and November–December 2005), Lebanon (May–June 2005) and Palestine twice (January 2005 and January 2006).
2. Interview with Sheikh Hasan Yousef, Ramallah, July 2005.
3. Interview with Ziad Dayyeh, Ramallah, July 2005.
4. Interview with J. Scott Carpenter, State Department, February 2006.
5. Abduljawad Saleh, for example, interview in Ramallah, July 2005.
6. Interview with Yamama Shalaldeh, Sair, July 2005.
7. Khaled Hroub, 'Hamas after Shaykh Yasin and Rantisi', *Journal of Palestine Studies*, vol. XXXIII, No. 4 (Summer 2004), 21–38 (27).
8. See Beverley Milton-Edwards, *Islamic Politics in Palestine*, London and New York: Tauris Academic Studies, 1996.
9. Interview with Ziad Dayyeh.
10. See Khalil Shikaki, 'The Future of Palestine', *Foreign Affairs*, vol. 83, no. 6, November/December 2004, pp. 45–60.

11. Interview with Ahmed Ghneim, Ramallah, July 2005.
12. Khalil Shikaki, p. 47.
13. Lindsey Hilsum, 'Arafat's Heir', 30 January 2006. http://www.channel4.com/news/special-reports/special-reports-storypage.jsp?id=1612#followOn.
14. Interview with Mustapha Barghouti, Ramallah, July 2005.

4. Syria and Lebanon: Party Problems

1. http://amarji.blogspot.com.
2. Cited in Derek Hopwood, *Syria 1945–1986: Politics and Society*, London: Unwin Hyman, 1988, p. 87.
3. Patrick Seale, *Assad: The Struggle for the Middle East*, Los Angeles: University of California Press, 1988, p. 61.
4. Seale, *Assad*, p. 85.
5. Raymond Hinnebusch, *Syria: Revolution From Above*, London and New York: Routledge, 2001, p. 81.
6. El Khazen, 'Political parties in post-war Lebanon: parties in search of partisans', *Middle East Journal*, vol. 57, no. 4, Autumn 2003, 605–24, p. 605.
7. Farid el Khazen, 'Political parties in post-war Lebanon', p. 624.
8. See Chapter 5.
9. This is an appropriate place to acknowledge the quality of informed discussion of Lebanese politics carried out online in blogs such as Across the Bay, Lebanese Political Journal, the Head Heeb, Al-Hiwar and others.
10. The Druze are a small Muslim sect mainly confined to mountain regions of Lebanon and Syria. Some Muslims consider them not to be Muslims (a view similar to that held by some of the Alawites, and by some Sunni extremists, of the Shia).
11. See, for example, Robert Fisk, *Pity the Nation*, New York: Athaneum, 1990; Farid el Khazen, *The Breakdown of the State in Lebanon 1967–1976*, London: I.B.Tauris, 2000.
12. Farid el Khazen, *The Breakdown of the State in Lebanon*, pp. 9–10.
13. Farid el Khazen, *The Breakdown of the State*, p. 10.
14. Judith Palmer Harik, *Hizballah: The Changing Face of Terrorism*, London and New York: I.B.Tauris, 2005.
15. Rodger Shanahan, *The Shi'a of Lebanon: Clans, Parties and Clerics*, London and New York: Tauris Academic Studies, 2005, p. 126.
16. Rodger Shanahan, *The Shi'a of Lebanon*, p. 119.
17. Harik, *Hizballah*, pp. 108–9.
18. El Khazen, 'Political parties in post-war Lebanon', p. 618
19. El Khazen, 'Political parties in post-war Lebanon', p. 617.

5. Jordan and Morocco: The Authority of the Legitimate King

1. See 'Jordan's King of Disguise', BBC News, 30 July 2001.
2. One particularly valubale exception to this is Michael C. Hudson, who wrote with some optimism in his *Arab Politics: The Search for Legitimacy*, New Haven: Yale University Press, 1977, of the positive prospects for modernization in the monarchies of the Gulf and beyond.

3. The book in question is Fred Halliday, *Arabia without Sultans*, Harmondsworth: Penguin Books, 1974.

4. For one of Sharif's less distinguished works, but one whose *New York Times* description typifies this mythology, see the made for-TV movie *Harem* (1986): 'The classy made-for-TV *Harem* managed to get away with plot devices that dated back to the days of Rudolph Valentino. Nancy Travis heads the cast as Jessica Gray, a turn-of-the-century American woman who is kidnapped and ensconced in the harem of Turkish Sultan Hasan (Omar Sharif). http://movies2.nytimes.com/gst/movies/movie.html?v_id=130357.

5. David Holden and Richard Johns, *The House of Saud*, London and Sydney: Pan Books, 1982.

6. See Lisa Wedeen, *Ambiguities of Domination*, Chicago: University of Chicago Press, 1999.

7. M. Elaine Combs-Schilling, 'Performing monarchy, staging nation', in Rahma Bourqia and Susan Gilson Miller (eds) *In the Shadow of the Sultan: Culture, Power, and Politics in Morocco*, Cambridge, MA: Harvard University Press, 1999 (176–214), p. 177.

8. Henry Mufson, Jr, *Religion and Power in Morocco*, New Haven and London: Yale University Press, 1993, p. 148.

9. Andrew Rathmell and Kirsten Schulze, 'Political reform in the Gulf: the case of Qatar', *Middle Eastern Studies*, vol. 36, no. 4, October 2000, pp. 47–74.

10. Rathmell and Schulze, 'Political reform', p. 60.

11. Fathallah El Rhazi, *Alternance et Democratie*, Oujda: Edition El Joussour, 2000.

12. Bruce Maddy-Weitzman, 'Women, Islam and the Moroccan state: the struggle over the personal status law', *Middle East Journal*, vol. 59, no. 3, Summer 2005, pp. 393–410 (p. 402).

13. Maddy-Weitzman, 'Women, Islam and the Moroccan state', p. 403.

14. Maddy-Weitzman, 'Women, Islam and the Moroccan state', p. 406.

15. John Waterbury, *The Commander of the Faithful: The Moroccan Political Elite – A Study in Segmented Politics*, New York: Columbia University Press, 1970, p. 31.

6. Oman: Tradition and Change

1. Fredrik Barth, *Sohar: Culture and Society in an Omani Town*, Baltimore: The John Hopkins University Press, 1983, p. 98.

2. See Richard Sennett, *The Fall of Public Man: On the Social Psychology of Capitalism*, New York: Alfred A. Knopf, 1977.

3. Barth, *Sohar,* p. 118.

4. Barth, *Sohar,* p. 254.

5. S. Oman's elected national assembly, created in 1994 to replace the appointed State Consultative Council.

6. State Department Country Report: Oman, February 2005 (http://www.state.gov/r/pa/ei/bgn/35834.htm).

7. Michael Herb, 'Princes and parliaments in the Arab world', *Middle East Journal*, vol. 58, no. 3, Summer 2004, p. 378.

8. Herb, 'Princes and parliaments', p. 378.

9. These include a range of senior and long-serving Omani officials, *majlis*

members past and present, various erstwhile British and American ambassadors and leading members of the business community.

10. Uri Rabi, 'Majlis al-shura and majlis al-dawla: weaving old practices and new realities in the process of state formation in Oman', *Middle Eastern Studies*, vol. 38, no. 4, October 2002, p.47.

11. Interview with Salem al-Ghattami, Muscat, 21 February 2005.

12. See, for example, the International Press Institute's World Freedom Report for 2003 (http://www.freemedia.at/wpfr/Mena/oman.htm).

13. Basic Statute of the State Article 33 (http://www.omanet.om/english/government/basiclaw/rights.asp?cat=gov&subcat=blaw).

14. Off-the-record interview, Muscat, 18 October 2003.

15. Off-the-record conversations with Omani officials.

16. See *Majlis a-dawla* Basic Statute of the State Article 58 (http://www.omanet.om/english/government/basiclaw/council.asp?cat=gov&subcat=blaw); see also Public Rights and Duties Articles 15 to 40 (http://www.omanet.om/english/government/basiclaw/rights.asp?cat=gov&subcat=blaw).

17. See, for example, John E. Peterson, 'Oman: three and a half decades of change and development', *Middle East Policy*, vol. 11, no. 2, Summer 2004, p. 134.

18. Interview with Dr Fawzia al-Farsi, Muscat, 20 February 2005.

19. See http://www.omanet.om/english/government/majlis.asp?cat=gov.

20. Interview with Dr Sharifa bint Khalfan al-Yahyai, Muscat, 21 February 2005.

21. Interview with Dr Rawya bint Saud Albusaidi, Muscat, 2 March 2005.

7. Dubai: The Airport State

1. See Marc Augé, *Non-Places: Introduction to an Anthropology of Supermodernity*, London: Verso Books, 1995.

2. Jonathan Raban, *Arabia*, London: Picador, 1979.

3. Raban, *Arabia*, p. 172.

4. Raban, *Arabia*, p. 197.

5. See Frauke Heard-Bey, *From Trucial States to United Arab Emirates*, London and New York: Longman, 1996, p. 242.

6. Heard-Bey, *From Trucial States*, p. 242.

7. Heard-Bey, *From Trucial States*, p. 243.

8. Heard-Bey, *From Trucial States*, p. 255.

9. See Thomas Lippman, *Inside the Mirage: America's Fragile Partnership with Saudi Arabia*, Boulder, CO: Westview Press, 2004.

10. Rosemarie Said Zahlan, *The Origins of the United Arab Emirates*, New York: St Martin's Press, 1978, p. 159.

11. Zahlan, *The Origins*, p. 158.

12. Zahlan, *The Origins*, p. 158.

13. Heard-Bey, *From Trucial States*, p. 258.

14. Michael Field, *The Merchants*, London: John Murray, 1984, p. 61.

15. See, for example, Jamila Verghese, *Her Gold and Her Body*, New Delhi: Vikas Publishing House, 1980, or, for a more conventionally academic study, Ranjana Sheel, *The Political Economy of Dowry*, New Delhi: Manohar 1999. Interestingly, Sheel suggests that contemporary dowry practices in India are far from faithful enactments of Hindu tradition but rather 'invented traditions' in the same sense

as those identified by Hobsbawm and others in their study of European 'traditions'. The same might also usefully be said of the so-called 'religious' traditions that limit the freedom of women in many Arab countries.

16. Field, *The Merchants*, p. 63.
17. Muhammad al-Murr, *Dubai Tales*, translated from the Arabic by Peter Clark, London and Boston: Forest Books, 1991, p. 10.
18. Muhammad al Murr, *Dubai Tales*, p. 13.
19. Heard-Bey, *From Trucial States*, p. 261.
20. Ali Parsa and Ramin Keivani, 'The Hormuz Corridor: building a cross-border region between Iran and the United Arab Emirates', in Saskia Sassen (ed.), *Global Networks, Linked Cities*, New York and London: Routledge, 2002, p. 194.
21. David Hirst, 'Dubai, a sheikhdom happy to embrace globalisation', in *Le Monde Diplomatique* (English Edition), February 2001, http://mondediplo.com/2001/02/06dubai.
22. Field, *The Merchants*, p. 60.
23. See also, for example, Hirst, 'Dubai, a sheikhdom', who refers to '"Maktum Inc"', as some call it'.
24. Field, *The Merchants*, p. 60.
25. Heard-Bey, *From Trucial States*, p. 260.
26. This was an important theme in the first report, *Arab Human Development Report 2002: Creating Opportunities for Future Generations*, New York: United Nations Publications, 2002, and the main subject of the second, *Arab Human Development Report 2003: Building a Knowledge Society*, New York, United Nations Publications, 2003. Both are available online at http://www.undp.org/rbas/ahdr/.
27. Lee Smith, 'The Road to Tech Mecca', *Wired*, http://wired.com/wired/archive/12.07/dubai_pr.html
28. Saskia Sassen, *Globalization and its Discontents*, New York: The New Press, 1998, p. 178.
29. Sassen, *Globalization and its Discontents*, p. 180.
30. Hirst, 'Dubai, a sheikhdom'.
31. Raban, *Arabia*, p. 168.
32. Sassen, *Globalization and its Discontents*, p. xxxii.
33. Sassen, *Globalization and its Discontents*, p. xxxiii.
34. According to figures used by the Dubai Development and Investment Authority, only 18 per cent of the population of Dubai are citizens of the UAE. See www.datadubai.com/population.htm. Allowing for citizens of Persian, Baluchi and other origins, one has to assume that the 'indigenous' Arab population, with tribal affiliation, will be considerably smaller than this. The government does not publish analysis of its population by ethnicity.

8. Turkey: Islamists in Power

1. Olivier Roy, *The Failure of Political Islam*, London: I.B.Tauris, 1999.
2. Erdogan was initially ineligible to be elected to parliament, let alone serve as prime minister, because of an earlier conviction for which he served time in prison, arising from an occasion on which he famously recited the words of a

provocatively 'Islamic' song: 'Our mosques are our helmets, our minarets are our bayonets'.
3. Interview with Lakhdar Brahimi, October 2004.
4. Nicole Pope and Hugh Pope, *Turkey Unveiled: A History of Modern Turkey*, Woodstock and New York: The Overlook Press, 2004, p. 141.
5. Interview with Admiral Biren, 2005.
6. Ilter, Turan, *The Justice and Development Party: The First Year in Power*, Turkish Industrialists' and Businessmen's Association, p. 2.
7. Interview with Cengis Cedar, 2005.
8. Orhan Pamuk, *Guardian*, 29 October 2005.
9. Pope and Pope, *Turkey Unveiled*, p. 183.

9. Iraq: Democracy under Occupation, Revisited

1. See, for example, Seymour Hersh, *Chain of Commmand*, London: Penguin Books, 2005; George Packer, *The Assassin's Gate: America in Iraq*, New York: Farrar, Strauss & Giroux, 2005.
2. Richard Perle, PBS *Frontline* Interview <http://www.pbs.org/wgbh/pages/frontline/ shows/truth/interviews/perle.html>
3. Laith Kubba, *Frontline* interview <http://www.pbs.org/wgbh/pages/frontline/shows/truth/interviews/kubba.html>
4. Elie Kedourie, *Democracy and Arab Political Culture*, Washington DC: Washington Institute for Near East Policy, 1992, pp. 27–8.
5. Eric Davis, *Memories of State: Politics, History and Collective Identity in Modern Iraq*, Berkeley: University of California Press, 2005.
6. Kedourie, *Democracy and Arab Political Culture*, pp. 29.
7. Matthew Elliott, *'Independent Iraq': The Monarchy and the British Influence 1941–1958*, London: Tauris Academic Studies, 1997, p. 6.
8. Elliott, *Independent Iraq*, p. 23.
9. Adeed Dawisha, 'Democratic attitudes and practices in Iraq, 1921–1958, *Middle East Journal*, vol. 59, no. 1, Winter 2005, pp. 11–30 (p. 29).
10. Kedourie, *Democracy and Arab Political Culture*, p. 34.
11. Davis, *Memories of State*, p. 75.
12. Davis, *Memories of State*, p. 75. Davis refers here to Benedict Anderson's famous idea of a national identity facilitated by substantial literacy and the spread of print journalism.
13. Davis, *Memories of State*, pp. 75–6.
14. The term is Eric Hobsbawm's and refers to the retrospective creation (blending myth and evidence) of a story that legitimizes the present in terms of its roots in the past. The 'invention of tradition' was crucial to the formation of numerous European nations, providing them with coherent and accessible national histories in which to ground their modern statehood.
15. George Packer, *The Assassin's Gate: America in Iraq*, New York: Farrar, Strauss & Giroux, 2005, p. 98.
16. Toby Dodge, *Inventing Iraq*, London: Hurst, 2003, p. 159.
17. Dodge, *Inventing Iraq*, p. 158.
18. Faleh A. Jabar, *The Shiite Movement in Iraq*, London: Saqi Books, 2003, p. 34.

19. Peter and Marion-Farouk Sluglett, 'The historiography of modern Iraq', *American History Review*, December 1991, pp. 1412–3, cited in Jabar, p. 35.

20. Riverbend, Baghdad Burning, 26 August 2003.

21. Larry Diamond, 'What went wrong in Iraq', *Foreign Affairs*, September/October 2004.

22. Isobel Coleman, 'The payoff from women's rights', *Foreign Affairs*, May/June 2004.

23. Larry Diamond, *Squandered Victory: The American Occupation and the Bungled Effort to Bring Democracy to Iraq*, New York: Times Books, 2005, p. 44.

24. Diamond, *Squandered Victory*, p. 40.

25. Diamond, *Squandered Victory*, p. 327.

26. Diamond, *Squandered Victory*, p. 328.

27. Edward Djerejian, 'One man, one vote, one time is not democracy', *New Perspectives Quarterly*, September 1996.

28. Reuel Marc Gerecht, *The Islamic Paradox: Shiite Clerics, Sunni Fundamentalists, and the Coming of Arab Democracy*, Washington DC: AEI Press, 2004, p. 36.

29. Gerecht, *The Islamic Paradox*, pp. 37–8.

30. Reuel Marc Gerecht, 'The birth of democracy', in Gary Rosen (ed.) *The Right War? The Conservative Debate on Iraq*, Cambridge: Cambridge University Press, 2005, p. 241.

Conclusion

1. Marc Lynch, *Voices of the New Arab Public: Iraq, Al-Jazeera and Middle East Politics Today*, New York: Columbia University Press, 2006.

Index